Arab Nationalism

Arab Nationalism:
A History

Nation and State in the Arab World

Youssef M. Choueiri

Copyright © Youssef Choueiri 2000

The right of Youssef Choueiri to be identified as author of this work has been asserted in accordance with the Copyright, Designs and Patents Act 1988.

First published 2000

2 4 6 8 10 9 7 5 3 1

Blackwell Publishers Ltd
108 Cowley Road
Oxford OX4 1JF
UK

Blackwell Publishers Inc.
350 Main Street
Malden, Massachusetts 02148
USA

British Library Cataloguing in Publication Data
A CIP catalogue record for this book is available from the British Library

Library of Congress Cataloging-in-Publication Data
Choueiri, Youssef M., 1948–
    Arab nationalism / Youssef Choueiri.
        p.   cm.
Includes bibliographical references and index.
ISBN 0-631-21728-2 (alk. paper)—ISBN 0-631-21729-0 (pbk. : alk. paper)
    1. Nationalism—Arab countries—History—19th century.   2. Nationalism—Arab countries—History—20th century.   3. Arab countries—Politics and government—19th century.   4. Arab countries—Politics and government—20th century.   I. Title.
    DS62.7.C46   2000
        320.54′089927—dc21
                                                                        00-009406

Typeset in 10.5/12 pt Galliard
by SetSystems Ltd, Saffron Walden, Essex
Printed in Great Britain by Biddles Ltd,
www.biddles.co.uk

This book is printed on acid-free paper.

Contents

Preface

The population of the Arab world is calculated to reach over 300 million by the end of the year 2000. In 1990 the Arab population figure stood at 221 million, denoting an annual growth rate of 3 per cent, compared to 1.7 per cent at the global level and 0.5 per cent in the advanced countries. Moreover, the accelerating rate of migration from the rural areas to the cities has, over the last decade or so, led to the transformation of the Arab world from a predominantly rural to an urban society, with 55 per cent of its inhabitants living in over-crowded cities.

Straddling the continents of Asia and Africa, and stretching along the Mediterranean coastline from Morocco to Syria, its geography lends it a vital strategic importance, and renders its human and material resources of immediate concern to an emerging international order driven by economic prosperity, the principle of human rights and globalization of knowledge. Containing the largest reserves of oil, the engine of modern life, it has often been the site of European rivalries and super-power efforts to link its destiny to an external scheme of things. Its long history since the dawn of time, tells the story of the first civilizations that humankind fashioned out of its environment and went on to organize the earliest urban centres and build imperial states in the agrarian age. By devising an intricate system of writing, which made the alphabet a medium of communi-cation of different cultures, its inhabitants embraced monotheism as the common religion uniting different continents and ways of life.

Riven by conflict and rival interests, it nevertheless brought together its newly independent states under the umbrella of the Arab League, founded in 1945.

As the Arab world enters the twenty-first century, it still teems with political problems and human dilemmas waiting to be resolved. Ranging from the Arab-Israeli conflict to economic development, not to mention the entitlement of its men and women to exercise their full democratic rights, these dilemmas of accumulated frustrations and aspirations deserve to be told or revisited in their historical and contemporary dimensions.

This book aspires to tell the story of a particular political endeavour, which since the nineteenth century has sought to restructure or unify the Arab world in a number of ways and according to a variety of methods. Its scope is perhaps somewhat ambitious, given the minute details one has to go into in order to bring out a certain historical background or keep abreast of the march of events as they relentlessly press forward.

Thus, without belittling the task that lies ahead, it is felt that there is still an urgent need for a comprehensive study of Arab nationalism, both as an historical movement and a doctrine. No academic work has so far dealt with this subject in its entire history, which spans more than a century. Moreover, the persistence of scholarly disagreement as to the date of its exact origins, political nature and intellectual significance, necessitates a fresh look at the subject.

As an historical event, Arab nationalism emerged as a result of the convergence of socio-economic and political factors towards the end of the nineteenth century. However, there are a number of indications which suggest that the collapse of the Ottoman empire by the end of World War I constituted the major event that paved the way for the emergence of a concrete drive for Arab unity. Nevertheless, the nineteenth century did witness the rise of a certain type of protonationalism or Arab cultural awakening.

The total collapse of the Ottoman Empire was followed by the failure of various local Arab movements to achieve full independence, or devise viable economic growth. Indeed, in one single decade (1920–30), one Arab rebellion after another was either utterly defeated or achieved partial and ephemeral success. This was the case in Syria, Iraq, Egypt, the Sudan, Tunisia and Morocco. This series of failures provided a suitable environment for the rise of a more radical doctrine.

Arab nationalism represented a movement that aspired to meet a new situation in which all the Arab world had become the target of European colonial penetration. This happened at a time when almost all foreign powers became either unreliable or lukewarm allies. The Arabs were, more or less, left to fend for themselves and work out a new strategy capable of checking the intensification of European domination. It was thus perceived that earlier attempts, which aimed at achieving the independence of certain Arab countries, lacked both a comprehensive vision and a proper organizational framework that transcended local and regional boundaries.

Advocated by an ambitious generation of middle-class intellectuals and professional elites, the idea of Arab unity became within two decades a powerful weapon which threatened the entrenched interests of old style notables, large merchants and landowners. From being a political movement concerned with articulating the necessity of Arab unity, it developed into a popular current armed with a modern programme of action. Arab nationalism reached its heyday in the 1950s and '60s, changing in the process the outlook of an entire Arab generation.

A study of nationalism presupposes an analysis of the conditions and historical transformations which made its emergence possible. It is thus envisaged that cultural, economic and political developments in the nineteenth century constitute a significant threshold in the generation of Arab Nationalism, and have to be included in delineating the dynamics of this movement. It is against this background that the present study is divided into three distinct phases: the cultural, the political and the social.

Thus, chapter 1 introduces nationalism by means of analysing its western theories, while chapter 2 offers a survey of Arab history as perceived by a number of Arab historians who, for the first time, tried to cover the entire history of the Arab nation.

The cultural phase, extending from approximately 1800 to 1900, witnessed the rediscovery of Arabic civilization as a glorious golden age. A new literary Arabic language was consequently forged to represent an autonomous cultural identity within the world of Islam in general, and the Ottoman empire in particular. It was also in the nineteenth century that the concept of the fatherland as a well-defined territorial entity began to be propagated. This was a conscious and rational endeavour undertaken to create a new form of human organization.

The second phase, extending from 1900 to 1945, had an eminently political character. In this stage the concept of the fatherland became associated with self-determination, independence and the active participation of indigenous elites in deciding its general well-being. These two phases are the subject of chapter 3.

Chapters 4 and 5 delineate the theoretical articulations of a new generation of Arab activists and members of the intelligentsia. By doing so, western theories discussed in chapter 1 are revisited and tested with a view to pinpointing Arab contributions to our understanding of nationalist movements.

In its third phase (1945–73) Arab nationalism acquired widespread popular support and succeeded in implementing its own radical programme. Henceforth, Arab nationalism became associated with socialism, one-party rule and the struggle for the liberation of Palestine. It thus asserted itself as a triumphant movement, eclipsing all other ideologies throughout the Arab world. This is the subject of chapter 6.

In chapter 7, it is argued that the Arab world stands at the threshold of a fourth phase in which both nationalism and democracy have resurfaced in a fresh encounter. It is an encounter that is played out against the resurgence of Islamist notions of state and nation as well as the thrust of a novel wave of globalization.

The study of Arab nationalism is thus considered to be bound up with the development of the modern and contemporary Arab world. By focusing attention on the drive for Arab unity, social reform and economic growth, one is able to gauge the pace of change in Arab societies, on the one hand, and assess its implications for the future, on the other. Furthermore, such a study, by tracing the history of various Arab nationalist currents, aims to discover their viability in an Arab world made up of independent states.

Acknowledgements

I would like to thank the following colleagues and friends, who in their own ways, made the completion of this study possible: Derek Hopwood, Khayr al-Din Haseeb, 'Abdul Karim Rafeq, Raghid al-Sulh and Tim Niblock.

I acknowledge with gratitude the responses of the five anonymous readers who offered their advice with generous and liberal scholarly insights.

I owe a great debt of gratitude to my wife, Amal, for her unfailing patience and encouragement.

It is with great pleasure that I single out Tessa Harvey of Blackwell Publishers, for her decision to commission this book and see it through its various stages.

Last but not least, I would like to thank Sheila Westcott for word-processing the typescript.

Youssef Choueiri
Exeter
24 March 2000

Glossary

Adnanites	Collective name given to northern, as opposed to southern, Arabian tribes.
Al-'Ahd	'The covenant': a clandestine pan-Arabist society formed by Arab officers in the Ottoman army shortly before World War I.
'Asabiyya	Tribal or group solidarity.
Ba'th	Renaissance or resurrection: the name of the political party founded by Michel 'Aflaq and Salah al-Din al-Baytar in the 1940s.
Hizb	Political party or faction.
Al-fatat	"The young Arab" founded in 1911 in Paris as a secret society opposed to turkification. It adopted a programme of Arab separatism after 1915.
Iltizam	Tax-farming.
Kharijites	Seceders. An extreme Muslim sect of the first Islamic century.
Mülkiye	An Ottoman college for civil servants founded in 1859 in Istanbul.
Al-Muhajirun	Meccan migrants who accompanied the Prophet on his flight to Medina in 622 AD or joined him at a later date.
Nadi	club.
Nahda	Renaissance.
Qahtanids	Collective name of southern Arabian tribes, considered to be the ancestors of pure Arabians.

Al-Qahtaniyya	Pan-Arabist society founded in 1909 in Istanbul.
Quraysh	The most prestigious Arabian tribe, composed of a number of clans, including that of the Prophet Muhʔammad, Banu Hashim.
Qusayy	Founder of Quraysh as the foremost Arabian tribe.
Sharif	Descendant of the Prophet.
Sufi	Muslim mystic or ascetic.
Tali'a	Vanguard.
Tanzimat	Reorganization; Ottoman reform movement.
Umma	Community, nation.
Watan	Homeland or fatherland.

1

Nationalism and its Theories

It is generally agreed in the world of western scholarship that the study of nationalism has over the last three decades or so been the subject of genuine scrutiny. Although debates still abound as to the precise characteristics of nationalism, or its function in the contemporary world, most scholars recognize its crucial historical significance.

A number of studies, published in the Anglo-Saxon world,[1] testify to this preoccupation with a political and cultural phenomenon that seems to be the hallmark of modernity itself. In other words, it has become virtually impossible to ignore the simple fact that our political world has been functioning for at least two centuries on the basis of particular units known as nation-states.[2] These nation-states are then perceived to have arisen, first of all, in the European context, and represent as a result 'historical' or 'continuous' nations. The historical development of England, France and Spain are invariably cited as the forerunners in this field.[3]

The most common explanation of the rise of the nation-state is often based on the idea of the decline of other older associations, such as feudalism, the church, or the city-state. This decline is then said to be the result of the steady ascendancy of a centralizing state bent on carrying out a sweeping programme of modernization, or the advent of capitalism as an agency of homogeneous change across social and economic barriers. Hence, this centralized state is assumed to have brought under its uniform jurisdiction one well-defined national territory, creating thereby, with the onset of capitalism, a unified national market. Moreover, universal languages, such as Latin, were dropped in favour of local vernaculars, and the urban-based middle classes, imbued with a spirit of rational investments and profit calculations, gained the upper hand at the expense of old-style rural landlords.

Thus, the birth of the nation-state announces and solidifies uniformity in political organization, economic activity and cultural growth. This uniformity is daily reproduced by the rational organization of one army, one police force, one bureaucracy, and one law supervising and governing all citizens enjoying equal rights and duties. All barriers, be they social or religious, were removed, and a new political space was created so that citizens could compete according to their talents and merits rather than inheritance or origin. In other words, status in society is to be earned rather than ascribed. It is in this respect that laws are supposed to derive from the will of free citizens who had discarded the divine rights of kings or religiously-sanctified injunctions.

Whatever the peculiar historical circumstances which occasioned the genesis of the modern nation-state, it has now become fairly common to accept the universality of such a phenomenon. Its common characteristics, cutting across continents and cultures, can be summarized as follows:

1. The nation occupies a territorially-delimited space in possession of a juridical personality recognized in international law.
2. The state, while ensuring the perpetual sovereignty of such a nation, enjoys an independent existence that is sanctioned by the popular will. It thus governs in the name, and is itself the product, of civil society. Being representative of civil society rather than religion or the divine right of kings, it operates an *ipso facto* separation between the political and the religious. This separation could take the form of outright secularization of politics or some other related procedure.
3. The welfare of the members of the nation, treated as autonomous individuals, is an acquired responsibility of the state, with particular reference to education, social security and defence.
4. Democracy is therefore taken to be a natural corollary of the unification of the nation into one single modern state.

Approaches to nationalism, be they positive or negative in their appreciation of its implications, tend to accept this salient feature of modernity either enthusiastically, reluctantly or despairingly. Consequently, one could classify scholars into three categories: unbelievers, believers and agnostics. Unbelievers, needless to say, reveal in their criticism a certain anger at the turn of historical events, sometimes wishing to turn the clock back, but more often than not, considering nationalism a heretical aberration of a refined sense of patriotism exclusively engendered by western Europe or Anglo-Saxon culture.

There is thus an unbridgeable gap between Anglo-Saxon patriotism and other forms of nationalism. Believers only see different shades of nationalism, which when viewed sympathetically, combine to produce, so to speak, a wonderful rainbow testifying to humankind's ingenuity. Agnostics are in a league of their own, endeavouring to enumerate the inevitable socio-economic and political factors which made the nation a product of a long historical process, on the one hand, and trying, on the other hand, to underline the contingency of the same phenomenon and its possible disappearance at an undefined date.

The World of Unbelief and Negative Approaches

Lord Acton (1834–1903) could be said to have initiated a negative attitude towards nationalism in an essay published in 1862.[4] In this essay, Acton goes out of his way to highlight the distinction between Teutonic and Latin nations. According to his theory, it is countries with a Latin culture that tend to fall prey to revolutions or witness sudden changes in government and politics. This Latin spirit of extremist measures is contrasted with the culture of Teutonic countries (i.e. England and Germany and perhaps the United States) which is moderate, measured and calculating.

Acton considered nationalism (or the principle of nationality) to be an unfortunate development of the modern era. He correctly observed that this principle was a recent phenomenon born out of the democratic spirit of the age. He defined it as the theory which sees the nation as being commensurate with its language and its ardent desire to bring the language-based community under one single political roof. However, he deemed such a desire detrimental both to the enjoyment of liberty and the growth of civilization.

In this sense, his ideal community was modelled on the British imperial experience whereby different racial, linguistic and religious groups lived under the authority of one benevolent state. This imperial state, multi-cultural and multi-lingual, was the best guarantee of liberty and the ideal social structure. It is the state rather than the nation which ought to regulate society and its vital institutions.

By the first half of the twentieth century, nationalism had become one of the most salient features of the political scene throughout the world. It was thus perceived to be worthy of historical treatment and meticulous scholarship. Hence, a number of historians turned their attention to nationalism in order to chronicle in a precise chronological sequence its rise and evolution.[5]

It was also in this period that a more refined interpretation of the principle of nationality had developed with a view to explaining its varieties and divergent outcomes. This was made all the more imperative by the rise of fascist and semi-fascist parties in central and eastern Europe professing the gospel of nationalism. By refining their theories, historians and political scientists reintroduced Acton's binary version on a much wider scale. It was now the difference between the Anglo-Saxon culture and the rest of the world which accounted for the mild and extreme varieties.

In his mature diagnosis of the varieties of nationalism, Hans Kohn, writing in 1955, in the preface to his concise study *Nationalism: its Meaning and History*, (revised edition, 1965) informs the reader:

> Nationalism has been one of the determining forces in modern history. It originated in eighteenth-century Western Europe; during the nineteenth century it spread all over Europe; in the twentieth century it has become a world-wide movement, and its importance in Asia and Africa is growing with every year. But nationalism is not the same in all countries and at all times. It is a historical phenomenon and thus determined by the political ideas and the social structure of the various lands where it takes root.[6]

Hence, these political ideas and social structures lead to 'different forms' of nationalism and have to be accorded their due weight in unlocking the secret of a movement that meant for the modern and contemporary world what religion had been for the world of Christianity in the thirteenth century.

Rousseau's Passion

Seeking the roots of nationalism, Kohn demonstrates its modernity by referring to older loyalties based on empire or city-state. Henceforward, common civilization was reduced to national civilization, and the general and the universal became the peculiar expression of national identities. Nevertheless, nationalism in its beginnings originated in a country that professed 'the liberty of man' and the freedom of the individual. This was seventeenth-century England. The Glorious Revolution of 1688 made the practice of all the positive qualities of political life both possible and enduring. Linked to the emergence of a vigorous English middle-class of traders, it expressed a new spirit of freedom, justice and tolerance which embodied democracy in the institutions of the nation. This tolerant English nationalism was best exemplified in the political philosophy of John Locke (1632–1704).

Locke simply expressed a new 'national spirit' which opposed 'the authoritarian absolution of King and Church'. Furthermore, the movement of liberal English nationalism:

> became known abroad through the intermediary of French thinkers, and was absorbed and transformed into the general consciousness of eighteenth century Western mankind through the genius of French rational thought and the clarity of the French language.[7]

However, it was in New England that a more advanced nation was born, deriving its ideals and constitution from the principles of the mother-country and the Age of Enlightenment. The North American colonies which were to become the United States of America developed a heightened sense of their destiny enshrined in the entitlement of all individuals to certain inalienable rights: life, liberty and the pursuit of happiness.[8]

According to Kohn, French nationalism was initially closely associated with the tradition of English liberty and American tolerance. However, 'the fertile and unstable mind of Rousseau' (1712–78) injected a new pernicious element which was to poison the body politic of the French Revolution. Calling for emotional bonds of national loyalty and a patriotism tinged with religious fervour, he advocated the cause of 'common men' whereby peasantries and the lower classes became the locus of the nation's general will and the expression of its noble soul. Thus, Rousseau's 'tremendous influence' subverted the course of the French Revolution in 1789, leading to an exaggerated emphasis on the active participation of the ordinary citizen in the management of his nation state. In other words, the privacy of the individual, a central tenet of the glorious Revolution, was shattered and replaced with 'an aroused national will'.[9]

In this sense, Rousseau's concept of the general will, coupled with the excessive centralization of the French Revolution and its 'pseudo-religious creed' mark a turning point in the evolution of nationalism. The rest of Kohn's narration of the nationalist phenomenon is governed by this binary division between the enlightened Anglo-Saxon nationalism and a degenerate form that was destined to spread throughout the world. The orderly evolution of the English system of government, be it national or imperial, becomes at the hands of Kohn an oddity rather than a pattern of development. Almost all other societies practise a distorted version of nationalist politics that is either constitutionally flawed or socially fraught with war and bloodshed. The destructive force of nationalism is thus asserted as an inherent characteristic of modern nations and tolerated at the same time as an inevitable evil.

Kant's Guilt

In Kohn's version it was the French philosopher Jean-Jacques Rousseau who exercised his pernicious influence upon succeeding generations of violent nationalists. In a more vigorous and sustained attack on nationalism, another scholar, writing in the second half of the twentieth century, turned to the German philosopher Immanuel Kant (1724–1804) to apportion the highest degree of guilt.

According to Elie Kedourie the guilt belongs to Kant's idea of autonomy and the categorical imperative which stresses the individual's self-determining capacity to formulate his own moral freedom. This assertion of the human will emerged to coincide with the breakdown of traditional institutions and community habits whereby petty officials, young men and artisans began to look for an alternative scheme of things. Hence, the philosophical, social and political realms, hitherto kept separate and differentiated, interlocked to activate a long-drawn process of unfortunate nationalist agitation.

What constitutes the most damning aspects of nationalism is its defiance of the natural order of things. Here Kedourie relies for his arguments on the conservative approach to politics made into a philosophical system by Oakshott. This process was set in motion by what Kant assigned to the individual in his ceaseless search for perfection, and the adoption of the idea of progress as the unlimited horizon of human endeavour. Whenever ethical doctrines enter the political realm, as Kant and his followers attempted to achieve, far-reaching consequences follow. The price of being an autonomous individual is excessive freedom that never flinches from pursuing its own political ends. These ends, espoused by restless young or marginal men, often culminate in terrorist acts, assassination attempts and mindless violence. Based on the erroneous idea of a new style of politics, and in which principles override compromise and divergent interests, the French Revolution made terrorism part of its doctrinal nationalism, aided and abetted by another pernicious revolution of ideas, that of Kant and his imaginative disciple Johann Gotelieb Fichte (1762–1814).[10]

In the wake of Prussia's defeat by Napoleon, Fichte delivered in 1807–08 his celebrated *Addresses to the German Nation*. In them, Fichte called on the German nation to undertake the leadership of the world by reasserting the purity of its language and perfection of its culture. Resisting Napoleon was for Fichte a mere opportunity to reaffirm German superiority despite temporary setbacks and military defeat.

Kant differentiated between things-in-themselves, which are inaccessible to human knowledge, and the Phenomenal World, which is the realm of appearances and contingencies. Over and above these two levels, morality springs from an inner law and which forms its own criteria of good and evil. Fichte took the moral dimension one step further, turning it in the process into a dynamic force. Thus, consciousness became the ruling principle which is embodied in a universal ego capable of illuminating the systemic order of nature and society. This single consciousness imposes coherence by envisaging existence as an organic whole rather than disparate or disconnected parts. Thenceforward, the individual became part of a much larger unity, the unity of national society. Love of fatherland conjoins 'the eternal and the divine' and liberates both the individual and society. To realize oneself, one must struggle in order to maintain life in its original diversity and national cultures. Moreover, one of the most decisive factors in striving to maintain diverse cultures is the conservation of one's language. Fichte's emphasis on the purity of language and its centrality in defining the characteristics of a nation, leads Kedourie to conclude:

> This emphasis on language transformed it into what it had seldom been before, into a political issue for which men are ready to kill and exterminate each other.[11]

Nevertheless, Kedourie condemns the German variety of nationalism, on the one hand, and praises the patriotism of the British and the Americans on the other. He contends that patriotism is shorn of 'a particular doctrine of the state or of the individual's relation to it'. It is, therefore, simply love of one's country and committed loyalty to its various institutions. In this scheme of things, British or American nationalism is an inexact appellation. The repugnant label should only be attached to German culture and its subsequent transmutations in the rest of the world.'[12] To Kedourie, nationalism outside Europe is a derivative doctrine, entirely alien to the traditions and histories of Asia and Africa. It is, moreover, artificially constructed either by imposition or imitation: its inevitable outcome is destruction, brutal murder and persecution of minorities.

The period of imitation is initiated by a handful of western-educated young men, who are 'marginal' by the mere fact of defying the norms of their indigenous societies. Their education and marginality propel them towards a European scheme of things. At first, they are inclined to cooperate with their European masters and join them in the management of their own country. However, an imperial government imposes its own colonial rules and acts according to its own priorities. Consequently, it finds itself unable or constrained to employ and promote its native parvenues, particularly if it is to remain faithful to policies of merit and achieved qualification. Shunned by his original society and rejected by scrupulous European masters, the marginal man develops his own ideology to resolve a purely personal dilemma. Nationalism enters the scene as the direct expression of frustrated ambitions and becomes the outcry of a suppressed and downtrodden nation. As they turned into revolutionary idealists, these marginal men proceeded to impose on their societies an alien creed dripping in blood.[13]

The World of Positive Belief

Lord Acton's negative view of nationalism was to a large measure a reaction to the liberal and favourable appraisal of the principle of nationality, both in its Continental and British varieties. As a matter of fact, his article, published in 1862, can be read as a rebuttal of the nationalist current advocated by revolutionary activists, such as the Italian Giuseppe Mazzini (1805–72), and the utilitarian philosopher, John Stuart Mill (1806–73).

It was during this period that the movement for Italian unification was reaching its climax. A year earlier (1861), Mill had published *Considerations on Representative Government*, which treated the freedom of the individual in conjunction with the self-determination of the nation. Lord Acton refers to both the activities of Mazzini and the ideas of Mill as examples of a new evil wave. In his article he equated 'the theories of equality, Communism, and nationality' as being subversive. He connected the first with the name of Rousseau, the second with that of Baboeuf and the third as the most pernicious, with that of Mazzini. He thus quotes in the same breath a statement by Mill and alludes to Mazzini who is said to have given to the principle of nationality 'the element in which its strength resides'.[14]

Mill's wrong diagnosis is perceived to be his contention that 'it is in general a necessary condition of free institutions that the boundaries of governments should coincide in the main with those of nationalities'.[15]

It is, nevertheless, apparent that Mill envisages the principle of nationality to be an integral part of forming a democratic state or what he termed 'representative government'. His discussion of what came to be known as the theory of nationalism, albeit brief and qualified, was a highly positive one. His discussion opens with the following:

> A portion of mankind may be said to constitute a Nationality if they are united among themselves by common sympathies which do not exist between them and any others – which make them co-operate with each other more willingly than with other people, desire to be under the same government, and desire that it should be government by themselves or a portion of themselves exclusively.[16]

While Mill's assessment of nationalism was measured and hedged by a number of qualifications, the French scholar Ernest Renan (1823–90) devoted to the same principle one of his most eloquent and memorable public lectures. His most quoted metaphor: 'a nation's existence is . . . a daily plebiscite' has become synonymous with the definition of nationalism in both its negative and positive aspects. However, Renan's concept of the principle of nationality converges in its main thrust with that of Mill. Both, for example, dwell on the relevance of race, language, geography and religious loyalties in the generation of nationalism, only to conclude that these were mere contributory factors.

To Mill, the strongest cause which serves to generate a feeling of nationality is 'identity of political antecedents', these antecedents are then said to include 'the possession of a national history, and consequent community of recollections; collective pride and humiliation, pleasure and regret, connected with the same incidents in the past'.[17] To Renan, the heroic past of one's nation is deemed to be 'the social capital upon which one bases a national idea'. But Renan goes on to place a higher premium on suffering and sacrifice rather than pride or pleasure. This is all the more so because, as he contends, in the universe of national memories 'griefs are of more value than triumphs, for they impose duties, and require a common effort'.[18]

Delivered at the Sorbonne on 11 March 1882, Renan's lecture has echoes of the Franco-Prussian war of 1870 and the subsequent annexation of French Alsace-Lorraine. His exclusion of language, race and religion as the determinants of nationality is more absolute than Mill's numerous qualifications. However, both can be safely placed in the liberal camp which asserted the prior formation of the nation as a precondition of political life and organisation.

A Question of Dignity

By and large, positive approaches consider the creation of the nation to have preceded the movement of nationalism. In this sense, the contributions of the British scholar Anthony D. Smith to the study of nationalism fall within the same tradition. Smith, perhaps more than any other scholar, has devoted his entire career to the elucidation of the historical and sociological background of nationalism. His numerous works on the subject reveal a sympathetic and somewhat over-enthusiastic evaluation of the nationalist phenomenon and its implications for the modern world.

In his first major publication, *Theories of Nationalism*,[19] he reviews all the major approaches to nationalism, only to find them wanting in more than one respect. His main criticism centres on theories advanced by Elie Kedourie, Ernest Gellner and the American modernization school. Moreover, he thought the time had come to offer a fresh methodological approach that was pitched at a higher level than the narrative and chronological general studies. To him, nationalism has been one of the most influential of the various doctrinal constellations that have vied for men's loyalties since the erosion of traditional religions.[20] Hence Kohn's distinction between western and eastern nationalism is rejected and nationalism is affirmed as the incarnation of common human problems.

The binary opposition between good and bad nationalism was given its most articulate form by the political philosopher John Plamenatz (1912–75). Born in Montenegro, but educated in England since early age, Plamenatz seems to have been in an ideal position to delineate and delimit the political boundaries of two separate concepts. The title of his article, 'Two types of nationalism' sums up the difference.[21] His distinction is based on the notion of differentiating between a people with a high level of culture and education and one with meagre cultural resources. In the first case, nationalism is western (more precisely English and French), progressive, liberal and the characteristic of culturally well-equipped people. The examples of England and France inspired the Germans and Italians who already possessed the requisite ideas and skills for national regeneration, and all they needed was to construct national states to express the new stage of their development. The second type, embracing the Slavs and later the Asians and Africans, was distinguished from the outset by a felt inadequacy in all fields of national and cultural construction. This type is therefore illiberal, not in an inherent sense, but simply as a result of 'conditions unpropitious to freedom'. These unpropitious conditions are related to the fact that leaders or rulers who take it upon themselves to create a nation or transform it, to provide it with skills, ideas and values it did not have before, are impatient of opposition. Their task, they think is urgent, and they will not tolerate obstructive criticism, taking it for granted that it is for them to decide when it is obstructive.[22]

However, Plamenatz goes on to set against this illiberalism some liberating outcomes: old authorities are destroyed, the grip of the family over the individual is loosened, new opportunities and occupations are created, and scientific ideas are propagated. More importantly, the individual is introduced to the liberating concept of deliberate change as part of human society.

Thus, the negativity of eastern nationalism is thought to be a temporary and transitional phase, destined in due course to be transformed into a badge of dignity, adequacy and democracy. In other words, eastern nationalism is the reaction of backwardness and the struggle of the weak to be developed and able to join the community of western civilized nations.

This mildly sympathetic view of authoritarian nationalism, which Ernest Gellner termed 'the sad reflections of a Montenegrin in Oxford,[23] lies beyond Kedourie's vehement condemnation of nationalism in all its varieties.

Although Smith reserves his severest strictures for the modernization theorists (Daniel Lerner, K. W. Deutsch), his sociological approach is firmly situated within the intricate and profound nexus of relationships between types of nationalism and the process of modernization.[24] His most sustained and fruitful engagement turns out to be with Gellner's diagnosis of nationalism as the true inventor of the nation, nationalism being a mere expression of a society's transition from the agricultural to the industrial age.

Gellner's tidal wave of industrialization which sweeps across the globe, creating in the process a novel configuration of culture, language and science, is modified to include nations which had hardly entered the industrial age. In this way, one could speak of a pre-industrial and an industrializing variety of nationalism.

Adumbrating a concept which he later developed into a full-blown theory, Smith differentiates between nations as the product of a prior religio-ethnic unity and the modern nationalism of nation-states. In this respect, what the French word 'ethnie' denotes is this first type of 'nation', embracing 'cultural distinctiveness and territorial contiguity'. Ancient 'nationalism' is, therefore, ethnically based and has as its main purpose the preservation of a cultural group against foreign rule or occupation. Set against this is the polycentric nationalism of modern times dating back to the French Revolution.[25]

This differentiation between ancient and modern nationalism is offered as a necessary clarification in order to separate 'national sentiment' from 'nationalism', the former being the hallmark of ancient ethnic groups, and the latter denoting a concept of modernity. Polycentric nationalism is, then, defined as:

> an ideological movement, for the attainment and maintenance of self-government and independence on behalf of a group, some of whose members conceive it to constitute an actual or potential 'nation' like others.[26]

On the other hand, the nation is said to be:

> a large, vertically integrated and territorially mobile group featuring common citizenship rights and collective sentiment together with one (or more) common characteristic(s) which differentiate its members from those of similar groups with whom they stand in relations of alliance or conflict.[27]

Although Smith does not stipulate a pre-existent nation for all types of nationalism, the thrust of his argument leads one to believe otherwise. Moreover, despite his sociological extrapolations, Smith is primarily concerned to demonstrate how 'nationalism' has replaced 'religion' as the new legitimating system of values whereby the 'scientific state' plays the role of the midwife ushering in an age of rationalism and secularism.

This shift to psychological history is confirmed by Smith's other major work, *The Ethnic Origins of Nations*.[28] This is a historical *tour de force* that reaches into the earliest written records of humankind in order to unearth the ethnic substratum of almost all existing nations. By doing so, the text attempts to chart a middle course between two schools of nationalism: the perennialist and the modernist.

The first, which represents a minority strand within the world of scholarship, asserts the permanent existence of the nation since the dawn of history. It thus postulates objective attributes such as language, race, territory and religion as being 'primordial ties' which underlie human loyalties throughout the ages. Nations are simple natural phenomena in the same way geography and kinship affiliations are supposed to be. The best known example of such a view is John Armstrong's *Nations before Nationalism*,[29] which sought to demonstrate the central role of ethnic identities in the formation of modern nations or nationalism itself.

The second, or modernist school, theorizes the nation as a by-product of modern conditions, and the advent of capitalism as a new system of economic and social organization. While some stress the economic conditions to explain the rise of modern nations, and others allude to the importance of political factors and the availability of a modernizing central authority, they all agree on the contingent and recent appearance of the nation. In other words, nationalism is neither inherent in human nature, nor is it deep-rooted in history. The works of Ernest Gellner, Benedict Anderson, John Breuilly and Eric Hobsbawm dominate this particular school which will be discussed in more detail in the next section.

Armstrong's book, alluded to above, acts as the point of departure for Smith's historical investigations. Whereas Armstrong sought to establish a direct link between ethnic identities and nationalism, Smith takes a more circumspect approach, considering 'ethnic polities' of the ancient and medieval world as a mere cultural base for the emergence of nationalism.[30]

However, this balancing act between perennialists and modernists turns out to be a difficult position to sustain. No sooner does Smith start to walk his tightrope than he begins to slide steadfastly into a perennialist mode. After all, the title of his book leaves no room for any other course of action, inscribing as it does the rise of the nations into their 'ethnic origins'. By retaining Armstrong's conceptual units of analysis – myth, symbol and memory – and generalizing them to embrace all major ethnic groups of the known historical record, Smith identifies the constituents of his *ethnie* or ethnic community as the solid base of nations. Hence, whatever changes have been wrought by modern factors, these take place 'within a pre-existing framework of collective loyalties and identities, which has conditioned the changes as much as they have influenced the framework'.[31]

The advent of nationalism in the modern world was thus conditioned by centuries-old historical developments having the collective ethnic identities at their core. Those *ethnies* which managed to survive and weathered the storm of dissolution and disappearance were transformed into modern nations. This happened as a result of a triple revolution, which was initially confined to western Europe: a revolution in the realm of the division of labour, a revolution in administration, and a revolution in cultural organization.[32]

Briefly stated, the first revolution meant the end of feudalism and the emergence of a capitalist system which brought about a more advanced level of economic integration within single national territories. Merchants, artisans and peasantries were thus brought together and turned into 'a potentially mobile workforce', with the state acting as a binding power linking 'various regional and urban elites to each other in a common economic fate'. With the development of military techniques in artillery and warfare, the state was able to exert effective administrative control. This second revolution brought about the new type of 'rational state', whereby professional armies, bureaucracies and technical experts became the hallmark of modern organization. The third revolution in the cultural and educational fields created 'a standard mode of communication' and ensured a vivid identification with the community and the birth of a 'unified national consciousness'.[33]

This triple revolution signalled the emergence of the territorial nation-state. Transplanted into the rest of the world in the nineteenth and twentieth centuries, the territorial dimension became ethnically based. The binary division of western and eastern nationalisms, first adumbrated by Hans Kohn, is adopted by Smith in his analysis as being the territorial and the ethnic. However, ethnic nationalism loses most of its negative aspects, and emerges in Smith's text as a fully legitimate framework capable of creating homogeneity, cultural unity and common citizenship.

In elaborating the complex pathways to nationalism, Smith makes a number of concessions to the modernist school, without, however, relinquishing his basic agreement with the perennialists. In this sense, modern nations turn out to be not as 'modern' as prevalent scholarship would lead us to assume. If one excludes the novel democratic principle of including all citizens in the national community, Smith argues that 'modern nations and nationalism have only extended and deepened the meanings and scope of older ethnic concepts and structures'.[34] Thus, the nation is a mere extension of a pre-existing *ethnie*.

Both nations and *ethnies* have the same ends, while they might differ in the means at their disposal. This difference, which encompasses sociological and anthropological ctegories, is clarified thus:

> the means have quite patently changed. Formerly, priests and scribes were the guardians and conduits of ethnic 'myth-symbol complexes', of ethnic memory from generation to generation. Now it is more likely to be intellectuals and professionals who rediscover and transmit to future generations the myths and symbols of modern nations, with the bourgeoisie and military replacing aristocracies as the power underpinning ethnic expansion and penetration.[35]

In other words, nationalism ensures the survival of a particular ethnic group by embarking on a journey of historical rediscovery, be it imagined or real.

The Agnostics or Reluctantly Neutral

At the hands of Smith scribes and priests perform the same functions as their modern counterparts: intellectuals and professionals. The identity of the social carriers may vary, but the message they transmit is encoded in almost identical scripts, and very easily deciphered by antiquarians and modernists alike. Not so for Gellner. Once a new socio-economic system appears on the scene, all codes of behaviour, values and culture have to change accordingly.

The agrarian age had its priests and scribes who performed a function prescribed by clearly-defined rules of conduct and a language that was inaccessible to the majority of the community. This specialized clerical group enters into competition or alliance with the central state which is dominated by a small ruling stratum. Horizontally stratified, the ruling minority does not favour cultural homogeneity; on the contrary, permanent divisions of cultural differences are inscribed into the fabric of society as part of deliberate policy, thereby averting friction or ambiguity of status. Beyond the realm of the state and the clergy, small peasant communities eke out an existence with no interest in high culture or common bonds of loyalty. Their role is to pay taxes, obey orders and accept inequality as being inevitable and natural. In other words, such a society is rigidly bound and composed of horizontally segregated layers of ruling and literate minorities who extract taxes and dispense justice in a community of agricultural producers.[36]

No fusion of state and culture, the aim of nationalism, is thus either possible or desirable. Although the clerisy, in opposition to the military rulers, may aspire to spread their high culture throughout society, such as the 'ulama' in Islam, they invariably fail to change prevalent conditions. It is only in industrial society that prescribed stratification is overturned and social mobility becomes the normal feature of daily life. Under such circumstances, high culture pervades society, creating the feasible congruence of the political and national units. The age of nationalism has arrived.[37]

The new society is rational, mobile, egalitarian and obsessed with innovation. It sustains itself by an enormous capacity for permanent growth and high productivity based on a refined division of labour. In a sense, modern society is organized according to standard criteria which mirror to a large extent the way a modern army is trained, producing recruits with basic common qualifications such as literacy, numeracy and familiarity with essential technical skills. Such training of all actual or potential citizens is linked to a unique modern ideal: 'the principle of universal and centrally guaranteed education'.[38]

It is this particular feature of universal, standardized education, which operates and fosters a context-free language of communication, that acts as the hallmark of the national state. Consequently nationalism is simply an outcome of the desire of the state to marry its own culture. By doing so it begets nationalism which in turn acts as a strong bond that holds together state and culture. But this is a marriage with a difference: by taking its culture into its own bosom under conditions of modern economic organization it cannot but diffuse it throughout society in order to ensure its material and political survival. The unified measure of 'fact' proffered by Kant or Hume is but an expression of this new state of affairs and is analogous to the anonymous action of a moral state.

From being hierarchically organized, agrarian society was transformed into a horizontally-based nation in which all citizens stand in direct relationship to the state without prescribed mediation rooted in a system of feudal patronage. Uniformity of status, at least in theory, is guaranteed by the education system:

> the employability, dignity, security and self-respect of individuals, typically, and for the majority of men[39] now hinges on their *education*; and the limits of the culture within which they were educated are also the limits of the world within which they can, morally and professionally, breathe. A man's education is by far his most precious investment, and in effect confers his identity on him. Modern man is not loyal to a monarch or a land or a faith, whatever he may say, but to a culture.[40]

This school-transmitted, state-administered culture is the hallmark of the age of transition to industrialism, with nationalism acting as the glue that binds culture and polity. Furthermore, the process of industrialization was first confined to its European core, but with colonialism and imperial conquests it spread throughout the globe engendering different reactions under specific conditions. However, the age of nationalism became an integral part of modern society.[41]

It is perhaps appropriate at this juncture to allude to the controversial nature of Gellner's industrial society and its link with the rise of nationalism. A number of scholars have raised objections to confining nationalism to the industrial age, contending that some nationalisms, such as the Greek, the German and the Indian varieties, emerged in societies which could hardly be classified as industrial.[42] Although Gellner's use of the term is open to charges of reductionism, functionalism and Eurocentrism, it seems that his industrial age could be interpreted to refer to two separate but complementary phases: (1)

the underlying pre-conditions of industrialization; and (2) industrialization proper.

The first phase embraces the emergence of a new culture or ethos
which has rationality in its broad Weberian sense at its core. It includes
orderliness, efficiency, and above all, a common conceptual currency.
It is a common conceptual currency that purports to locate all facts
'within a single continuous logical space' and 'one single language
describes the world and is internally unitary'. Furthermore, this act of
equalizing and homogenizing facts means 'the breaking up of all
complexes into their constituent parts'. Rationality is then that '*esprit
d'analyse*' which underpins Weber's notion of means-ends efficiency
and symmetry of treatment. Both Kant and Hume are credited with
coining this currency.[43]

The second phase is that of industrialization proper, in the sense of
manufacturing enterprises, advanced technologies and a refined division of labour.

Thus, societies which are exposed to the impact of the second
phase begin to formulate their reactions by adopting the formulations
of the first phase as they look forward to an industrial age of their
own. In the age of nationalism, nations are engendered to comply
with different social conditions. Nationalism precedes the nation and
acts as its progenitor by using and redefining whatever cultural funds
and historical memories it is able to select and transform. However,
such selection and invention does not imply either the contingency or
artificiality of nationalism. On the contrary, the nationalist principle
'has very deep roots in our shared current condition, is not at all
contingent, and will not easily be denied.'[44]

More importantly, nationalism is the culture of urban-based groups
who aspire to impose their version of high culture as opposed to the
low culture of the countryside. Gellner's model in this instance is
largely based on his highly controversial analysis of high and low
Islam. High Islam is urban, scripturalist, reformist and imbued with a
sense of sobriety and rationality. By contrast, low Islam is rural,
superstitious, tribal, and tied to the idea of saint cults. In rural Islam,
holy lineages and their rural shrines function as mediators between
man and God, whereas urban Islam with its scripturalism defines in
the modern world the identity of a nation, as it did in Algeria, doing
away with tribal and other sectional divisions (pp. 73, 75–81).

Thus nationalism accompanies the establishment of centralized
authority, requires an effective education system, and is a by-product
of the diffusion of market relations. As to its future trajectory, it may
lose its sharpness as industrialism matures and establishes its standard
norms and homogenous rhythms throughout society, but nationalism

as the badge of a modern world is here to stay for a long time to come.

Although Anderson's principal arguments[45] are in basic agreement with Gellner's diagnosis, his is a more romantic account, seeing nationalism almost in religious terms, in spite of his frequent references to 'print-capitalism'. Thus nationalism becomes a high ideal that leads certain persons to sacrifice their lives for it. It is, moreover, a powerful energetic agent capable of generating an abstract notion of the nation.

The ability of nationalism to attain high levels of idealism and abstraction is substantiated by its creation of an 'imagined community'. This imagined community is the nation of the modern world, replacing universalist conceptions of religion with concrete, yet no less forceful, images of national narratives involving simultaneously individuals across their territorial units. It is this fertile imagination, born as a result of the advent of the printed word and its propagation, that lends time its linear propensity, doing away with the old idea of cyclical happenings rotating within a cosmic order of repetitive circularity whereby the cosmos, monarchical authority and religious rectitude speak the same universal language. It is now the vernacular of the community that takes precedence and proceeds to thrive, embodying itself in novels that mirror the reconfigured boundaries of a territory clearly delineated on modern maps. The novel, the newspaper and the demarcated map are the by-products of 'print-capitalism' and the birth of a secular concept of time.[46]

In this scheme of things economic change, embodied in a system of capitalism, made possible the dissemination of books and newspapers as emblems of a new secular culture. Although capitalism involved different operations and the production of numerous commodities, it was the industry of 'book-publishing' at the dawn of the modern age which heralded the birth of mass consumption, whereby the new creed of protestantism contracted a coalition with print-capitalism to wage its 'battle for men's minds'. The erosion of Latin and its 'sacred imagined community' paved the way for the adoption of national vernaculars, which gradually acquired standardized forms through print. As these newly printed languages acquired fixity and visibility, they made possible the emergence of the idea of a deep-rooted, historically ancient nation. However, what Gellner termed 'industrialism', Anderson calls 'capitalism', and it is the emergence of this new species that generates nationalism and ultimately the nation-state.[47]

In his account of nationalism, Anderson is anxious to avoid a eurocentric version whereby Creole movements of national liberation in North and Latin America are deemed to have pioneered this type of politics.[48] By doing so, he almost demolishes his own argument in so much as he assigns priority to the establishment of distinct administrative units which acted as the locus of national consciousness in North or South America. It is true that Benjamin Franklin (1706–90) is cited as the pioneering entrepreneur of newspaper publishing, and some provincial newspapers are mentioned in the context of wider developments, but this is hardly the same as saying that print-capitalism or industrialism ushered in nationalism in the Americas.

Thus, Anderson's contribution to the study of nationalism has been misunderstood by a number of scholars. What he wished to stress above all was the pioneering role of the Americas in the emergence of nationalism. In other words, it was the New World, rather than old Europe, that 'invented' nationalism and launched it on to the world stage. The American revolutionary wars between 1776 and 1825, and which embraced both the North and the South, heralded the birth of new nations, and consequently the modern nation-state as we know it today.[49] In the revised edition of his book, Anderson laments the fact that in many of the notices of *Imagined Communities* this different American perspective is lost sight of, so much so that 'Eurocentric provincialism remained quite undisturbed, and that the crucial chapter on the originating Americas was largely ignored'.[50]

To Breuilly[51] nationalism is 'a form of politics' which is mainly concerned with the capture of power as well as the establishment of a legitimate state. Thus, by analysing nationalism one does not duplicate the nationalists' propensity to tabulate the characteristics of national identity, nor is it illuminating to study ideological doctrines in their abstract formulations. It is rather political action and organization as practised and carried out by agents of a new and modern type state that should receive extensive treatment. And it is to the modern state that Breuilly devotes the bulk of his book, whereby the nations of Europe, Asia and Africa are diagnosed as they emerged into the world of nationalism.

Hence, nationalism is situated within modernity and analysed as a product of struggles for power by social groups that are brought into existence by policies of modernization. Ideology enters the scene, not as an independent force, but is itself a 'constituent' of political action. Nationalism uses ideology as a justification of its practices. It translates the abstract nature of ideology through symbolism and ceremonial. By the use of symbols, such as personality cults, or in ceremonies, re-enacting and celebrating glorious movements of national history, it makes the nation a palpable object.

To Breuilly, it was in Europe that nationalism began its long journey which eventually encircled the whole globe. This journey of nationalism has its roots in the early monarchical policies of centralization, leading in due course, and beginning with the eighteenth century, to modernization and secularization. However, it is the opposition generated by these policies of modernization and centralization that marks the birth of nationalist movements. Opposition politics is thus the form which nationalism embodies in its encounter with the institutions of a modern state. Such an opposition may assume three different forms:

> A nationalist opposition can seek to break away from the present state (separation), to reform it in a nationalist direction (reform), or to unify it with other states (unification).

However, Breuilly exhibits an ambivalent attitude towards his subject which is the result of seeing nationalism as simply a form of political action. His discussion of the Italian and German unification movements is a case in point. He is at pains to show that unification came about as a result of political ambitions and actions rather than a well co-ordinated nationalist policy. As a matter of fact, he succeeds in showing how meagre and inconsequential nationalism figured in the process of unification in comparison to the political will of Cavour or Bismarck.[52]

Finally, E. J. Hobsbawm's *Nations and Nationalism since 1780*[53] may serve as a conclusion to our survey. Hobsbawm's contribution to the study of nationalism resides in his differentiation between a golden age of nationalism, closely connected with the rise of liberalism in the nineteenth century, and a degenerate form largely associated with the second half of the twentieth century. In its golden age, nationalism was inclusive and essentially tolerant, aiming to create nations out of a motley of disparate communities and divergent social groups. Needless to say, this was the classical age of industrialization and the rise of the middle classes coupled with a vigorous trade union movement. After World War II, Hobsbawm asserts, a sinister form of nationalism began to emerge centred on the notion of ethnicity and exclusive notions of communal self-determination. In other words, whereas for Smith the ethnic origins of nations preceded nationalism as we know it in the contemporary world, the sequence of development is inverted and what once seemed to be a positive process of development is reduced to a regrettable degeneration. It is for this reason that what appears to be a potent force is merely an illusion destined to be swept away by the tide of globalization and an international type of supranational institutions.[54]

In the course of theorizing nationalism, all the texts discussed above allude to Arab nationalism in one way or another. Except for Kedourie, their occasional references seem to be either neutral or largely appreciative of its modern connotations. However, this appreciation is sometimes marred by historical inaccuracies which are largely the result of relying on secondary sources.

Needless to say, Smith, Gellner, Breuilly and Hobsbawm consider Arab nationalism as a modern movement, generated and structured by the intrusion of the industrial world into the heart of the Ottoman empire.

Gellner perceives a direct corrolation between Islamic reformism and Arab nationalism. He even goes further by equating the two, thereby making them inseparable.[55] Smith, contrary to Gellner, sees the task of Arab nationalism riddled with difficulties stemming from the dispersed nature of the Arab world, historically, geographically, demographically and politically. Neither Islam nor language, according to Smith, have succeeded in countering 'these geo-political cleavages'. Thus Arab nationalism has so far failed to establish a clear direction based on territorial or ethnic norms of nationhood.[56]

Breuilly, on the other hand, deals with Arab nationalism as a separatist movement in the Ottoman Empire. It was, moreover, an 'anti-colonial movement' as well as a movement of 'unification'. Despite Breuilly's misgivings of attaching much importance to culture and intellectual interpretations, he is willing to concede 'the importance of nationalist intellectuals in Arab nationalism'.[57] However, while he correctly alludes to the central role of intellectuals, such as Michel 'Aflaq and Sati' al-Husri in the twentieth century, he ventures to make the following erroneous statement:

> the intellectual origins of Arab nationalism can, in fact, be understood in another way. The Maronite Christian community on which it was centred could use the concept of nationality as a way of overcoming its separation from the Muslim majority surrounding it. (p. 150)

While one could plausibly point to a number of Maronite individuals who espoused some sort of Arabism, 'the Maronite community', as such had no truck with Arab nationalism, exhibiting on numerous occasions an outright hostility towards its aims. However, Breuilly is on firmer ground when he goes on to highlight 'the limited development of nationalism' in the Arab territories prior to World War I (p. 154). He also correctly observes that Arab nationalism is still a strong movement despite its failure to achieve the concrete unification of its nation. (p. 286).

Finally, Hobsbawm contends that Arab nationalism 'is today identified with Islam' to the bewilderment of its friends and enemies alike. Its 'first hints' manifested themselves in the Ottoman Empire in the late nineteenth century. It was, moreover, a pan movement, akin to 'pan-Africanism' or 'pan-Latin Americanism' and has consequently to be classified as being 'supra-nationalist'.[58]

2
Narrating the Nation

How do the Arabs themselves perceive the history of their own nation? To what extent are the formation of the nation and the emergence of nationalism interlinked? Was the Arab nation the outcome of a nationalist movement bent on creating its own political identity, or did Arab nationalism develop in response to the prior existence of its nation?

By and large, Arab nationalists insist on the existence of their nation as an historical entity, long before the rise of a nationalist movement embodying the latent potentialities of a concrete human community. Thus, the nation had to exist in order for certain individuals and groups to become aware of its unique identity. One could summarize this particular formulation in the following manner:

The Arab nation came into being with the gradual elaboration of Arabic as a language of communication and the advent of Islam as a new culture and set of institutions. Thus the Arabic language and historical Islam constitute the cornerstone of the nation.

In this sense, Arab nationalism represents the Arabs' consciousness of their specific characteristics as well as their endeavour to build a modern state capable of representing the common will of the nation and all its constituent parts.

This elaborate scheme of differentiation is even carried further by some Arab nationalists. For example, one of the founding members of the Ba'th party, the Syrian Jalal al-Sayyid (1913–92), published in 1973 a book designed to show the relationship between the Arab nation and its nationalist movement.[1] In it, al-Sayyid distinguishes between three different entities: the Arab nation, Arab nationalism and the movement of Arab unity. Thus:

the Arab nation is that human collectivity which speaks the Arabic language, inhabits a territory called the Arab lands and has a voluntary and spontaneous feeling of belonging to that nation. (p. 49)

On the other hand,

> Arab nationalism is the sum total of characteristics, qualities and hallmarks which are exclusive to the collectivity called the Arab nation, [whereas] Arab unity is a modern notion, which stipulates that all disparate Arab countries should be formed into one single political system under one single state. (p 40)

Moreover, the movement of Arab unity is a transitory phenomenon, while the other two are eternal. Curiously, Arab nationalism is said to have been submerged in tribalism in pre-Islamic times, and in religion with the rise of Islam (pp. 75–6). Hence, Arab nationalism did not come into its own and manifest itself in its true identity until modern times (p. 142). In other words, both Arab nationalism and the movement of Arab unity are modern developments.

In my book *Arab History and the Nation-state 1820–1980*,[2] I put forward the idea that the advent of a new style of history – writing in the Arab World accompanied a modern sense of national awareness. This new style was particularly apparent in the production of books narrating the history of a particular Arab country in a non-annalistic and non-dynastic manner. It was a new genre of history-writing whereby historical data and events are organized according to a linear plan of continuous development. Thus, whereas classical and medieval chroniclers in the Arab/Islamic world, such as al-Tabari (d. 923), Ibn al-Athir (d. 1233), Ibn Khaldun (d. 1406) and al-Maqrizi (d. 1442), adhered to a scheme whereby events are grouped under a particular year or a dynasty, and irrespective of territorial boundaries or national allegiances, modern Arab historians adopted a well-defined national territory to act as the theatre or site of unfolding events. In this sense, it is the national territory itself, rather than other criteria, that lends events their significance and determines the manner of their distribution. Thus, the past acquired its own pattern of historical development, turning dynasties into mere expressions of the particular character of one's fatherland or *watan*. This was the case in Egypt and Syria in the second half of the nineteenth century and in most Arab countries in the first half of the twentieth.

It is in this context that one may offer the suggestion that local patriotism, focused on a particular Arab country, such as Egypt, Tunisia or Iraq, preceded the rise of pan-Arabism as a movement of national consciousness embracing the entire Arab world as we know it today. Nevertheless, this local patriotism was itself based on a common fund of Arab culture, values and certain glorious episodes of Islamic history and which could be associated with the national territory. Even when the pre-Islamic past of particular Arab countries (the Pharaohs of Egypt, the Canaanites of Syria and Lebanon, the Sumerians, Babylonians and Assyrians of Iraq) was appropriated as an integral part of the local national cultures, pan-Arabism did not flinch from widening its scope by incorporating this new element within its modern paradigm. This was done in the 1920s by postulating Arabia as the cradle of all the Semites who had migrated over the centuries and paved the way for the latest wave of Arab migration,[3] or by co-opting all pre-Islamic cultures of the Near East into an evolving Arab identity.

Lessons of History

One of the first modern histories of the Arab nation in contrast to a mere history of a particular Arab country, was written by an Arab nationalist activist of Palestinian origin in the late 1920s. The text in question was composed by Muhammad 'Izzat Darwazah (1887–1984) under the title *Lessons of Arab History: From Antiquity to the Present Time*.[4] It was intended to be used as a text book in primary or secondary schools, hence its direct and simplified language. However, its pioneering character is all the more apparent. be it in its general approach or pan-Arab purview.

Having secondary school pupils as its audience, the text depicts the various episodes of Arab history with a view to showing their interconnected nature and common background, along with the moral lesson to be deduced thereof.

Darwazah was born in the Palestinian city of Nablus, where he received his primary and secondary education. In his memoirs,[5] he gives a graphic and almost exhaustive description of his hometown at the end of the nineteenth century: its shops, mosques, residential quarters, orchards, industries and inhabitants. Moreover, he dwells at length on the social composition of the town, endeavouring to reveal the open conflict between what he calls 'the feudal families'[6] and the new generation of middle traders, functionaries, civil servants and teachers. In addition to Arabic, Darwazah learnt Turkish and French, but left school without going on to either Istanbul or Beirut to finish his education as was the custom of his generation. Instead, he joined the post office as a telegraphist, rising in due course to the position of district manager. More importantly, in 1916 he joined a secret society called the Young Arab Society or al-Fatat. This society developed as a result of the 1908 Young Turk revolution and the tension it generated between the various national communities of the Ottoman empire: Arabs, Turks, Armenians, Albanians, Serbs, Greeks and others.

Darwazah begins his narration with the origins of the Semites. Iraq, rather than Arabia, is considered to be the cradle of the Semitic race. The twin rivers, the Euphrates and Tigris overflowed their banks at an uncertain date and covered the entire Mesopotamian landscape with an enormous flood. In order to escape the fate of those who had already drowned, entire communities fled south into the Arabian peninsula and settled in it as their new homeland. Once in Arabia, and although they had previously tilled the land and were known for their farming skills, these migrant communities reverted to nomadism. Spreading out into the desert, these nomads formed themselves into tribal groups, with each tribe trying to secure for itself adequate pastureland. As their numbers multiplied, and water and land resources became scarce, they began to migrate once again into the south and the north, embracing in their migrations the Yemen, Iraq, Syria and Palestine. Having settled in these lands which were already inhabited by populations enjoying a high degree of urban and agrarian prosperity, they were gradually integrated into a new mode of life and developed with the passage of time into 'new nations' known to history as the Babylonians, Assyrians and Akkadians in Iraq, and the Phoenicians, Canaanites, Aramaeans and Hebrews in Syria and Palestine. As for those tribes which had stayed behind, they were eventually known as 'the Arabs'. They are all considered by historians to belong to 'the Semitic nations'.[7]

Having established the common origins of the ancient civilizations of the Near East,[8] he immediately highlights the fact that 'the inhabitants of Palestine, Iraq, Syria, Lebanon, Egypt, Tunisia, Algeria, Morocco, the Egyptian Sudan,[9] the Yemen, Najd and al-Hijaz,[10] nowadays speak the Arabic language'. While Arabic as a spoken language may vary widely in some of its idioms, there is one single literary language. Thanks to the Qur'an, modern schools, newspapers and books, standard Arabic acts as the common language of all the Arabs. Thus, common ethnic origins and a literary standard language establish at this initial stage of the narrative the implied unity of a nation and its subsequent development. This development unfolds along three interrelated periods embracing pre-Islamic Arabia, the rise and expansion of Islam and the modern Arab world. Each period had its own socio-economic, political and cultural character, with the common thread of Arab identity running through their differing fortunes.

Pre-Islamic Arabia includes the ancient civilization of the Yemen, and the states which were set up by the Arabs in southern Iraq, Jordan and Syria. The historian repeatedly draws the attention of his audience to the urban and settled characteristics of these states, in contrast to their nomadic and tribal roots. Hence, trade, agriculture and the organization of military forces, either independently or in alliance with the great imperial powers of the day (Byzantium and Persia) constituted the solid foundations of an ever-expanding community (pp. 58–73).[11]

The Rise of Islam

The rise of Islam is introduced against the background of the growing role of trade in both the Yemen and Western Arabia, particularly Mecca. Moreover, the historian underlines the significance of Mecca as a religious centre and the emergence of Quraysh as its most prestigious tribe under the leadership of Qusayy. This is said to have taken place some two hundred years before the birth of the Prophet Muhammad.[12] The emergence of Quraysh at the head of an alliance of various Arabian tribes signalled a shift in economic and political power from southern Arabia, dominated by the Qahtanids, who are said to be the original Arabs, in favour of the 'Adnanites, known to history as northern Arabized tribes (pp. 74–8).

Darwazah devotes eight 'lessons' of his history to the life and career of the Prophet Muhammad. He is shown to be a direct descendant of Qusayy, the founder of the fortunes of Mecca and consequently Quraysh. He, like his ancestor, grew up to be a trader and a trusted leader of men. His morality and trustworthiness attracted the attention of a wealthy Qurayshite widow, by the name of Khadija, who asked him 'to share in her trading activities'. He willingly accepted the offer and went on to make 'enormous profits'. As he confirmed her trust in him, she offered to be his wife and he agreed (pp. 79–81).

In his early forties, Muhammad was endowed by God with the gift of prophethood. He was commanded to call upon his community to foresake paganism and worship one single God. Henceforth, Qur'anic verses were revealed to him. At the beginning only a few people believed in his mission, whereas the majority turned against him. It was this mounting enmity of a commercial community, clinging to its pagan gods and their lucrative revenues, which convinced the Prophet to respond to the invitation of a delegation of the northern town of Yathrib. Yathrib, renamed Medina, was an agrarian settlement inhabited by warring Arab tribes as well as a number of Jewish clans.[13] This act of emigration, which was later adopted to mark the first year of the Muslim calendar,[14] is singled out by Darawazah as one of the most momentous events in the history of Islam. Its significance lies in the way the Prophet and his companions risked their lives for the sake of their mission. It was this mission which 'announced the advent of the glory of Islam and the Arabs' (pp. 82–5).

Once in Medina, the Prophet endeavoured to bring to an end the enmity between the two principal Arab tribes: the Aws and the Khazraj. A new community began to emerge composed of Meccan migrants (*al-muhajirun*) and Medinan supporters (*al-ansar*) or helpers. Darawazah concentrates on the religious, moral and economic ties which were woven by the Prophet as the leader of a united society. Thus:

> After the Prophet, Peace be upon him, had brought harmony between the Aws and the Khazraj and made the migrants and the helpers associate as brothers, he began to preach the message of Islam to the Arab tribes, and teach Muslims moral values such as truthfulness, honesty, the practice of prayer, alms-giving, cleanliness and veracity, calling upon them to refrain from vices such as drunkenness, gambling, stealing, lying, causing harm to others, hypocrisy, fraud, false testimony, calumny and defamation. The Arabs began to respond to his message, enlist under his banner and flock into God's religion in throngs. For they saw in his message and sayings truthfulness and in his deeds noble characteristics. Hence, their morals started to improve, their habits to become upright, and their coarseness was turned into kindness and civility". (pp. 85–6)

It was these characteristics which enabled the Prophet to conquer Mecca after eight years of his migration. The conquest of Mecca in 630 AD marked another watershed in the history of Islam and paved the way for the conversion of all the Arabs.

With the rise of the Umayyads, Darwazah signals a number of social, economic and political changes in the fortunes of Islam as an Arab and universal religion. Being an exercise in civic education and a tool of inculcating modern notions of government and national awareness, the text, unlike medieval Muslim chronicles, takes these changes for granted. It, moreover, adumbrates their significance as part of a progressive and inevitable march of historical events. Thus, the struggle between the fourth Caliph 'Ali and Mu'awiyah is depicted in neutral terms and without burdening the event with the curse of schism in the community as previous traditional Arab historians tended to do. In this sense, the emergence of the Kharijites, or seceders, who objected to Ali's conciliatory approach to the conflict is said to be a natural development related to the appearance of opposition or dissident groups in all political societies. So is the growing sect of Shi'ites who rallied to the cause of 'Ali and his descendants as the only legitimate heirs to the Prophet. Another Shi'ite sect, the Isma'ilis, are also introduced, but who more properly belong to the successors of the Umayyads. More importantly, the extravagance and largesse of the Umayyads, in contrast to the moderation and simplicity of the early Caliphs, are attributed to difference in place and time. The early Arabs were sons of the desert, lived the lives of nomads, and expanded most of their energies in wars of conquest. By contrast, the Umayyads established their capital in one of the most advanced urban centres and in countries which had been governed by the great Pharaonic dynasties, as well as the Phoenicians, the Greeks and the Romans. Moreover, the kings of these conquered lands had had servants, slaves, palaces, chamberlains, clerks, ministers, minted currency, and built schools, temples, churches and libraries. The Umayyads, along with the Arabs, seeing their subjects were used to a refined urban life, were impelled to follow suit (pp. 129–34).

Whereas the Umayyad dynasty lost its power as a result of internal quarrels, the 'Abbasids began their relentless decline the moment they allowed Turkic elements to dominate their army and Persian bureaucrats to run the central administration. This decline was, moreover, a long, drawn-out process which did not reveal its full implications until the Ottomans established themselves as the masters of the Arab world following their defeat of the Mamluks in 1516 and 1517 (pp. 149–50).

The Modern Age

Napoleon's invasion of Egypt and Syria at the end of the eighteenth century is implicitly introduced as the beginning of the modern history of the Arabs.

The invasion is explained in terms of a wider Anglo-French rivalry to gain the upper hand in Europe and the East. Competition to secure new markets, and consequently increase trade, is said to lie behind this rivalry. The French were defeated by a combination of British naval power, Ottoman military resistance and popular opposition. Nevertheless, Napoleon's brief excursion alerted the Muslims to the meaning of 'liberty' and its benefits. Publications and learned studies by scholars who had accompanied Napoleon on his expedition began to make Egyptians aware of the importance of their culture (pp. 183–6).

Nevertheless, Darwazah links the rise of modern Arabism to the historical experiences of Greater Syria. According to him, Syria was

Map 2.1   The Arab Empire, 632–750 AD:
from Spain to the borders of China

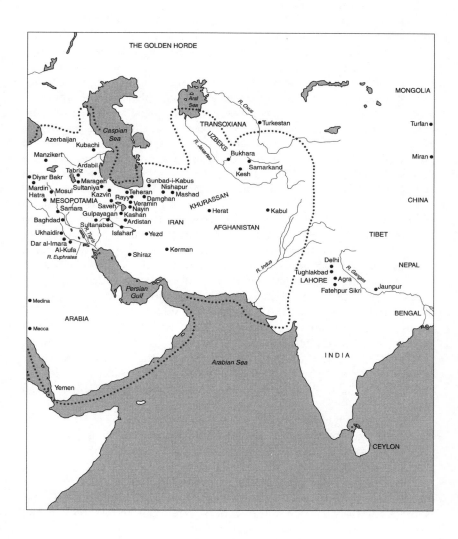

THE GOLDEN HORDE

MONGOLIA

Azerbaijan
Kubachi
Caspian
Sea
TRANSOXIANA
R. Oxus
Turkestan
Turfan
Aral
Sea
UZBEKS
R. Jaxartes
Miran
Manzikert
Ardabil
Tabriz
Diyar Bakr
Mardin
Hatra
Mosul
Sultaniya
MESOPOTAMIA
Samara
Baghdad
Ukhaidir
Dar al-Imara
Al-Kufa
R. Euphrates
Kazvin
Rayy
Saveh
Gulpayagan
Sultanabad
R. Tigris
Isfahan
Teheran
Damghan
Veramin
Nayin
Kashan
Ardistan
Gunbad-i-Kabus
Nishapur
Mashad
KHURASSAN
Herat
Kabul
CHINA
Bukhara
Samarkand
Kesh
IRAN
AFGHANISTAN
TIBET
Yezd
Kerman
Shiraz
R. Indus
NEPAL
Delhi
Tughlakbad
LAHORE
Agra
Fatehpur Sikri
Jaunpur
Persian
Gulf
BENGAL
Medina
ARABIA
Mecca
Arabian Sea
INDIA
Yemen
CEYLON

ideally placed to initiate the movement of Arab renaissance: it boasted a bustling urban life brought about by the intelligence and energy of its inhabitants and their commercial and cultural interaction with various European communities.[15]

However, 'the real Arab renaissance in Syria did not become fully apparent until the proclamation of the constitution' of 1908. It was only then that the Arabs of Syria began to articulate their national demands. These included the adoption of Arabic, rather than Turkish, as the official language of Syria; the building of a network of schools; the establishment of representative local councils; and the appointment of Arabs to all official posts in Syria. In order to ensure the achievement of these demands, associations were founded and Syrian deputies in the Ottoman parliament in Istanbul consistently voiced their support of this programme (p. 207). However, the leaders of the Young Turks, Tal'at (1874–1921), Enver (1881–1922) and Jamal (1872–1922) showed no particular interest in Arab demands.

The outbreak of World War I only served to accelerate an inevitable outcome. The Ottoman state entered the war against Britain and its allies. To make matters worse, Jamal Pasha, a person known for 'his cruelty' and hatred of the Arabs, was appointed Supreme Commander of the Fourth Ottoman Army and Governor of Syria. His acts of cruelty included the arrest and execution of leading lights of the Arab renaissance. Thus, these arrests and executions of prominent Syrian leaders in 1915 and 1916 were yet another painful reminder of the gulf that separated Arabs and Turks. It was at this juncture that the descendant of the Prophet, Sharif Husayn of Mecca (1854–1931), came to the conclusion that the Arabs were more worthy of the Caliphate and fully entitled to their political independence. Thus, the Arab revolt was proclaimed on 10 June 1916 (pp. 206–8).

Having sketched the trajectory of a wide range of historical events, stretching back over two thousand years, Darwazah brings his narration to its logical conclusion by indicating a number of moral and practical lessons.

Towards the beginning of his narration, the cultural unity of the Arabs was simply assumed to consist of a common language which has as its point of reference a noble book, the Qur'an. Moreover, the modern period, with its schools, newspapers and books, has facilitated the spread and learning of standard Arabic, as opposed to varying dialects (p. 2). In the conclusion the existence of 'an ancient' Arab nation with a glorious pre-Islamic past which Islam strengthened and superseded by becoming its great achievement, is taken for granted. However, the lessons of history are said to reveal moments of astounding cultural and material accomplishment, and other moments of weakness and degradation. Nations prosper as a result of high morals, devotion to one's duty and sincerity in word and deed. Bad habits of selfishness, greed and false ambition invariably lead to rapid decline and loss of good government. Nowadays, the text continues, the Arab nation has fallen far behind 'Western nations in science, power and civilization'. It has, moreover, become the victim of direct foreign rule. Hence the obligations upon the shoulders of young men[16] had to include an entire programme of moral and national rejuvenation (pp. 216–17).

Thus ends the first modern history of the Arab nation on a note of moral exhortation and rectitude.

Darwish al-Miqdadi: The Nation in History

Darwish al-Miqdadi's *History of the Arab Nation*,[17] published in four successive editions between 1931 and 1939, belongs to an Arab nationalist trend that leaves ample room for local loyalties and allegiances. Its flexible stance, associated with the thought of the first systematic Arab nationalist writer, Sati' al-Husri (1879–1968), allowed it to posit the case for Arab unity in a manner that combined *Wataniyyah* (local patriotism) and *qawmiyya* (nationalism or pan-Arabism), judging both, once properly evaluated, to be complementary rather than mutually exclusive. It was officially approved by the Iraqi Ministry of Education to be used as a textbook in the secondary schools.[18]

Al-Miqdadi (1898–1961) was born in the village of Tibat Bani Sa'b, in the district of Tulkarm, Palestine. He received his education at the Ottoman Islamic College and the American University of Beirut, specializing in history, literature and sociology. He was to spend the rest of his life in various posts associated with teaching and educational administration. After his graduation (1922), he first worked in Jerusalem before moving to Iraq in 1927 where he joined the Teachers' Higher Training College. He was involved during this period in propagating nationalist ideas, working in close cooperation with Sati' al-Husri who dominated the Iraqi education system at the time. He also became a founding member of the Futuwwah Youth Organisation headed by Sami Shawkat, who replaced al-Husri as Director General of Education in 1933. The last revised edition of his text, to which references are being made here, was banned by the British authorities in 1941, following the failure of Rashid 'Ali al-Kaylani's revolt. As to the author's fate, he was arrested and spent four years in prison. In 1946 he was appointed Director of the Arab Bureau in Jerusalem. From 1948 to 1950 he taught history at the University of Damascus. However, between 1950 and 1961 he was employed by the Education Department of Kuwait. It was during those years that he wrote another history book, but its scope was much reduced and confined to Kuwait itself.

It is perhaps this last book that gives us an appropriate perspective in dealing with his *History of the Arab Nation*. It is, therefore, apt at this juncture to ask the following questions. How does al-Miqdadi organize his theoretical vision of his Umma? What particular elements enter into his historical structure? To what extent does he succeed in arguing the case for Arab unity on the basis of one single state, be it in the past, the present, or the future?

Historical Structures

The text itself is divided into four separate parts.[19] The first part treats the history of pre-Islamic Arabs, the formative period of Islam, the Arab conquests, the foundation of the Umayyad and 'Abbasid dynasties, the Crusades and the cultural and literary contributions of the 'Abbasid period as well as the topography of Baghdad (pp. 1–293). The second part deals exclusively with Islamic Spain down to the fall of Granada in 1492 (pp. 299–331), while the third part concentrates on 'Arab Africa' stretching from Egypt to Morocco (pp. 337–51). The fourth and final part returns to what al-Miqdadi terms throughout his text *al-jazira al-'arabiyya* or the Arabian peninsula, and which includes in his definition Arabia proper, in addition to Greater Syria and Iraq (pp. 355–81).

This novel definition of the Arabian Peninsula is remarkable for a number of reasons. It seems that al-Miqdadi demarcated such a large geographic entity in order to construct his own definition of the origins and development of the Arab nation. Thus, the Arabian peninsula is said to be composed of three interlinked organs, each with its own function and operating as 'one living body' or organism. The Fertile Crescent is said to be the head of this body having two wings, Iraq and Syria (*bilad al-sham*), while the coastal regions, extending from the Gulf of 'Aqaba to the Gulf of Basra, constitute the limbs of the body. The heart is located in the hinterland, particularly the region of Najd. It is this heart that the author considers to be the birthplace of the Semites 'from the days of the Babylonians down to the period of the Wahhabites' (pp. 2–5).

Such a biological analogy is clearly weighted in favour of Syria and

Iraq. Whereas Arabia provides 'the heart and the limbs', or the primary material and the blood that circulates in the veins of the modern Arabs, the Fertile Crescent represents the seat of the intellect and the perceptive power of the nation. Although Egypt, the Sudan and North Africa are considered an integral part of the Arab nation, their history does not figure in the text until 336 pages have been devoted to this 'living organism'.

Having postulated the birth of the Arab nation as a biological entity, al-Miqdadi proceeds to narrate its early growth, maturity and degeneration. Nevertheless, this same organism is deemed capable of self-renewal and regeneration. Hence the title of the final part: the cycle of apathy and that of awakening (*dawr al-ghafla wa dawr al-yaqza*).

Al-Miqdadi's historical configurations are tightly controlled throughout the text by two dominant themes: the role of the Arabs as state-builders and as creators of a flourishing civilization. Consequently, the narration of events is carried forward by the twin ideas of state-building and cultural creation. In one sense, the Arabs emerge as one national group worthy of independence, sovereignty and freedom. However, this positivity is achieved at the expense of forging political unity crowned by the institutions of one national state.

The functional units of al-Miqdadi's historical analysis allow him to use past precedents for the sake of overcoming the shortcomings of the present. After all, in 1939 only four Arab states had a semblance of independence: North Yemen, Saudi Arabia, Iraq and Egypt.

State-building is shown to be a characteristic of Arab history long before the rise of Islam. Thus it is explicitly stated that the state built by Hammurabi (d. 1750 BC) in Iraq and the dynasty of the Hyksos which ruled lower Egypt from about the eighteenth to the sixteenth century BC were both founded by Semitic emigrants from the heart of Arabia (pp. 7–8). He also dedicates a separate chapter to 'the trading states'. These include Petra, Palmyra and the Yemenite Kingdoms. Zenobia (267–272 AD), the Queen of Palmyra (Tadmur), is celebrated in these words:

> She was renowned for her courage, patriotism and beauty: she was brown of complexion, had black eyes, pearl teeth and was well-built. She used to wear the helmet on her head and a suit of armour plate on her chest, riding horses, girding on her sword, reviewing troops and fighting the enemy. In addition to Arabic, she was fluent in Aramaic, Latin and Greek. She also administered the affairs of her Kingdom in person. This is Zenobia, the heroine of the Arab desert who led her people to glory ... When her husband died she proclaimed her

country's independence, expelled the Romans and extended the borders of her state to the extremities of Iraq and to the north of Syria (pp. 12–13).

Although Zenobia failed in her endeavours, the legacy she left behind is held up to posterity as an example of Arab patriotism and institution-building. It is also worth noting that this celebration of the feats of an Arab woman fits into a general modernist view that al-Miqdadi is anxious to inculcate. Throughout his text, he chooses an opportune moment or a relevant event to announce the role of Arab women as full partners in conquests, socio-cultural affairs and even political activities (pp. 32, 110, 130, 180, 189, 209–10, 261, 294). Describing the social conditions of the Bedouins in pre-Islamic Arabia he states:

> As far as woman was concerned, she enjoyed a great deal of freedom: she used to practise numerous activities in her household ranging from spinning and weaving to cooking and treating her guests with hospitality. She also used to choose her own husband while her father did not force her to marry someone she did not love. (p. 32)

As for Muhammad, he is deemed to have 'enacted laws which enhanced the status of woman and bestowed on her rights which are in some aspects wider than those enjoyed by Western woman' (p. 110). Having demonstrated the ability of an Arab woman to lead an army in battle and conduct the affairs of a well-organized state, he gives another example from the Islamic period. In the course of discussing the political activities and beliefs of the Kharijites, he singles out the revolt of Shabib b. Yazid b. Nu'aym of Shayban (Shabib al-Shaybani) against the forces of the governor of Iraq, al-Hajjaj, in 76 H/695–7. Relying on the work of 'Abd al-Qahir al-Baghdadi (d. 429/1037), *al-Farq bayna al-firaq*, he mentions a raid on Kufa in which Shabib led an army composed of one thousand men and 200 women. Amongst his troops there was his mother Ghazala[20] and his wife Juhayza. Upon Shabib's entry 'into the mosque of Kufa, his mother Ghazala went forward, ascended the pulpit and addressed the congregation. The followers of Shabib used to say that a woman had the right to be caliph'. The school pupils are also informed that upon Shabib's death, his mother took over the leadership and went on fighting until she was killed along with Juhayza. He concludes this section by emphasizing that 'the history of the Kharijites was full of heroism, courage and faith' (p. 181).

The decline of the status of Arab women is attributed to the 'Abbasid practice of polygamy, particularly by marrying foreign women, a fact which affected 'the upbringing of children and weakened their national affiliation'. Moreover, al-Miqdadi contends that the habit of wearing the veil was originally a Persian one, becoming widespread only during the same 'Abbasid period. But 'it is not one of the customs of the Arabs, and Islam does not impose it on woman' (p. 210). This novel idea is amplified in another passage, and woman's freedom and independence of mind are emphatically defended as an integral part of Arab traditions and Islamic culture (p. 262). The veil is explicitly shown to be harmful and of foreign origin, whereas polygamy served to weaken both the 'Abbasid state and family (p. 294).

By showing the positive aspects of Arab culture and its open-mindedness towards women, al-Miqdadi amalgamates pre-Islamic and Islamic history into one single unit. The Arabs had a developed civilization and administered complicated state structures in both periods. The age of *jahiliyya* loses its decadent and primitive connotations, and is rendered one of prosperity and high cultural values. He thus gives as irrefutable evidence the fact that in ancient Yemen the Arabs 'had their own organised states' ruled by kings whose main aim was to 'build cities, palaces and dams' (p. 17). The Lakhmids of al-Hira, the Ghassanids of Syria and the Kindites of Yamama are all considered to have established their own states before the rise of Islam (pp. 12–22). A chapter is devoted to Mecca and Yathrib entitled: The Centres of Civilisation in the Hijaz (pp. 23–8).

Islam itself emerges as a response to a crisis in Arab society characterized by the collapse of their states and the loss of trade – the basis of their civilization; facing the constant rivalry of Byzantium and Persia, the Arabs tried various solutions to their dilemma, but to no avail.

It was in Mecca, a city riven by social conditions, pitting greedy merchants and usurers against poor and downtrodden masses, that the economic crisis was exacerbated by a spiritual longing for a higher order of things. At this juncture Muhammad enters the scene, combining in his character and teachings the mission of a saviour and the qualities of a consummate statesman. The Prophet's career interrupts the numerical order of al-Miqdadi's chapters whereby the title of this section is the only one in the text that is printed in bold face. The headings read:

Our High Ideal
Muhammad
Our Prophet and Guide

then a subheading sums up Muhammad's achievements:

> The founder of our great Arab State, the unifier of our nation, our national hero and social reformer. (p. 48)

Lessons of History and Temporal Distances

Although al-Miqdadi's text presents facts and events in a manner that does not violate the broad rules of historical objectivity, its educational and national purpose is not lost sight of. Indeed, pupils were being moulded to embrace the virtues of modern citizenship, national unity and service to the fatherland. One of the first lessons is derived from the intermittent quarrels between the two Arab vassal Kingdoms of the Lakhmids and the Ghassanids. Had these kinsmen cooperated with each other, al-Miqdadi avers, the Sassanians and the Byzantines would have not managed to establish their hegemony over the Fertile Crescent. Hence, 'foreign rule endures in a country as a result of divisions amongst its people' (p. 20).

History also teaches modern Arabs that a small but well-organized group could overcome much more numerous enemies and establish its dominance under a capable leader. This was the case of Muhammad during the Medinan phase of his struggle. Furthermore, al-Miqdadi draws an analogy between the rise of Medina as the centre of a vast state and that of Rome, 'which used to be a mere collection of small villages until its rulers turned it into the capital of a mighty empire' (p. 92).

The battle of al-Qadisiyya, in which the Arabs scored a decisive victory over the Persian army in 637, is another illustration of the crucial impact a steadfast belief yields in bringing about the triumph of a small group over a much larger one driven by force rather than conviction (p. 129).

Arab history, al-Miqdadi asserts, did not always produce a glowing record of glorious deeds. Under such circumstances the historian interrupts the flow of events in order to stage a timely intervention designed to neutralize the negative connotations of his factual data. The internecine rivalry between the Hashemites and the Umayyads is invested with neutrality by referring to its pre-Islamic origins, on the one hand, and pronouncing the followers of both to be 'our forefathers', on the other. Consequently, studying their differences means an exercise in learning the lesson of avoiding 'the harmful effects of conflict' on pan-Arabism. The text underlines this message in these words: 'We are Arab first and foremost and our aim is to unite the community of the Arabs. Our motto is: "in the name of the Arabs we live and in their name we die". Nowadays every nation is proud of its nationalism and traditions' (pp. 159–60). Similarly, the tragedy of Karbala' is said to have been an inevitable occurrence, given the strong beliefs and values of the people involved. Each party felt that if it succumbed to an unacceptable authority, it would be answerable for its actions to God and the people. Everyone wishes, al-Miqdadi asserts, that this and other divisive events did not take place. However, historical conditions, determined by the ethos of a certain community made the conflict unavoidable (p. 127). In this example and the previous one, al-Miqdadi manages to draw a proper moral lesson and establish a certain temporal distance between his age and that of his Arab ancestors; he even does not shy away from alluding to some positive characteristics possessed by the arch-enemies of the Arabs. The fall of the Umayyads is thus explicitly attributed to the tribal rivalries of the Arabs who, unlike the Persians, were not imbued with a healthy respect for the individual irrespective of his social status (p. 198).

Temporal distances, established by al-Miqdadi at the relevant juncture of events, are mainly meant to subsume religion under his modern notion of nationalism. Thus the policy of 'Umar b. al-Khattab to expel non-Muslims from 'the heart of Arabia' was dictated by a desire to create a harmonious society. Since religion constituted in those days 'the distinguishing feature between peoples', his expulsions have to be understood within this particular historical context. However, this temporal distance is partially undermined when immediately in the second sentence the text justifies 'Umar's decision by pointing to the exchange of populations between Greece and Turkey after World War I (p. 147).

Institutions, as well as historical events, originate at a particular time in order to meet, or respond to, the needs of the moment. In this sense, the Caliphate figures in the text as a human device forged 'to protect religion, despite the fact that in the Qur'an there are no explicit stipulations pertaining to the Caliphate or the Caliphs'. In another passage, al-Miqdadi explains that the Caliph was selected by a limited number of people, namely the helpers and the emigrants. Although the Umma had a say in electing its leader, this procedure was rarely adhered to, particularly upon the appointment of 'Umar b. al-Khattab and 'Uthman (pp. 178, 202).

Towards the end of his text, al-Miqdadi discusses the modern emergence of Arab nationalism by referring to a number of movements, individuals and events. Napoleon's invasion of Egypt and Syria is followed by the rise of Muhammad 'Alī, the revolt of the Wahhabi-

tes, the foundation of local and missionary schools and the rise of an
enlightened Arab intelligentsia. Both Muhammad 'Ali's policies and
Wahhabism, despite 'the Albanian origins' and personal ambitions of
the former and 'the Islamic overtones' of the latter, restored a certain
sense of Arab greatness. Nevertheless, the outbreak of World War I
exposed the weaknesses and shallow nature of Arab nationalism. In
fact, Arab nationalism at the time was confined to a few youth
associations, while 'the common people had no knowledge of Arab
nationalism, and thought that to rebel against the caliph was a
forbidden act' (p. 369).

Throughout the text, the Arab nation is dealt with as a historical
entity composed of countries, states and cultural traditions. It is these
structures which lend al-Miqdadi's narrative its significance and unity
of purpose. The text's modernism is demonstrated by an approach
that seeks to build a viable national community with a glorious
historical record. Rivalries, bloody encounters and setbacks are either
explained on the basis of peculiar social and political junctures, or as a
result of overwhelming odds exemplified by western expansionism.
The text succeeds in achieving its intention without turning into a
cheap piece of propaganda. However, the unity of the Arabs emerges
as a cultural and national enterprise as well as a political possibility, be
it in the past or the future.

Notwithstanding its broad scope and fair treatment of varied political differences and dynastic conflict, the text is to a large extent the
product of its Iraqi environment. Iraq, both as a state and a country,
can be seen as the determining factor in the interpretation of events
in an almost neutral tone.

Iraq, moreover, is privileged throughout its history. It is the cradle
of civilization. The Arab conquests first take place on its territory and
continue to work out their ramifications by means of sustaining a
continuous narration of Iraqi events, showing both its gradual conquest and organization under one authority. Moreover, of all the Arab
cities, only Baghdad is made the subject of detailed description
(pp. 286–93). The last chapter of the text (pp. 379–81) is devoted to
the history of Iraq from 1920 down to the author's time. After
achieving independence, the reader is told, Iraq became a member of
the League of Nations, and was recognized by all states. The text
concludes by highlighting Iraq's achievements which made it an
example to 'all Arab nations'. The hopes of the Arabs are thus pinned
on Iraq in order to attain total freedom and comprehensive unity'

An Egyptian Perspective

Shafiq Ghurbal (1894–1961) was perhaps the first Arab historian to offer a novel interpretation of the rise of the Arab nation: he dealt with its history as a modern entity, rather than an ever-recurring phenomenon continuously reproducing itself and thereby expressing deep cultural and material roots. This he did in a series of lectures delivered to an audience of research students at the Arab League's Institute of Higher Arab Studies. The Institute was founded by the veteran pan-Arabist educationist Sati' al-Husri in 1953 to stimulate 'nationalist awakening' and articulate a coherent 'theory of Arabism'. It included students from all over the Arab world and drew on the expertise and contributions of well-established scholars in the field of humanities. Upon the retirement of its founder in 1957, he was succeeded by Ghurbal as its second Director, and he remained in his post until his death in 1961. Before his appointment, Ghurbal had already established himself as the doyen of Egyptian historians and as an articulate exponent of Egypt's modern emergence as a nation in its own right.

Ghurbal was a professionally-trained historian[21] who enjoyed a long university career and was appointed several times as Under-Secretary for Education by various Egyptian prime ministers. With the advent of a new regime in 1952, Ghurbal began to shift his attention to wider pan-Arab issues in a systematic manner.[22]

Subtitled 'A general survey of the historical factors in the establishment of the Arab Nation as it is today',[23] these lectures were delivered and later published in book form against the background of the newly-formed merger between Syria and Egypt in 1958. Their principal thrust treats the ramifications of the Ottoman reform movement in the nineteenth century and the accompanying movement of European expansionism. The Ottoman reforms are seen as a response to an internal crisis of a 'traditional' imperial system and the various pressures of military defeats inflicted by European powers.

In 1960, most major Arab countries had achieved their independence or were on the verge of doing so. Despite the rising tide of Arab nationalism and the 1958 Syro-Egyptian unity under the leadership of President Jamal 'Abd al-Nasir (Nasser), the emergence of separate, independent Arab states continued to be the order of the day. Ghurbal attempts to strike a balance between the existence of different Arab entities and their affiliation to 'one single nation', by tracing their historical development under the auspices of the

Ottoman empire and the recent formation of an all-encompassing Arab identity.

Thus, he divides his topic into three parts. In Part I, a general survey of the Arab world in its current state of affairs is offered to show the diversity and unity of 'a nation' in the process of its transformation (pp.7–65). In Part II a comparative survey of Ottoman and European history is conducted to explain how the internal disintegration of the Ottoman state and the evolution of Europe into a concert of nation-states rendered the traditional Islamic system of government an obsolete thing of the past (pp. 69–118). In Part III, the emergence of the Arab world as a national entity is shown to be the result of a multifaceted process that began to unfold by the end of the eighteenth century (pp. 121–51).

Unlike Syrian and Iraqi Arab nationalists, whose countries did not escape Ottoman rule until the end of World War I, Egyptian and North African nationalists, who had to contend with direct European colonialism since Napoleon's invasion of Egypt in 1798, tend to have a more charitable view of the Ottoman Empire. Moreover, their Arab nationalist aspirations are distinguished by a more nuanced awareness of provincial differences and local conditions within the Arab world as an overarching entity.[24] Consequently, Ghurbal's history goes out of its way to place the Ottoman empire within the same tradition of all medieval Islamic polities.

His parallel exposition of things Ottoman and European between 1400 and 1800 is meant to show how two systems which had operated under similar conditions and degrees of organization began to diverge once a new European movement was set in motion.

Hence, in the fifteenth and sixteenth centuries the European age of exploration and discoveries had reached its climax, with dire consequences for the Arabs. The Europeans were finally able 'to bypass and encircle the Arab world'. And it was during this age of discoveries that the Arabs were placed on the defensive, 'representing a bygone era, rather than being participants in the building of a new one' (pp. 70–1).

The great Muslim states, the Ottomans, the Safavids of Persia and the Mughals of India, and which were formed in the sixteenth century, were highly conservative by their inherited background. They generally rejected modernization except under exceptional circumstances and only became more amenable to change when confronted with overwhelming external pressure. Change was thus externally-induced. During this period Europe witnessed the emergence of political units in the form of nation-states; the Reformation; secularism; the scientific revolution; the Dutch, the English, the French and the American

Revolutions; the Industrial Revolution; the birth of new systems of social thought; scientific theories and experiments; and sweeping social movements. In all these momentous developments, Ghurbal asserts, the Arabs were simply provoked recipients or alien parties to the initial impulses of modernity (p. 71).

Ghurbal's allusion to the emerging modern world order is meant to underline the fact that in both Europe and the Ottoman empire, 'the traditional way of life' was undermined and replaced by a new order but with different consequences. Whereas the West took the initiative and embarked on a policy of expansion, the Islamic world was caught up in a different position and forced to respond to a novel set of priorities. It had, for example, to redefine its relations with the outside world in non-religious terms, thereby discarding its outmoded idea of dividing societies into the Abode of Islam and the Abode of War (*dar al-Islam wa dar al-harb*). More importantly, by the end of the eighteenth century, the idea of re-establishing the state as 'a national polity' in control of 'all vital instruments of governance and domination', and 'subordinating everything to one single will', began to gain ground. However, this trend was at that stage confined to officials of the central authority, hardly touching traditional communities which continued to cluster around functional groups of warriors, religious leaders, artisans, peasant farmers and merchants (pp. 79–81).

Moreover, European states were not averse to the fall and utter disappearance of the Ottoman Empire. Russia meddled in its Balkan possessions and coveted an unimpeded access to the Black Sea, in addition to the burning desire of its czars to 'liberate' Constantinople, recreate 'the third Rome' and become the true heirs to the Byzantine Empire. Austria, having freed Hungary from Ottoman rule, aspired to increase its economic and political clout in the Balkans, a policy which brought it into conflict with Russia, particularly over Serbia, and helped to precipitate World War I. Furthermore, Russia claimed to be the protector of Orthodox Christians in the Ottoman Empire, Austria did the same, asserting its right to be considered the protector of the Empire's Roman Catholics, with France laying claim to an older privilege, running back to the days of the Crusades. France, moreover, had long-established commercial interests in the Mediterranean, whereas Britain had become in the seventeenth and eighteenth centuries an expanding imperial power, aspiring as France did, to monopolize the trade routes between India and the Ottoman state. Thus the Ottoman state began to lose its grip on the economy, and foreign powers had succeeded in establishing direct relationships with its non-Muslim communities and sects (pp. 82–5).

The movement of official reforms, initiated by the central Ottoman authority, Muhammad 'Ali of Egypt and the Bey of Tunisia in the nineteenth century, was not the only response to this situation. The other response sprang from the ranks of the various Ottoman communities and peoples who sought to ameliorate their economic and cultural conditions. Although the reform movement was non-nationalist at its official level, or Islamic in its wider dimensions, 'national awareness' was destined to prevail, to the extent that the Ottoman establishment itself ended up placing the principle of Turkish national interest above all other principles (pp. 85–6).

It is at this juncture that Ghurbal chooses to refute the assumption that 'the spread of national consciousness' among the Ottoman Turks, Arabs, Greeks, Serbs and Armenians was a 'mere imitation' of European nationalist movements:

> This idea of imitation is an illusion, because in order for the Greek to become aware of his Greekness, or the Egyptian of his Egyptianness, he does not need to imitate, for example, the way the English perceives his Englishness. What influenced the Egyptian or the Greek were the conditions of reorganization on a national basis. Only by creating this particular aspect of reorganising national life did Europe set a precedent for us. (p. 187)

At first it was thought that military reform was the key to recovery, in addition to a revamped diplomatic service with permanent missions in major European capitals. This new policy was initiated by Sultan Selim III (r. 1789–1807). However, the repercussions of Napoleon's invasion of Ottoman Egypt and the wider implications of the French Revolution created a conservative backlash which was exploited by the Janissaries and religious students, leading to the downfall of the reformist Sultan and his subsequent assassination. Mahmud II (r. 1808–39) fared better, but had to proceed more cautiously. His reign coincided with the establishment of a new religious movement in Arabia, known as Wahhabism, and the rise to power of an enterprising reformist in Egypt, Muhammad 'Ali (r. 1805–48). And it was to Muhammad 'Ali that the Ottoman Sultan turned for military assistance against the fundamentalism of Wahhabism. Having captured the Sa'udi capital Dar'a in 1818, the Egyptian forces remained in Western Arabia and along the Red Sea coast until 1840 when they were evicted by European armed intervention (pp. 91–2).

Although Muhammad 'Ali did not carry out his wide-ranging reforms on the basis of nationalist affiliation, he did appreciate the strategic and material advantages of placing the bulk of the Arab world under Egyptian administration. However, his ambitions were aborted by a combination of Ottoman resistance, local revolts and the inter-

vention of European powers. Nevertheless, by the death of Mahmud
II in 1839, the Ottoman Empire had witnessed an unprecedented
degree of centralization, characterized by the building of a new model
army along European lines and the liquidation of provincial chieftains
and semi-feudal lords.

The Ottoman reform movement gained momentum under the two
sultans 'Abdulmajid (1839–61) and 'Abdulaziz (1861–76). It was
during this period that new measures were implemented to turn the
empire into a modern state ruling all its subjects with equality, and
irrespective of race, religion or nationality. At the time Europe was
being transformed into a machine which in its turn created a single
financial world market. Germany and Italy were unified and Austria
became a dual monarchy with Hungary in 1867. Russia continued its
aggressive foreign policy, while the Napoleonic empire was recreated
in the person of Napoleon III.

European ascendancy made itself felt throughout the world, subordinating in its wake states and cultures stretching from China and
Japan to Morocco and the Ottoman Empire. Non-Europeans developed a sense of attraction and repulsion towards this new civilisation.
However, their being appreciative or censorious did not make much
difference: they always ended up by adopting its means for doing
things (pp. 95–6).

The reign of Khedive Isma'il of Egypt and that of the Ottoman
Sultan, 'Abdulaziz, share a number of similarities. Both witnessed 'the
introduction of the instruments of European financial transactions'
into an arena which was still operating according to an old scheme of
things. Its consequences were the collapse of public finances and the
ruin of landowners and merchants. This led in due course to the
demand of accountable governments and parliamentary systems. Civilian notables as well as military officers and elements of the intelligentsia were in the forefront of this liberal movement. By the time
Sultan Abdulhamid ascended the throne in 1876 the 'liberal' movement was in full swing: it culminated in the promulgation of an
Ottoman Constitution based on a parliamentary system of government and the establishment of a House of Parliament in Egypt. The
parliamentary Ottoman experiment was abruptly suspended in the
wake of the outbreak of hostilities between the Sultan and the Russian
Czar. Following the defeat of the Ottoman army, the 1878 Congress
of Berlin hastened 'the gradual liquidation' of the Ottoman state.
Having shown signs of independence, Khedive Isma'il was deposed
by the Sultan at the instigation of both Britain and France in June
1879. For some obscure reason, Urabi's revolt in 1881–2 is alluded
to but not discussed (p. 111).

'Abdulhamid's aim, according to Ghurbal, was to build a state supported by two pillars: Ottomanism and Islamism. Ottomanism was conceived as a bond which would unite all the disparate 'races' of the empire as equal subjects under one authority. He did so in order to ward off the danger of nationalist movements which were certain to break up the empire into its constituent parts. 'Abdulhamid was thus opposed to Turkish, Arab, Albanian or any other nationalism. Islamism, on the other hand, represented an earnest response to a genuine general Muslim feeling which increasingly tended to rally around the Ottoman empire as the embodiment of the Islamic caliphate. Moreover, the Sultan encouraged Islamism as a useful political tool which he could use in his dealing with those European powers which had Muslim subjects under their domination.[25] Both trends, Ghurbal asserts, were to be shortly swept away by the rising tide of nationalism (pp. 106–8).

'Abdulhamid's policies did, however, achieve an unprecedented level of modernization, particularly in education, administration and the military field. Hand in hand with modernization went a tendency towards 'absolute rule'. Thus, the 1908 revolution broke out in the name of Liberty, Equality and Fraternity, and was received with enthusiastic acclamation throughout the Ottoman lands. However, immediately after the restoration of the Constitution, Austria announced its annexation of Bosnia-Herzegovina, Ferdinand, the Prince of Bulgaria, proclaimed himself an independent King, the war in the Balkans reared its head in 1912 and 1913, and Italy launched its invasion of Libya in 1911. All of these events took place within a short period and at a time when the transition from absolutism to constitutional rule was still in its early days. No wonder the Committee of Union and Progress (CUP), which represented the Young Turks and had planned the revolution in the first place, became greatly alarmed by the nationalist demands of their Ottoman subjects. Some CUP members suspected foreign interference motivated by the desire to weaken the empire further. While others, more moderate, conceded the validity of nationalist demands in principle, but maintained that it was the wrong time to consider such far-reaching proposals (pp. 114–15).

In this respect, Ghurbal is less vehement than either Miqdadi or Darwazah, in his condemnation of Ottoman brutality. Nevertheless, he does see a growing Turkish tendency to put down local rebellions by force of arms, or ban legitimate political associations and banish Arab leaders into exile. The tragedy was that both Arah nationalists and the CUP government failed to resolve their differences in the Ottoman parliament, and had to resort to extra parliamentary means (pp. 115–16).

The onset of the Great War between the European powers left the Ottoman state no choice but to fight on the side of Germany. It could not have done otherwise, with Russia, Britain and France holding in subordination millions of Arab and non-Arab Muslims, and scheming to carve out its remaining African and Asian provinces.[26] Ottoman defeat unravelled 'Abdulhamid's legacy of Ottomanism and Islamism, leading to the rise of a vigorous nationalist movement under the leadership of Ataturk. By and large, the Arab provinces remained loyal to the Ottoman state, and numerous Arab soldiers and officers fought in the ranks of the Ottoman armed forces. Only the Sharif of Mecca was in open revolt against the Sultan, while other Arabian leaders were either pro-Ottoman or preferred to chart a neutral course (pp. 116–117)

The end of the war ushered in the full rigour of British and French domination of the Arab world.

How did Arab nationalism figure in this historical context?

Its emergence, Ghurbal asserts, should not be confined to Syria and Lebanon and the programme of certain Arab societies associated with these two countries. Arab national identity developed at parallel levels throughout the Arab world. It did so with the disappearance of 'rogue and adventurous military chiefs' and their armed bands, and their replacement by a more stable system of governance. This tended to stabilize local systems of government and served to define the territorial borders of various Arab provinces. The recruitment of local soldiers and officers, instead of Mamluks and mercenaries, constituted 'the most important factor in the construction of Arab nationalist consciousness'. Moreover, the settlement of tribal groups and bedouins on agricultural lands was another important factor in creating common and stable bonds of citizenship. The adoption of the concept of citizenship, on the basis of equality before the laws of one single fatherland, created national bonds which cut across sectarian and social differences. Modern means of communication and the creation of a uniform system of education and administration facilitated the unification of different regions and their eventual national homogeneity. Finally, reactions against European penetration in all Arab countries, and the fact that some ruling families were non-Arab in origin, or as a result of the turkification policies of the Ottoman government, generated a nationalist awareness of unmistakeable Arab character. These different currents flowing in parallel directions in separate Arab countries between 1800 and 1945, converged after World War II, and made possible the participation of the emancipated Arab communities in the building of a new 'Arab society' (pp. 148–51). Thus, Arab nationalism was of recent origins and had to be understood against the background of modernity and its late arrival in the Arab world.

Ghurbal's modernist approach, centred on the dichotomy between medieval institutions and the advent of a modern type of organisation, has much to recommend it. Moreover, it possesses elements which are in affinity with a Gellnerian theory of nationalism.

Islam and Arabism[27]

In 1984, almost a quarter of a century after Ghurbal's delivery of his lectures at the Institute of Higher Arab Studies in Cairo, a completely different version of the Arab nation's history was published.

It is in this context that the most recent history on the genesis of 'the Arab nation' is discussed.[28]

A historian by profession, widely renowned for his studies on early Islamic history, and academically acclaimed for his pioneering works on classical Arabic historiography, al-Duri was born in the city of Baghdad in 1919. He obtained an honours degree in history from the University of London (1940), and worked for his Ph.D. under the supervision of the highly respected orientalist, Hamilton Gibb. Back in his country, al-Duri taught history, published numerous books, acted as dean of the Faculty of Arts and Sciences of the University of Baghdad and became president of the same institution between 1963 and 1968. He eventually left Baghdad and took up a new professorship of history at the Jordanian University in Amman.

Formally trained in early Islamic history, al-Duri did not depart from his preferred subject until the late 1950s. In 1958, the monarchical regime in Iraq was abolished under the impact of a radical revolutionary tide, spearheaded by the army In the ensuing struggle for power various political parties and groups, espousing ideologies ranging from Communism to nationalism, were pitted against each other.

In a sense, al-Duri's interpretation of 'the historical formation of the Arab nation' was initially formed during those years. Two monographs of his, published in 1960 and 1965, on 'the historical roots' of Arab nationalism and Arab socialism respectively, testify to this assumption. However, these were preliminary statements produced on the spur of the moment in order to counter hostile accusations and reassert the deep-rooted existence of both Arab nationalism and socialism in the Islamic heritage of the nation.[29]

Thus, al-Duri posits the historical formation of his nation as the result of three successive stages, ethnic, cultural and political.

The ethnic stage had its 'formative elements' in pre-Islamic Arabia. Arabia's geography determined to a large extent the distribution of its inhabitants and their way of life. Lying along trade routes between the Mediterranean and the Indian subcontinent, it witnessed the birth of an active merchant class both in Yemen and the south-west regions, with Mecca acting as a nodal point. In regions which received sufficient rainfall sedentary life flourished in agricultural settlements and villages. However, in the desert and steppe regions nomadic or semi-nomadic patterns predominated. It was from the last areas that the great migrations from south to north generally originated (pp. 15–21).

Nomadism implied a certain uniformity of economic activity and moral values, with the tribe acting as its social structure and ultimate support. This tribal organization persisted even when the tribe became a sedentary association of farmers and peasants. The meagre resources of the desert tended to create strong bonds of loyalty, so that the social group could muster all its capabilities in the face of adversity. On rare occasions the tribes would coalesce into larger confederations either to wage a military campaign or to deal with the effects of natural calamities, such as drought or famine (p. 21)

All tribes claimed 'common descent' and origins. Consequently, a heightened interest in genealogies established itself and was transmitted down the generations throughout the medium of poetry. These genealogical traditions, orally transmitted, conceived of the Arabs as 'a race' divided into two broad ethnic branches: the 'Adnanites of the North and the Qahtanids of the South. The first branch was the one which spread Arabic as a unifying linguistic factor throughout the Peninsula and beyond (pp. 21–4).

The international trade routes, criss-crossing Arabia in various directions, were of immediate benefit to the tribes: transported in caravans, this traffic became dependent on tribal protection which had to be paid for in commissions. Towns rose or disappeared according to the safety of a particular trade route or its diversion elsewhere. More importantly, this commercial activity kept Arabia in constant contact with the outside world, on the one hand, and tended to create permanent social and economic links between its various regions, on the other (pp. 24–6).

In the three centuries preceding the rise of Islam, Arabia became, directly or indirectly, the theatre of the rivalry between three powerful imperial states: Persia, Byzantium and the Southern Yemenite Kingdom of Himyar. Both the Persian and Byzantine empires set up 'Arab principalities' along northern Arabia to keep Bedouin tribes in check. Some of these principalities had kings of their own. The Himyarite state, having converted to Judaism, was dismantled by a Byzantine-sponsored Abyssinian invasion in 525 AD. Moreover, the leader of the Abyssinian expedition, Abraha, attempted to invade Mecca in order to place the western trade route under his control. His failure, al-Duri concludes, sharpened the ambitions of Mecca's masters, the Quraysh-ites, and gave rise to a wave of 'Arab awareness' in western Arabia (pp. 27–8).

The Sasanian Persians, in their turn, coveted the trade of the Gulf region, entered into alliance with the Jewish tribes in Western Arabia, and finally occupied Yemen and remained there until the advent of Islam. These rivalries pitting one imperial power against another allowed Mecca to emerge as the principal trading and cultural centre of the Arabs. This was particularly the case after the gradual disappearance of all the foreign-sponsored 'Arab principalities' by the turn of the seventh century.

At first, Mecca under the leadership of its principal tribe, Quraysh, tried to chart a neutral course, avoiding to embroil its fortunes in the rivalries of the two great powers. It concentrated instead on turning its shrine, the Ka'ba, into a focal point of spiritual worship for all the tribes. Quraysh, acting as its custodian, assumed the role of arbiter in tribal conflict, endeavouring at the same time to promote trade and ensure the prevalence of peaceful co-existence amongst warring factions. Before long, paganism began to be diluted by the emergence of the notion of one god towering above all other idols and deities. Thus, the first hints of monotheism were manifesting themselves throughout Arabia. In the sixth century, poetry flourished and became the medium of expressing group feeling or tribal loyalties. A common literary language slowly emerged, and by the sixth century the Arabic script was being used for writing purposes, thereby replacing the older Himyarite and Aramaic scripts (pp. 29–32).

The emergence of Mecca as the centre of Arabian culture and economic power, coupled with the establishment of an inter-tribal alliance under the leadership of Quraysh, encouraged a sense of ethnic solidarity throughout Arabia. This solidarity, buttressed by the proliferation of local fairs and trading activities, was exemplified in the adoption of Arabic as the medium of communication and literary expression. Moreover, the tribe as a socio-political unit was being gradually transformed by a mode of sedentary life and the pursuit of commercial gain. Social differentiations based on status and wealth made their appearance and 'individualism' became part of a new social order. However, ethnic allegiance and genealogical pride were not fundamentally altered or dislodged. It was Islam that operated a fundamental change in the life of the Arabs (pp. 32–3).

Thus, from being an ethnically-based community, Islam turned the Arabs into a nation based on cultural affiliation. Fostered in an urban environment, Islam treated nomadism as an anomaly. In the following centuries both Islam and the Arabic language were to constitute the underlying foundations of the Arab nation as a cultural entity. Islamization and Arabization of conquered territories developed in tandem. However, not all conquered lands were Arabized in spite of their Islamization.

In lands in which Aramaic was widespread, and already had settlements of Arab tribes prior to the conquests, such as Syria and Iraq, Arabization was comprehensive and fairly easy. As for Egypt, continuous and successive Arab migrations into its urban and rural regions, after the eighth century, contributed to its permanent Arabization. The same phenomenon can be observed in North Africa, in addition to the migration of a new wave of Arabian tribes in the eleventh century. Spain, Iran and Punjab escaped this dual effect, owing to their vigorous local cultures, the relatively isolated nature of Arab settlements, and. more importantly, rural areas were left to their own devices. Furthermore, Arabization rendered former ethnic affiliations almost redundant, leading in the process to the articulation of a new concept of Arabism centred on Arabic and Islam. This movement found its culmination in the 'Abbasid period (750–1250) and established the permanent characteristics of the nation (pp. 37–75).

This cultural identity was thus the product of a vigorous urban milieu centred on a chain of cities teeming with the economic activities of merchants, artisans, bankers and notables. The cities became huge social magnets for the rural areas, acting as outlets for their produce and markets for purchasing goods and necessities. The state itself was, moreover, an important vehicle of Arabization. Its expanding administrative structures, economic activities and military services required a standard and common medium of communication. Standard Arabic gradually replaced other languages and became the official language of administration as well as literary expression (pp. 56–7, 60–1).

In the early Islamic period, al-Duri asserts, purely Arab urban centres[30] initiated a cultural movement based on studies related to the elaboration of Islam as a religion and way of life. Exegesis of the Qur'an, the career of the Prophet, the science of jurisprudence (*fiqh*) were first to emerge and formed part of a wider cultural domain – poetry, philosophy, history and geneology. It was at a later date that Arabized students of Islam and its language made their contributions. Moreover, these cultural activities had an immediate practical purpose related to the proper rights and duties of the members of the community. By the end of the first Islamic century Persian religious notions and Hellenistic ideas and translations began to circulate and gain importance. Whereas the 'Abbasid caliphs sponsored translations of Greek texts dealing with medicine, philosophy and astronomy, translations of literary and religious works of Persian origin were promoted by state officials and administrators (pp. 83–92).

It is at this juncture that al-Duri chooses to situate the culmination of the cultural formation of the Arab nation. The reappearance of a Persian literary tradition, dubbed the *shu'ubiyya* by its opponents led the Arab and Arabized elite to reassert a cultural identity which rehabilitated pre-Islamic Arabia as the cradle of all virtues. It was in this response to a Persian-inspired movement that Arabism finally articulated a coherent vision of its cultural identity.

According to al-Duri, the resurgence of Persian culture, straddling the eighth and ninth centuries, brought the pre-Islamic Arab heritage back into the foreground of cultural and political debates. Arabic reasserted itself as the 'fundamental bond' endowing its speakers with an identity of their own. Furthermore, as non-Islamic concepts of Manichaean, Mazdakaean and Zoroastrian provenance permeated intellectual circles of state secretaries, Arab and Arabized writers and historians re-established the direct link between Islam and Arabism. Furthermore, as the 'Abbasid state increased its reliance on foreign troops of Turkish descent, the Arabs, as the first builders of the Islamic state, were alerted to the implications of this step to their interests and identity This coincided in the ninth and tenth centuries with the rapid dissolution of tribal units and the evolution of urban societies whereby tribal notables gave way to merchants and bankers who formed the backbone of a nascent 'commercial bourgeoisie'. Under an economy based on trade, market forces and urban expansion, a large-scale movement of immigration from the rural areas took place. City life became more complicated and social differentiations glaringly apparent. Consequently, new forms of professional and trade organizations emerged and spread, in addition to youth confederations imbued with a spirit of martial arts and valour (pp. 90–8).

However, the institutions of the 'Abbasid state, led by the Caliphate, failed to accommodate these social transformations and economic activities. This was clearly demonstrated by the eruption of ethnic conflicts pitting Arabs against Persian or turkic elements. The Caliphate itself became increasingly authoritarian and deeply isolated from its Arab origins. It was under these conditions that the 'Abbasid state began to break up into its constituent parts, whereby local dynasties sprouted and mushroomed. Although the Caliphate attempted to revive its fortunes by espousing the cause of popular and youth organizations such as the Futuwwah, sponsored and supported by Caliph al-Nasir (1180–1225), the Mongol invasion of 1258 put an end to the experiment. Baghdad was occupied and the Caliphate suffered a mortal blow (pp. 98–100, 118–19).

Nevertheless, by the time of the Mongol invasion, al-Duri avers, 'the Arab nation' had been fully formed in its cultural identity. This cultural consciousness, based on the Arabic language and the close links between Arabism and Islam, re-emerged in modern times to launch Arabism on its political course.

Thus, the awakening of the Arabs to their political identity took almost six centuries to stir itself into action. No convincing arguments are offered to justify this long period of gestation. Although al-Duri does allude to the emergence of a socio-economic system of 'military feudalism' and the subsequent blockage of trade routes between the Arab lands and the outside world (pp. 123–4), considering both as possible causes of complete stagnation, the yawning gap of almost six centuries still cries for an explanation.

In one sense, al-Duri's approach suggests certain affinities with Smith's analysis in his work *The Ethnic Origins of Nations* (see chapter 1). Both contend that modern nations are formed on the basis of a developed sense of ethnic identity. However, whereas Smith sees ethnicity as a cultural compound formed out of a common fund of historical memories and values, al-Duri postulates a higher phase whereby ethnicity is subsumed by a social and cultural identity. Hence, the modern phase becomes almost redundant, in the sense that the nation is merely dormant and awaiting the opportune moment to recover its consciousness.

That said, al-Duri's diagnosis of the Ottoman reform movement does offer a nuanced and highly sophisticated interpretation of its implications for his third stage. Apart from demonstrating the inevitable decline of the Ottoman empire, and irrespective of the great efforts of its sultans and statesmen, he underlines the close links between Islamic reformism, on the one hand, and modern Arabism, on the other. However, along with Darwazah, Miqdadi and Ghurbal, al-Duri follows the uneven development of Arabism through the prism of local patriotisms.

In other words, al-Duri refocuses the scope of his investigation by enumerating the fortunes of various movements in their local articulation and confinement to particular Arab countries (Egypt, Tunisia, Syria and so forth). By doing so, he showed how Arabism had to rehearse its characteristics, based on language and Islam, in each Arab country before transforming itself into a pan-movement. Furthermore, 'this awakening of self-awareness' had once more to retraverse the vast distance of its ethnic and cultural history before it could negotiate its way to a political platform (chapters 6 and 7).

Smith's triple revolution in the spheres of the division of labour, administration and culture[31] is mirrored in al-Duri's meticulous description of the reform movement in the nineteenth and early twentieth centuries.[32] More importantly, European ascendancy in the military, commercial and industria fields accelerated the decline of the Ottoman Empire. Embarking on a programme of military and administrative reforms, the empire enacted a series of measures which resulted in the abolition of military feudalism and the introduction of private ownership of vast tracts of land. This led in its turn to the expansion of a new class of landowning notables who cultivated cash crops for the international market. The two Ottoman Sultans Selim III (r. 1789–1807) and Mahmud II (r. 1808–39), together with Muhammad 'Ali in Egypt, initiated this movement of centralization and modernization which was initially confined to military reform, but soon widened to embrace the education system, land and commercial laws. After 1839, the gates of the Ottoman imperial domains, including the Arab Provinces, were flung wide open to the products and industrial commodities of western Europe. Consequently, local industries and crafts began to lose ground. Moreover, foreign banks, private investment companies and western governments turned their attention to projects that were deemed essential to trade. Hence, the building of the Suez Canal, harbours, railways and river navigation systems – all meant to serve expanding western interests. It was under these circumstances that Muslim merchants were increasingly squeezed out of their international operations and tended to concentrate their efforts on local trading activities. A 'new middle class', composed of local agents, Christian in background, versed in Western languages and enjoying the protection of foreign consuls, emerged side by side with a Muslim landholding class. As Muslim merchants made investment in land their prime objective, they began to develop a sense of their own collective interests. The education system itself spawned a new generation of Western-educated officers, engineers and teachers (pp. 123–86).

Social and economic changes triggered innumerable cultural activities ranging from producing modern Arab dictionaries to publishing newspapers. Cultural revival was followed by the growth of an organized Arab movement. Between 1908 and 1916, Arab intellectuals and leaders articulated ideas and put forward demands which expressed their sense of a separate community with a distinct character. Sharif Husayn's revolt against the Ottomans in 1916 simply confirmed this state of affairs and launched the Arab nation as a political entity on to its preordained destiny (pp. 189–276).

Perhaps the significance of this most recent history of the Arab nation lies in its attempt to situate Islam at the heart of Arabism, thereby obliterating the slightest doubt as to the symbiotic nature of their association.

3

Cultural and Political Arabism

Nationalism, be it in the Middle East or Europe, is a modern phenomenon engendered by the disintegration of feudalism, the rise of a new middle class and the twin revolutions: the French and the Industrial.

Moreover, it is a process rather than an event. Nationalism enters the field as a political choice and becomes an integral part of creating, imagining and developing the nation. This process of creating the nation is often articulated in its abstract version by a cultural elite armed with a literary national language and having at its disposal a modern system of propagation and education. In this sense, Benedict Anderson's depiction of the nation as 'an imagined community', made possible by the advent of print-capitalism,[1] coupled with Eric Hobsbawm's notion of 'the nation as novelty',[2] and Gellner's definition of nationalism as 'a theory of political legitimacy' in the industrial age,[3] offer the most plausible and cogent argument for the modernity of our subject.

Be that as it may, most students of modern nationalism affirm its comparatively recent emergence, on the one hand, and the fact that it constitutes a definite break with the past, on the other. In this respect, Arab nationalism is considered a child of the modern world and closely affiliated with a worldwide movement.

As an historical process, Arab nationalism, or more correctly, Arabism, emerged as a result of the convergence of socio-economic and political factors in the nineteenth century. It was, however, confined at this stage to a broad awareness of a cultural identity that had to be cherished and reformed.

Ever since the destruction of the 'Abbasid Caliphate by the Mongols in 1258, the decline of the Arabs as a political and military force

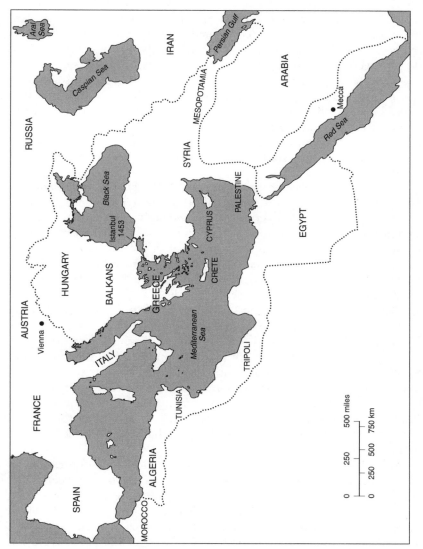

Map 3.1 Arab lands under Ottoman rule, 1683

in the Islamic world began to accelerate (see chapter 2). Although some ruling Arab families managed to survive in a reconstituted environment, dominated by Turkic, Persian and Mamluk dynasties, the Arabs' role as defenders and custodians of the new faith was being steadily eroded in favour of more energetic ethnic groups and communities. However, Arabic continued to be studied and used as a religious and legal language, and individuals claiming noble Arab descent were highly revered and accorded special privileges.

As we have seen, in modern Arabic history-writing and literature this period, extending approximately from 1258 to 1800, is normally judged to be 'the dark ages' of Arab civilization. In other words, despite the fact that Islamic power and culture continued to flourish during these centuries, reaching new heights under the Ottoman and Safavid empires, the Arabs were eclipsed as either state-builders or military leaders.

It is for these reasons that once an Arab dynasty or personality established an autonomous principality, no matter how precarious or short-lived, signs of recovery were immediately cited and accorded a significant function in historical developments. In other words, movements that were built upon purely religious or local dynastic ambitions became auspicious portents of a general pan-Arabist revival. For example, the revivalist Wahhabi movement, which originated in central Arabia in the 1740s, was seen in this light.[4]

Named after its founder, Muhammad b. 'Abd al-Wahhab (1703–87), and adopted as a political ideology by a local chieftain, Muhammad Ibn Sa'ud (d. 1765), it was based on puritan principles, calling for the absolute unity of God in opposition to the worship of Saints or the veneration of holy men and Sufis. Nevertheless, the fact that it was led by two Arab personalities who aimed at unifying local tribal groups under the banner of reviving the original message of Islam, denoted a resurgence of Arab vitality. It also demonstrated an implicit drive for independence by the challenge it posed to the authority of the Ottoman Sultans.

Wahhabism enjoyed widespread support until its suppression by Muhammad 'Ali (1805–48), the governor of Egypt, between 1812 and 1818. It did not re-emerge as a dynamic force until the early twentieth century. It was this movement, led by Al-Sa'ud, which established the Kingdom of Saudi Arabia in 1932.

This early conflict between regional powers in the Arab world has repeated itself, in one form or another, down to the present time. Although Egypt at the time was still nominally under Ottoman suzerainty, its dynamic ruler, Muhammad 'Ali, introduced the first comprehensive programme of modernization in the Arab world. His

policies paved the way for the rise of an indigenous elite that made
the entertainment of an independent path of development a concrete
possibility.

Other examples include the rise of local governors of Arab origin
who, while continuing to pay homage to the Ottoman Sultanate,
went to great lengths to consolidate their provincial power and local
economic base. The Syrian 'Azm family, ruling Damascus from 1724
to 1780, was deemed as such.[5] Even an earlier dynasty, based on the
Ma'n family which had a sound Arab genealogy, was deemed to be
another portentous indication. This was especially the case with the
advent to power of Fakhr al-Din II (1585–1635), who tried to form
an anti-Ottoman alliance with the grandduchy of Tuscany and Spain,
but failed in his endeavours. Between 1750 and 1775 an Arab chief,
Shaykh Zahir al-'Umar, set up an autonomous rule in the Palestinian
town of Acre and its surrounding areas. His aim was the establishment
of direct links with foreign traders who were eager to purchase cash
crops. Shaykh Zahir forged an alliance with another anti-Ottoman
rebel, 'Ali Bey of Egypt, as well as the Russian government. However,
the end of the war between Russia and the Ottoman Empire and the
conclusion of the Treaty of Küchük Kaynarja in 1774 heralded his
downfall one year later. Nevertheless, Shaykh Zahir's rule in southern
Syria could be interpreted as either an incipient Palestinian autonomous movement or an early Arabist defiance of Ottoman authority.[6]

Moreover, in Morocco, which did not form part of the Ottoman
Empire, as well as in Yemen and along the fringes of the Arabian
peninsula, dynasties claiming Arab descent, with strong local interests,
were also a prominent feature of this period.

As the Ottoman Empire underwent a process of reform, in order to
reverse its decline, local dynasties with deep-rooted Arab traditions
began to appear and sustain themselves in power. These reforms,
initiated by Sultan Selim III (1789–1807), and supported by a group
of army officers, diplomats and interpreters, gave the Arab subjects of
the empire the opportunity to engage in a wide-ranging programme
of modernization. Such a programme granted their privileged elite
direct access to modern institutions, legitimating at the same time
European ideas of government and citizenship.

The Ottoman Background and European Rivalry

Between 1516 and 1574 the Arab world was gradually integrated into
the Ottoman empire. It was initially this integration which halted the
disintegration of Arab societies, stabilized their administrative struc-

tures and made possible their reemergence as independent states. In other words, the Ottoman Empire, by the very nature of its flexible and adaptable administrative system,[7] created the objective conditions which eventually led to the crystallisation of separate political entities in the Arab world. The flexibility of the system was represented by a local administration which allowed ample room for local customs and traditions to persist and endure. What the Ottoman authorities needed first and foremost were strong, but loyal, local rulers in order to secure the regular collection of taxes, to protect strategic routes or ward off foreign intervention.

And it was only in the period of direct European economic and military influence that 'independence movements' became a viable option. Independence in this case denoted secession or detachment from the Empire. However, this viability was often brought about at a high price – that of total dependence and gradual integration into a world market dominated by the industrial nations. Arab reformers saw clearly this dilemma. Hence the insistence of most of their leaders on maintaining the integrity of imperial domains within a decentralized system of administration. Thus, the fact that the Empire was structurally 'flexible and adaptable' before the onset of modernization and its accompanying drive for centralization, created local reactions which ranged from conservatism to outright rebellion.

It may well be that at the popular level things were different. Although there are many indications that the Arabs of Western Asia had their misgivings about 'the Turks' as a ruling elite, the bond of religion served to dampen schemes for outright independence. However, the mere fact of repeated attempts by a number of local rulers and religious leaders to defy the Ottoman Sultanate served to recast its legitimacy in a conditional frame of reference. The legitimacy of the Sultanate became problematic and had to be re-established in conjunction with the drive for reforms. By linking its survival with its new political programmes it was now expected to act according to a set of practical and concrete policies. Once expectations were raised to a new level, deliverance of promises placed the Sultanate face to face with the actual performance of the states it was trying to emulate, i.e. the European powers. Hence, the Sultanate had to deliver military victories, introduce a fair system of taxation, set up a network of schools and colleges to teach new scientific and historical subjects, and reform the judicial system to comply with the norms of proper procedures and meticulous attention to complaints. Most importantly, it had to include its newly-formed intelligentsia, bureaucratic and merchant elite in its deliberations and decision-making.

The Ottomans responded by offering a number of theoretical and practical formulas which found their most eloquent expression in the Noble Rescript of 1839. All Ottomans, irrespective of race, religion or nationality, were to be 'citizens' of a new order known as 'the Ottoman fatherland'. The system of taxation known as tax-farming or *iltizan* was to be abolished and replaced with one fair set of consistent rules and procedures. Military service was the duty and right of all subjects, be they Christian, Jewish or Muslim. Commerce, private enterprise, and economic prosperity were pronounced to be the essence of civilized life. Education was to be made available to all children as an obligation of an enlightened state. Furthermore, communities and their representatives would be called upon to join newly-formed local councils to manage their domestic affairs. In 1856 and 1864, these reforms began to be introduced as a comprehensive programme promulgated by a new generation of reformers.

In the 1830s, the protracted struggle against the challenge of the Egyptian Viceroy, Muhammad 'Ali, whose forces had occupied Greater Syria and defeated the Ottoman army in more than one engagement, served to accentuate the need for a more radical programme of reforms than hitherto being contemplated. Between 1789 and 1838 reforms in the Ottoman state were restricted to the military and administrative sphere with a clear drive to limit the material power of local potentates and autonomous notables who had begun to erode the authority of the state, depriving it of much needed revenues. Thus, after a number of abortive attempts, the Janissaries, representing the degenerate military regression of a once formidable force, were finally liquidated in 1826. A new army, modelled on European lines, was set up and trained according to western techniques of organization and deployment. But within a few years, the Sultan's new army was deemed too weak to defeat the Greek insurrection. Consequently, the Ottoman governor of Egypt, who had begun his military reforms much earlier, was called upon to save the empire from a secessionist revolt. In 1827, at the battle of Navarino, the Ottoman and Egyptian fleets were destroyed by a European coalition of British and French naval forces. Almost two decades earlier, the same Sultan Mahmud II had to implore his Egyptian vassal to save Arabia from the rising tide of a new religious movement, Wahhabism. This he duly accomplished, securing the hinterland of Arabia for the Ottoman Empire up to World War I.

Both both the Ottoman Sultan and Muhammad 'Ali were operating within an emerging international balance of power in which Britain, France, Russia and Austria figured as local interested parties. Britain and France craved markets for their industrial goods and both looked upon the Ottoman empire as a fertile source of primary and agricultural products. Moreover, their rivalries drove them to secure for themselves spheres of influence and favourable terms of trade and direct involvement in domestic affairs. Napoleon's invasion of Egypt and Syria had alerted Britain to potential French threats to its Indian and Near Eastern theatre of operation, a fact which made Ottoman and British interests draw together in order to defeat French ambitions. This Anglo-Ottoman rapprochement survived the temporary inconvenience of the Greek insurrection which disrupted a long-term strategy based on safeguarding the integrity of the Ottoman Empire as a national British policy. It was in this context that while France surreptitiously welcomed Muhammad 'Ali's foray into Syria, Britain became increasingly alarmed at the prospect of finding the Ottoman state drifting towards dependency on Russian offers of assistance to stave off military defeat, while France strengthened its position in the wake of repeated Egyptian victories.

However, both Britain and the Ottoman state were to suffer from the law of unexpected consequences. Having defeated Napoleon's army and forced the French to evacuate Egypt in 1801, they created in both Egypt and Syria a vacuum of power into which Muhammad 'Ali stepped and filled with his Albanian contingent and the support of local forces. The former lords of Egypt, the Mameluks, had become discredited as a result of their internal squabbles and consequent defeat at the hands of Napoleon's army. In Syria, the intervention of the Ottoman army, the brief ascendancy of a local ruler, al-Jazzar (1775–1804), and the decisive role played by the British fleet under Sydney Smith, unleashed a new struggle for power among various social and religious groups. After 1811, Muhammad 'Ali began his systematic plan of reform, inspired by the efforts of the reformist Ottoman Sultan Salim III (1789–1807) and the military performance of the most advanced armies of his day, the British and the French. For a brief period between 1801 and 1807, it looked as though Egypt might become a republican theocracy, run by its energetic popular religious leader, 'Umar Makram, but it was not to be. Muhammad 'Ali proceeded to place the religious establishment under his control, depriving it at the same time of its vast landed properties and tax privileges. He did the same with the wealth and properties of the Mameluk class which he, moreover, physically liquidated in the massacre of 1811.

Responding to the request of the Sultan, Muhammad 'Ali used his Albanian forces to defeat the Wahhabites of Arabia between 1811 and 1817. Having tasted victory on a large scale, he next turned his attention to the Sudan, which he duly occupied between 1821 and 1824. In the meantime, he had forged a new army out of local

Egyptian peasants. This turned out to be a momentous event. For it was the first time in centuries that native Egyptians were conscripted as soldiers, having been spared this arduous responsibility by a Turkic Mameluk institution dating back several centuries.

Despite the fact that the upper echelons of the Egyptian army continued to be manned by Turkish, Albanian and other alien elements, its rank and file became thoroughly Egyptianized. This entailed a number of consequences, the foremost of which was the gradual erosion of the Ottoman culture of the ruling elite and the emergence of Arabic as the official language of state. At first, Turkish and Arabic were used, exemplified by the publication of a gazette in 1828 in which decrees in both languages were printed side by side.

The expanding bureaucracy had to rely more and more on Arabic-speaking subjects, particularly as the state took upon itself the responsibility of establishing a network of schools and sought to co-opt the religious establishment with its long-standing and exclusive reliance on Arabic as the language of instruction, legal transactions and rites of worship.

The decline of the Mameluk institution, which had reappeared in various forms under the Ottomans, following their occupation or annexation of Arab territories after 1516, serves in this respect as an index of the emergence of local national forces and elites who reclaimed Arabic as the language of administration and public affairs. Moreover, this decline indicated the growing necessity of building a new type of state which tended to weaken the entrenched authority of regional chieftains, tribal groups and private interests. In the wake of Napoleon's invasion, the Ottoman state itself intensified its efforts of centralization at the expense of local armies and communal forces. Muhammad 'Ali's Egyptian experiment made this scheme of things all the more desirable. The involvement of European armies in local disputes, or as a result of their own calculations, revealed the urgency of building new institutions capable of assimilating modern techniques and having the ability to operate according to a uniform plan of action.

While the Mameluk institution in Egypt was violently destroyed, first as a result of its defeat by Napoleon and then at the hands of Muhammad 'Ali who delivered the final blow, the same institution evolved in Tunisia in the course of the eighteenth and nineteenth centuries and was amalgamated into Tunisian society at large. However, in most instances, its liquidation was abrupt and accompanied by acts of resistance.

In Algeria, Iraq and Libya, the Mameluk institution, or its Ottoman variant in the shape of the Janissaries, came to a tragic end within five years of each other (1830–5). Within the same period, the old military forces in Syria, be they locally-based or imperially-trained, began to lose their Janissaries in 1826. The new Ottoman army, trained in the European manner, made its appearance in the province of Aleppo in 1830,[8] whereas Ibrahim Pasha's invasion of Syria in 1832 put an end to the structures of the old military institution.[9] In Morocco, Sultan Mawlay Hasan (1873–94) created a new modern army, trained by European instructors.

Thus, the collapse of the Mamluke and the imperial Janissary corps allowed local forces to emerge and assert their autonomy.

Moreover, although independence movements became viable for the first time, revolts against European domination were considered unacceptable and liable to cause irreparable damage to world trade and foreign interests. More importantly, the new international system did not look favourably upon such defiance which could result in excluding the European presence altogether.

In the wake of the 1878 Berlin Congress, the leading European powers began to work out a more controlled and manageable system. Each European power was, explicitly or implicitly, assigned a particular sphere of influence, either as a result of *de facto* reasons, or out of a sense of trying to satisfy as many legitimate competitors as possible. It was thought that such a political arrangement could serve to avoid a major conflagration, on the one hand, and help to control disruptive local forces, on the other. The Berlin Congress, for example, gave the French the right to control Tunisia (which they duly did in 1881), and allowed a free hand for Britain in Cyprus.

Thus, each local dispute or revolt seemed to call for greater European control. This invariably meant either the complete destruction of native institutions, as in Algeria, or nominal indigenous rule, tolerated to operate under strict supervision. In the last case, Tunisia after 1881, and Egypt after 1882, stand out as perfect cases in point. Whatever arrangement was reached or imposed the rules of the game were often taken for granted: open access by European powers either to sell their industrial products, purchase primary materials (grain, silk threads, cotton, tobacco, citrus fruits, etc), or gain freedom of settlement for their surplus population.

Moreover, wherever a state became bankrupt (Tunisia in 1869, Egypt in 1876), or was perceived to have failed to ward off popular defiance of its authority, one European power or another felt, or had to feel, obliged to intervene in order to restore what it conceived to be a normal state of affairs. This system did not operate as smoothly as it was intended and occasionally broke down, as in the Fashoda

Incident[10] in 1898. It finally became completely impractical with the outbreak of World War I.

During the same period, local national movements, wishing to win international support, began to offer themselves as the best guarantors of law and order. Provided they were allowed to run their own states, the argument went, they would in return act as reliable allies in a new system of liberal democracy and free market forces. It is in this context that the Egyptian nationalist leader Mustafa Kamil (1874–1908) toyed for a while with the idea of enlisting France's support and Ottoman goodwill in his drive to end British occupation of his country. However, France's retreat from Fashoda and the entente cordiale of 1904 between Paris and London dissipated his remaining illusions. Sharif Husayn's alliance with Great Britain in launching the 1916 Arab revolt can be seen in the same light. More often than not, these new approaches resulted in disappointment or by scaling down the original aim of these national movements.

Thus, the failure of liberal nationalist leaders to liberate their countries from foreign occupation, or the military defeats of local revolts by much superior European forces (Egypt in 1919, Iraq in 1920, Syria in 1926, Morocco in 1926 and so on) tended to give greater weight to state institutions within a particular administrative entity, on the one hand, and reinforce nationalist tendencies to break out of enforced political boundaries, on the other. Hence, the newly-accepted or reclaimed local state institutions became a legitimate political space for the activities of movements and leaders who were willing to pursue their national aims by a combination of popular pressure and diplomatic manoeuvres, and as the only official interlocutors of their colonial masters. By contrast, pan-Arabism tended to be the ideal solution or the last refuge of opposition forces. Moreover, the final articulation of political demands was couched in varied pan-Arabist versions.

Cultural Arabism

Cultural Arabism was born out of a tripartite encounter already alluded to: Ottoman reform, European models and Arab civilization. Cultural Arabism denoted a literary and ethnic movement that adapted 'the myths, memories, symbols and values' of Arab civilization to new conditions, endowing them 'with new meanings and new functions'.[11]

Thus, between 1800 and 1900, a sense of cultural and ethnic Arabism emerged and consolidated itself in Arab countries that were the direct theatre of Ottoman reform or European expansion. This applies in the main to Egypt, Greater Syria and Tunisia. Other Arab countries joined in this process at different levels or stages, a fact that explains the belatedness of political pan-Arabism in their historical development. This was particularly the case of Morocco, Algeria and the Arabian Peninsula. The absence of one factor, either Ottoman reform or direct European presence, accounts to a large extent for this uneven process of cultural Arabism.

Nevertheless, the rediscovery of Arabic civilization as a glorious golden age, coupled with an earnest desire to acquire knowledge of the modern European world, were the hallmarks of this cultural movement.

Thus, a configuration of social, institutional, economic and international events constitutes significant factors in the generation of Arabism. These historical conditions include the following:

1. The emergence of an Arab elite anxious to assert their interests and cultural credentials in a new political order.
2. Intense European rivalry for the acquisition of overseas possessions, as a result of modern transformations embodied in the Industrial and French Revolutions.
3. Ottoman endeavours of reform. Initially confined to military and administrative structures, these reforms encompassed by mid-nineteenth century state institutions, landownership, religious laws and social practices.

One of the most enduring legacies of the nineteenth century was the introduction of a new notion of citizenship, whereby political loyalty became centred on territorial dimensions. Cultural Arabism was fixed in this respect on the twin structures of a general Arab community and of a particular fatherland, with the Ottoman state acting as their political umbrella.

Three different social groups were granted this unprecedented opportunity to condition the emergence of cultural Arabism.

The first group consisted of religious scholars and prominent leaders who claimed descent from the Prophet Muhammad. This group had managed to survive the vicissitudes of decline visited upon their ethnic community by preserving their function as custodians of Arab culture and values.

This trend was first articulated, albeit in Islamic overtones, by Ahmad Ibn Taymiyya (1263–1328), a Hanbali jurist of the fourteenth century. It was this outstanding religious scholar who took up the idea of making the 'Ulama the legal and natural defenders of the community, following the demise of the Caliphate.[12] In this respect, the 'Ulama became the direct inheritors of the Prophet and the authentic representatives of their communities in the face of foreign dynasties and non-Arab ruling families. This idea, propagated in Syria, Egypt and Iraq, made Arab communities responsible for preserving their heritage and living according to their own original laws as embodied in the Qur'an and the Traditions of the Prophet.

Henceforth, most Sunni religious scholars thought of themselves in terms similar to those set down by Ibn Taymiyya. Thus, the study of Islamic law and its application required the twin disciplines of mastering the intricacies of the Arabic language and ascertaining the circumstances which occasioned particular injunctions and prescriptions in the Qur'an. Moreover, Arabic grammar, literature and history formed necessary auxiliary sciences in preparing oneself for guiding one's community or giving sound advice to the ruler of the day.

By teaching self-reliance, personal study and reasoning (*ijtihad*), this line of thought and practice manifested its most eloquent ramifications in the movement of Wahhabism which was inspired by the teachings of Ibn Taymiyya.

Echoes of the impact of this movement, despite its strict code of practice and puritanical principles, can be found in a chronicle of an Egyptian historian, who had witnessed Napoleon's invasion of Egypt in 1798. This was 'Abd al-Rahman al-Jabarti (1753–1825). Our historian was fiercely opposed to Muhammad 'Ali's policies and proud at the same time of his Arab origins and Egypt's long history. In his chronicle we come across allusions to the indigenous people of Egypt, subsumed under the name 'sons of the Arabs' (*abna' al-'arab*). To al-Jabarti, Egypt was inhabited or governed in the main by three different but interdependent sections: Ottomans, Mamluks (later replaced by Albanians and other minorities) and Egyptians or sons of the Arabs. It is noteworthy that al-Jabarti, in enumerating the holders of power in society, places the 'Ulama at the top of his list, following the Prophets and preceding in a descending order, kings and political rulers. Thus his 'ulama' are the elite of the elite, the heirs of the Prophets, and the followers of the true divine laws.[13]

Al-Jabarti's principal concern was the gradual decline of the 'ulama' both as a political and social force, brought about by the modernizing policies of Muhammad 'Ali. This was also the formidable task facing other Arab and Muslim scholars and statesmen as the era of reform, modernisation and European expansion was inaugurated by the Ottoman Tanzimat movement.

While resistance to reforms continued in one form or another, a number of religious leaders adopted a policy of accommodation, attempting to involve their colleagues in the process of modernization as being part of their religious duties. It is this new approach which gained ascendancy throughout the nineteenth century, despite the fierce opposition it encountered.

The second group included members of a new Christian intelligentsia based in Syria and Lebanon. Embracing teachers, journalists, editors, doctors and translators, this group disseminated its ideas by forming literary associations, publishing newspapers, and founding schools on modern European lines. The literary association, the newspaper and the school formed novel networks of communication and inculcation, acting as the mouthpiece of a new generation imbued with a sense of pride in a rediscovered Arab culture, and an enthusiastic response to western achievements in the fields of science, technology and education.

The third comprised a stratum of urban notables and landowners who entered the new institutions of a reformed Ottoman state either as civil servants, or representatives of their local communities. Members of this last group were destined to emerge in due course as leaders of political Arabism. In the meantime, the revivification of Arab culture enhanced their qualifications to assume wider responsibilities in an era of equality and fraternity.

By seeking to reconcile themselves and their immediate social circles to the new scheme of things, these groups adopted a twin-track policy: praising Arab historical achievements, on the one hand, and demonstrating the compatability of Arab cultural values, once purified and reinterpreted, with modern institutions, laws and cognitive knowledge, on the other. This journey of rediscovery entailed attaching central importance to the Arabic language as a medium of communication, and Arab ethnicity vouchsafed by a glorious golden age, to resume its role in history.

A new literary Arabic language was consequently forged to represent an autonomous cultural identity, capable at the same time of expressing the vocabulary and terminology of European civilization. The Arabic language was thus modernized and new terms were coined in order to convey the meaning of political ideas and institutions, or scientific innovations and philosophical concepts. Such a process could be seen, for example, in the attempt of Arab scholars to coin a term denoting the republican system of government in the wake of the French revolution, or the notion of democracy and parliamentary elections.

Hence, language became an instrument refurbished to understand the modern world, make it intelligible, and gain access to its novel secrets, be they intellectual, scientific or institutional.

This new language, which replaced the rhymed ornate prose of Mamluk and Ottoman official correspondence, or the semi-colloquialism of historical chronicles, arose out of the joint efforts of Syrian, Egyptian and Tunisian scholars. They were in the main teachers at newly established schools, editors of newspapers or journals, and civil servants working for modernising rulers.

In addition, new Arabic dictionaries were compiled in order to update and reinsert Arabic as part of a much wider cultural awakening. Both the Syro-Lebanese Butrus al-Bustani (1819–83) and Ahmad Faris al-Shidyaq (1805–87) compiled dictionaries for this purpose. The former also edited and published the first modern encyclopedia in Arabic, modelled on French and British versions.

In Egypt the multifaceted writings of the reformist teacher, translator and scholar Rifa'a Rafi' al-Tahtawi (1801–73) set the stage for the adoption of a new style of expression. It was further developed and given a solid articulate form by the Egyptian religious reformer, Muhammad 'Abduh (1849–1905), a disciple of Jamal al-Din al-Afghani (1838–97). By 1876, Egypt, in addition to Beirut, had become the foremost centre of Arabic literature, learning and journalism. It was thus in Egypt that the combined productions of Syrian and local writers endowed the Arabic language with its final and concrete modern form. Thus, in the age of reform, equality and citizenship, state structures were being forged to readjust to the new situation and ensure their legitimacy by using the language whose speakers they claimed to represent.

The emphasis on Arabic as an eloquent language embodied in literature, history, science and poetry went hand in hand with the rediscovery of the Arabs as an ethnic community in possession of cherished ideals and valid values. By doing so, these religious scholars and secular writers imperceptibly transformed the notion of Arabism, widening its scope so as to include by the turn of the twentieth century all Arabic-speaking communities.

We see this process at work in the works of al-Tahtawi who served Muhammad 'Ali and his successors. During his sojourn in France in the 1820s, al-Tahtawi learnt French as the Imam (prayer leader) of a student mission sent by his patron and began to appreciate the similarities and differences between Islamic and European civilizations. In 1834 he published his diaries in a book which was widely acclaimed for its comparative approach. It was called *Kitab takhlis al-ibriz fi talkhis Bariz.*

This Egyptian religious scholar was perhaps the first to consider the rise of Islam as the result of 'the national bond' which united the Arabs into one single body. This national bond manifested itself in the

Arabs' determination to assert their independence and constitute a civil association capable of creating a powerful state.[14]

Claiming descent from the Prophet Muhammad, al-Tahtawi mentions on more than one occasion the virtues of the Arabs, singling out their generosity, magnamimity, noble character, readiness to assist those in distress and fulfilment of promises and obligations. According to him, these characteristics were common to pagan, Christian and Jewish Arabs long before the advent of Islam.[15]

His pride in the Arabs was thus premissed on ethnic qualities that were strengthened by the new religion as conveyed in the Qur'an. It also makes him contend in his Paris diaries, mentioned above, that the liberty which the Franks (or European nations) sought was one of the traits of the Arabs in ancient times.

Such an emphasis on the ethnic virtues of the Arabs and their cultural achievements developed in the nineteenth century into an all-pervasive current. It was adopted, with slight variations or nuances, by both Muslim and Christian members of the intelligentsia, thereby creating an overarching bridge that made possible the creation of a neutral space claimed by two religious communities. This current, while embracing Muslim leaders such as the Egyptian educationist Muhammad 'Abduh (1849–1905), also became the hallmark of a group of Christian intellectuals in Syria and Lebanon.

This group, which included journalists, teachers, doctors and translators, disseminated its ideas by forming literary associations, publishing newspapers and magazines, and founding schools in which modern subjects and foreign languages were taught. They included Butrus al-Bustani (1819–83), Nasif al-Yaziji (1800–71), Salim Taqla (1849–92), Faris al-Shidyaq (1805–87) who converted to Islam, Ya'qub Sarruf (1852–1927), and Faris Nimr (1860–1952). One of the foremost propagators of the concept of a glorious Arabo-Islamic civilisation was the Syro-Lebanese Jurji Zaydan (1861–1914), who founded the magazine *al-Hilal*, wrote a history of Arabic literatures and authored numerous historical novels dealing with exemplary episodes of the Islamic past.

The Fatherland and Patriotism

While Arab ethnicity was highlighted irrespective of particular territorial locations, patriotic affiliations were often confined to a particular geographic unit, such as Egypt, Tunisia, Syria or Iraq.

It was in the nineteenth century, particularly after 1839, that the concept of the fatherland as a well-defined territory was propagated in the Arab world. This was a conscious and rational endeavour undertaken to create a new form of human organisation. The fatherland, limited to a particular Arab country, was positioned in the foreground as an integral territory and reference point. Patriotism served in this instance as a permanent marker in a world of flux and change. The territory which one stood upon was fixed and stabilized in order to make this firm ground a reliable foundation for social and economic reform. The idea of *Watan*, or the fatherland, introduced by Ottoman officials or their local associates, spread into various parts of the Islamic world, becoming a familiar and integral concept of the political vocabulary of Muslim and Christian Arabs alike.

Accordingly, national historical writings, centred on one particular Arab country, began to be written in order to offer a visible demonstration of the unfolding events over a single territory. The fatherland was celebrated in prose and poetry whereby its dynasties, geography and historical junctures were made to pulsate with meaningful messages, creating an ongoing dialogue with its inhabitants, and leading to ever stronger bonds of devotion. This shift from a religious or dynastic narrative to one built around a territory and its people denoted a secular dimension that was later incorporated by political Arabism. In this sense, religion became a dependent variable that had to be explained within the wider context of history itself. In other words, national identity grew out of the long history of a particular fatherland sharing a common fund of Arab cultural values.

Thus, it was in the period of the *tanzimat* or reforms that the idea of loving one's fatherland as a political duty began to gain currency. The Noble Rescript of Gülhane, officially proclaimed on 3 November, 1839 which promised to guarantee the security, honour and property of all Ottoman subjects, irrespective of race or religion, highlighted for the first time the importance of defending the fatherland. It furthermore made 'love of fatherland' a condition of introducing a fair system of justice and applying the rule of law in all economic and judicial transactions.

The Imperial Rescript mentioned above was soon afterwards translated into Arabic and distributed in Tunisia, Egypt, Iraq, Syria and other Ottoman Arab provinces.[16] Although the Ottoman authorities preferred to consider, and refer to, their entire empire as one single fatherland, it was the smaller autonomous or administrative units that became identified as such.

Tunisia was perhaps the first Arab country to be designated by its officials as a fatherland. The chronicle of one of its state officials, Ibn Abi al-Diyaf (1802–74) testifies to such an early maturation of the concept of national affiliation. Tunisia witnessed various reforms introduced by its local rulers after 1835. It followed a pattern similar to Egypt in the economic and social fields, but with a clear affinity with Ottoman imperial pronouncements and political terminology. The notion of considering one's administrative territory a fatherland was consequently adopted to refer to Tunisia as one single political unity, worthy of loyalty and admiration.

On the other hand, Greater Syria began to be identified as such from the early 1850s onwards. The reference to Egypt as a fatherland, and contrary to common belief, did not become firmly established until the disappearance of Muhammad 'Ali from the scene in 1849. Thus, the Egyptian educationist al-Tahtawi undertook to propagate such a concept in his school manuals, patriotic poems and magazine editorials in the second phase of his career, namely 1856–75.

By the first half of the twentieth century, the idea of loving one's fatherland had become an intrinsic part of political discourse through-out the Islamic world. As each Arab state gained its independence, its designation as a separate fatherland was taken for granted. Moreover, while references to the Arabs as 'a nation' or *umma*, were fairly frequent after 1900, referring to the Arab world as a fatherland remained a rarity until the late 1920s.

By redefining the fatherland to embrace a limited and less vague territory than the entire Ottoman Empire, the inhabitants of this newly imagined single political unit gained a sense of their particular national history, on the one hand, and reclaimed for the local culture its own language, on the other. Hence, using Arabic instead of Ottoman Turkish, in governmental decrees and official transactions became a political right of citizenship and an assertion of national identity. In Tunisia, for example, state officials decided to use Arabic instead of Turkish in their correspondence with the Ottoman Sultan-ate as early as 1838. According to Abi al-Diyaf, the Tunisian religious leader, Shaykh Ibrahim al-Riyahi (1766–1850) insisted on using Arabic so as to be able to put his signature to a text the meaning of which he would be able to understand.[17]

The Cultural and the Political

As we have seen, the rediscovery of Ibn Taymiyya was not confined to the circle of fundamentalist Wahhabites. On the contrary, his approach to Islam and its interpretation seems to have struck a resonant chord with a group of Islamic reformists who were at the same time imbued with a pan-Arabist spirit. This group consisted of prominent Muslim scholars scattered across the Arab world and beyond. They were fiercely opposed to popular practices of Islam, particularly exaggerated Sufi notions and superstitious beliefs. Their conception of Islam was thus derived from an emphasis on its pure Arab origins and the necessity of restating the message in a modern framework of rational attitudes to political and cultural problems. In this sense, they restored the Arab character of Islam as an intrinsic ingredient of its viability and compatability with the modern world. Consequently, signs of decline in science and industry, and traditional accretions of mystical beliefs, were considered the result of a process of adulteration, set in motion by the ascendancy of non-Arab ethnicities. The return to the practices and simple creed of the early Arab ancestors was, in this respect, a modernist attempt to relaunch Islam on a new course. It also led, by the nature of its remit, to direct confrontation with a variety of Islamic traditions, be they officially sanctioned or popularly upheld.

Ibn Taymiyya entered the scene, or was dragged into these controversies, as a representative of a strict line of religious dogma and a fierce defender of its Arab frame of reference. Moreover, his strictness and puritan orthodoxy went hand in hand with a firm adherence to the necessity of individual interpretation or *ijtihad*. In other words, all schools of law in Islam and the venerated opinions of their founders were mere personal interpretations that had no sanctity or infallibility in comparison with the original text, the Qur'an. Needless to say, Ibn Taymiyya's purpose was purely religious and could not have been otherwise, given the medieval culture of his times. He, moreover, considered faith and piety, irrespective of race or ethnic origin, to be the essence of Islam.[18]

Nevertheless, to Ibn Taymiyya, as to most of his fellow 'ulama, the inhabitants of the known world were divided into two main branches: Arabs and non-Arabs, or *'arab wa 'ajam*. The Arabs in their turn were either Bedouin or urban dwellers. The last were more perfect and better equipped to practise religion and conduct themselves in a civilized manner. The Prophet himself was an urban dweller, and his message was primarily addressed to his social group. Furthermore, the urban Arabs were endowed with unique qualities which differentiated them from other communities and made them superior in a number of ways. Within the world of urban Arabs themselves there was also a scale of preference: Quraysh, Muhammad's tribe, was the best of all tribes, and his clan, Banu Hashim, was the most excellent of all clans. In the same way Quraysh is ranged in its relation to the Arabs, so are the Arabs in their relation to other ethnic communities. Hence the innumerable sayings and statements attributed to the Prophet in urging his followers to venerate and love the Arabs (pp. 142–59).

According to Ibn Taymiyya, the Arabs deserved preference for the power of their perception, the eloquence of their language, the quality of their morality and the value of their deeds. However, these qualities were in a state of suspension until Islam managed to breathe new life into them. It is in this context that Ibn Taymiyya's analysis of the importance of Arabic as the key to understanding Islam stands out for its originality. To him 'the Arabic tongue is the symbol of Islam and its adherents, and language is one of the most distinguishing symbols of nations' (p. 203). He goes on to explain that when the early Muslims settled in Syria, Egypt, Iraq, the Maghreb and Khurasan, they began to acquaint the inhabitants of these countries with the Arabic language until it became their first tongue, 'be they Muslims or unbelievers'. It was only in Khurasan, in south-eastern Iran, that Arabic receded owing to the laxity of its settlers. No Muslim, Ibn Taymiyya insists, should use any other language, be it at home, work or school. The reason being the effect language exerts in shaping the mind, forming character and performing one's religious duties (pp. 202–6).

In this sense, Arabic ceases to be an ethnic attribute and is closely connected with the development of an independent religious and cultural identity. For Ibn Taymiyya was clearly aware that the Arabs were originally differentiated into three categories: speakers of Arabic, descendants of the Arabs,[19] and the inhabitants of the Arabian peninsula. Nowadays, he continues, those who are Arabs could be classified so either linguistically, ethnically or territorially (pp. 166–7).

Ibn Taymiyya's rediscovery in the eighteenth and nineteenth centuries took place against the background of growing Arab discontent with Ottoman authority. In Arabia, Wahhabism pushed his teaching in an extremist direction centred on excommunicating all Muslims who did not adhere to his strict Hanbali censorship of popular practices. By implication, Ottoman lax attitudes towards Sufi orders and claims to the Caliphate were condemned and delegitimized. In this sense, Arabism was implied but never espoused as a concept in its own right.

By contrast, in Damascus, Baghdad and Cairo a milder and more sophisticated version of Ibn Taymiyya's teachings was cultivated. The Yemeni scholar Muhammad ibn 'Ali al-Shawkani (1760–1835) was perhaps the first to highlight the implications of Ibn Taymiyya's works in the realms of religious revival and the duty of all Muslims to interpret their religion in accordance with social and economic circumstances. To that end, a return to the early sources was made an act of good practice superseding all subsequent contributions occasioned in the main by personal motivations.

By the second half of the nineteenth century Wahhabism was in abeyance, being confined to its original hinterland in central Arabia. This freed other religious circles and scholars to pursue their own agenda by using Ibn Taymiyya in an attempt to restore their status in an age of westernized reforms, on the one hand, and to reassert the relevance of Islam to creating a more balanced scheme of things, on the other. The Alusi family of Baghdad, spanning three generations – Nu'man Khayr al-Din (1836–99), 'Ali 'Ala al-Din (1860–1921) and Mahmud Shukri (1857–1924) – were amongst those who propagated a message of reform and rational deductions based on the methodology of Ibn Taymiyyah. In fact, Mahmud Shukri al-Alusi published in 1896 a three-volume study on the merits of the Arabs as an ethnic community with a developed cultural heritage long before the rise of Islam.[20] He also singled out the inherent capability of the Arabic language to be the medium of transmitting and expressing the modern scientific discourse.

This particular approach to rehabilitating the history of the Arabs in pre-Islamic times coincided with the emergence of the Amir 'Abd al-Qadir al-Jaza'iri (1807–83), as a hero of Algerian resistance against French occupation. Although he was defeated and sent into exile after 1847, his military exploits, political leadership and reformist approach to religion continued to inspire admiration throughout the Arab world. He himself was an admirer of Muhammad 'Ali's efforts to build a modern state equipped with an industrial infrastructure and a standing army. His short experiment at state-building (1832–47) revealed a willingness to introduce all available technological and material advances to strengthen his political independence as Algerians confronted a more superior foreign power. Detained in France for five years, he was finally released by Louis Napoleon III and allowed to travel abroad. After a brief sojourn in Anatolia, he finally settled in Damascus in 1855. Damascus was to remain for him, together with a large Algerian entourage, his preferred place of abode and centre of activities for the rest of his life.

Enjoying the patronage of both France and the Ottoman Sultan, 'Abd al-Qadir re-established himself in the old umayyad capital as a wealthy landowner, a renowned scholar and a patron of schools and mosques in his own right. By 1860, or following his humane efforts to save Damascene Christians from the onslaught of Druze forces during the same year, he was increasingly being mentioned as a possible head of an Arab Kingdom in Syria under French auspices.[21] It was, however, in 1877 that his name was put forward by a local group of notables to declare Syria's independence and establish a truly Arab state. According to the memoirs of one of these leaders, 'Abd al-

Qadir accepted their offer in principle, while at the same time wishing to maintain his recognition of the Ottoman Sultan as the spiritual representative of all Muslims. He, furthermore, stipulated that the 'Syrian people' should be given the opportunity to proclaim his election.[22]

This movement for independence was launched during the Russo-Ottoman war in 1877–8. Its leader, Ahmad al-Sulh, a resident of Beirut, was convinced that the Ottoman Empire was on the verge of collapse. He and other leading members in Greater Syria feared that Ottoman defeat in the war or the Empire's doomed fate might tempt more than one European power to annex Syria and turn it into another Algeria. In order to forestall such an outcome, they calculated that 'Abd al-Qadir, with his international reputation and well-known tolerance, would be a great asset at the head of an independent Arab Kingdom.

However, although the war ended in Ottoman defeat, it did not spell the end of the empire, nor did the European Great Powers at the 1878 Congress of Berlin broach the Ottoman sovereignty over Syria. Britain at the time was more interested un securing Egypt and the Suez Canal,[23] while France was realigning her forces to invade Tunisia. Moreover, the appointment of Midhat Pasha (1822–83) to the governorship of Syria seems to have defused the disaffection of Syrian notables. Midhat, as the architect of the first Ottoman constitution, was virtually exiled to Syria by Sultan 'Abdulhamid. He remained in his post for twenty months when on 1 August 1880 he was transferred to Izmir. But he remained long enough to re-establish Ottoman authority and earn the goodwill of the population. Three years later, 'Abd al-Qadir died, leaving behind him a cultural and political legacy which was partly revived by the son of another Algerian emigrant who had settled in Damascus in 1847. This was Tahir al-Jaza'iri (1852–1920).

Tahir's career as a teacher, educationist and librarian was launched under the direct patronage of Midhat Pasha. In addition to founding Syria's first library, the Zahiriyyah, for which he collected books and manuscripts throughout his active career, his direct interest in reviving Arab culture in all fields of learning, reveals the direct link between religious reform and the emergence of Arabism as an articulate national identity.

Prior to the 1908 Revolution in Istanbul, both Islamic reformists in Arab urban centres and Young Turks cooperated in their opposition to Sultan Abdulhamid. In Damascus this took the form of a literary and cultural circle organized by Tahir al-Jaza'iri and known as the senior circle. The first Arab members were, on the whole, second-rank 'ulama who had either been shunned by the Ottoman establishment, or had chosen to pursue an independent career. Others belonged to notable families who had lost political influence as a result of the autocratic rule of 'Abdulhamid. The latter group included Rafiq al-'Azm (1867–1925), whose family, as we have seen, rose to prominence in the eighteenth century. However, al-'Azm emigrated to Egypt in 1894 for family reasons. He later re-emerged as the co-founder the Ottoman Consultation Society in 1907. He, together with his colleague the Syrian reformist Rashid Rida (1865–1935), called for 'a constitutional and parliamentary regime' in an open Ottoman society regardless of race, religion or nationality. However, most of its branches were based in Arab countries. It was dissolved in the wake of the Young Turk revolution. Rafiq al-'Azm became in 1912 President of the Ottoman Party for Administrative Decentralisation (see below).

Side by side with the Senior Circle, there began to coalesce around Tahir al-Jaza'iri a junior circle of young students who were graduates of a modern secondary school, Maktab 'Anbar, which was established in 1893. Its curriculum comprised modern subjects, such as economics, world history and geography as well as chemistry, physics and geometry. However, its teachers were in the main Turks and used Turkish as the language of instruction. This was often a source of friction between Arab and Turkish students, and helped to reinforce calls for a more tolerant attitude towards Arab culture.[24] According to a member of the junior circle, these Arab students formed in 1903 a secret society which included Muhibb al-Din al-Khatib, 'Arif al-Shihabi, 'Uthman Mardam, Lutfi al-Haffar, Salih Qunbaz, Salah al-Din al-Qasimi and Rushdi al-Hakim. Their programme called for a system of decentralization in the empire whereby Arab rights would be guaranteed, and the adoption of Arabic as the official language in the Arab provinces.[25] From Damascus, the secret society widened its network of contacts to include other similar minded students, particularly in Beirut. Those contacted or recruited became at a later stage prominent members of other Arab societies.[26]

In 1906, a number of Arab students who had gone on to advanced studies in Istanbul decided to set up a society under the name of the Arab Renaissance (*al-Nahda al-'Arabiyya*). The founder of the society was Muhibb al-Din al-Khatib (1886–1969), a former member of the Junior Circle of Damascus and a law student. He also contacted two members of the Junior Circle, still resident in Damascus, Salah al-Din al-Qasim and Lutfi al-Haffar, to organize a branch of the Arab Renaissance Society in Damascus. Soon afterwards, the Syrian capital became its headquarters. Its main purpose was still that of the junior circle, but with a clear structure which ensured its continued operation until it was forced to merge with the CUP at the end of 1909. By that time, it had been carrying out its activities under the title the Syrian Renaissance Society when it was forced to drop its Arab appellation after the advent of the Young Turks to power in 1908. The Ottoman authorities forced its founders to change the name of the society under the pretext of complying with 'the law of associations' which forbade political parties to use ethnic designations.

The original Senior Circle of Tahir al-Jaza'iri brought together three different political strands in Ottoman Syria, and which could be said to represent a microcosm of other Arab provinces. These were: (1) Islamic reformism advocated by a group of middle 'ulama; (2) cultural Arabism, which shared a common interest with Islamic reformism, but differed from it in its emphasis on the modern dimension of national culture as an independent variable. Moreover, whereas Islamic reformism was a virtual monopoly of religious leaders, cultural Arabism was emerging as the ideology of professional groups who had enjoyed a secular education provided by newly-established state schools and aspired for a career either in the army or the bureaucracy;[27] (3) Young Turk modernism which emphasized a strict definition of Ottomanism based on the twin concepts of constitutionalism and centralization. Thus, the third group was less concerned with the niceties of cultural differences, and more interested in the survival of the Ottoman state and its fate as part of a system of intensifying European rivalries.

The Arab (later Syrian) Renaissance Society represented the culmination of a cultural movement which sought to forge an Arab identity within an overarching Ottoman framework. It also denotes the transition from cultural pursuits and literary interests to a more active political involvement in the struggle for a more solid basis of constitutional reform.

Salah al-Din al-Qasimi (1887–1916) embodied in his career and writings this transitional period in more than one sense. Born into a family of religious leaders, he initially espoused the cause of Islamic reform, joining Tahir al-Jaza'iri's circle of like-minded reformers. But unlike his father and elder brother, Salah al-Din departed from the family's tradition and chose to pursue a non-religious career. In 1914, he graduated from the local medical college which had opened its doors to members of his generation at the turn of the twentieth century. Hence, al-Qasimi's medical education, preceded by an intense interest in modern scientific subjects, governed his approach to politics as revealed in his public lectures and published writings.[28] He, moreover, acted as the most dynamic and recognizable symbol of the Arab Renaissance Society since its foundation. In his capacity as its first secretary, he represented the Society throughout its history and negotiated on its behalf in its dealings with prominent Ottoman authorities.

The aim of his Renaissance Society, as he saw it, was to achieve the happiness and prosperity of 'the Arab nation', and restore the wonder of a bygone Arab glory. Whereas al-Kawakibi wavered between an Arab identity and an Islamic reformist programme (see below), al-Qasimi resolved this tension by giving priority to nationalism as the expression of a new and more advanced phase of human history. In other words, al-Qasimi differentiated very clearly between a former phase in which religion figured as the most effective medium of achieving a nation's interests, and a more recent one whereby nationalism, by the sheer fact of 'evolutionary processes', made nationalism more beneficial and effective in ensuring the survival and progress of societies. In order to prove the effectiveness of nationalism in the modern age, he draws attention to and cites the example of the American and French Revolutions as well as the Italian and German unification movements. He, moreover, had no doubt that Rousseau, Kant and Fichte exerted as much influence on bringing about the new age of nationalism as prominent statesmen.[29]

However, like other Arabists of the period, al-Qasimi did not call for separation but close cooperation between two national communities: the Turks and the Arabs.

After 1905, political organizations began to proliferate in the Arab world. These were on the whole elite societies, set up by young men in the early stages of their careers. Their social profile included lawyers, journalists, army officers, medical doctors, teachers and administrators. Their grievances articulated in political terms and programmes centred on gaining greater autonomy for their respective national territorial units which they had identified as the locus of their immediate loyalties. This was as much true of the programme of the Young Tunisians, published in 1907, as that of the Party for Administrative Decentralisation in Syria. The reclamation of Arabic and its heritage figured figured as a common denominator in both North Africa and Arab Asia.[30]

In North Africa the phase of cultural Arabism dragged on well into the 1920s, at a time when political nationalism was already in the ascendant in the eastern part of the Arab world. By that time the model for liberation had become an independent separate state, and within what was being increasingly called 'the world of Arabism' (*bilad al-'uruba*).

According to Eliezer Tauber,[31] the Arab Renaissance Society 'may be considered the mother of the Arab societies' which were founded between 1908 and 1914. These included the following:

1   The Arab-Ottoman Fraternity (*al-Ikha' al-'Arabi al-uthmani*). It was founded shortly after the 1908 revolution by a number of Arab notables, resident in Istanbul and known for their conservative views. The Fraternity included both Muslim and Christian Arabs who felt the need to defend Arab interests and culture at a time when former aids of Sultan 'Abdulhamid who had been placed under arrest, were becoming the butt of ridicule in the press.[32] Its programme consisted of asserting the Arabs' attachment to the Ottoman Sultan and Empire, while at the same time stressing the need to preserve their dignity and improve their position. It called for measures to expand education in the Arab territories and announced the intention of its executive committee to publish three newspapers in Arabic, Turkish and French. It also wished to encourage Arabs in organizing societies for the promotion of commerce, industry and agriculture.[33]

The 'Law of societies',[34] which forced the Arab Renaissance Society to drop its 'ethnic' designation, was used to ban the new one following the counter-revolution in 1909.

2   It seems that the demise of the Arab-Ottoman fraternity prompted Arab students and army officers to set up a secret organization, the Qahtaniyya Society.[35] Its senior member was Salim al-Jaza'iri (1879–1916), a nephew of Tahir al-Jaza'iri and a graduate of the Military Academy and the Staff Academy in Istanbul. He was joined by 'Abd al-Hamid al-Zahrawi, who represented the city of Hama in the Ottoman Parliament, 'Aziz 'Ali al-Misri, an army officer of Egyptian origin, 'Abd al-Karim al-Khalil, a law student from what is today Southern Lebanon, and others. The society had a strict military discipline and had as its aim the promotion of Arabism within the context of the Ottoman state. However, it does not seem to have continued its secret activities beyond 1911.

3   There are strong indications that the members of the secret organization, the Qahtaniyya, decided to use a public, legally-recognised front to work for its Arab cause at a much wider level. Hence, al-Muntada al-Adabi or the literary club, was formed on 8 February 1910. One of its most prominent members was 'Abd al-Karim al-Khalil (see above). It recruited Arab members who were pursuing their higher education or various professional careers in the Ottoman capital. Arab scholars regard this society as the first organization to turn the Arab question into a truly national cause. Its members learnt the art of political lobbying and group pressure by seeking the endorsement of sympathetic Ottoman officials. It, moreover, set up

branches in a number of towns and cities in Arab Asia. Its aim was in line with the general mood of the time which stressed the co-operation of Arabs and Turks within 'the Ottoman nation'. The most prominent item on its agenda was concerned with unifying school curricula and establishing a teachers' college to train a new generation of Arab students in modern methods of education. It is worth noting in this respect that it included Egyptian educationists and public figures in its deliberative committee on education.[36] It, moreover, put on plays which had as their themes glorious episodes of Arab history, organized classes in Arabic and Turkish and invited writers and scholars to lecture on a variety of topics. Amongst those invited lecturers was the future theorist of Arab nationalism, Sati' al-Husri, but who was then a staunch Ottomanist. It even devised the first modern Arab flag, consisting of four horizontal white, black, green and red stripes. It also published a periodical which discussed various cultural and political issues related to the Arab cause. In March 1915, the Ottoman authorities banned the club and five months later executed its President, al-Khalil, along with a number of other Arab activists.

4   Perhaps the most important organization which emerged during this period was al-Fatat or to give its full name: Jam'iyyat al-Umma al-'Arabiyya al-Fatat – The Society of the Young Arab Nation. It was later abbreviated to the Young Arab Society. Its origins go back to the early days of the Young Turk Revolution, when 'Arab traitors' of 'Abdulhamid era (see above) were being denounced in the press and in public speeches. According to the memoirs of one of its founders, it was these insults to Arab dignity and national honour which led a group of Arab students to protect their national rights by following the example of the Young Turks who started out as a secret organization.[37] However, al-Fatat was not formally established until 1911, when 'Awni 'Abd al-Hadi and Muhammad Rustum went to Paris to continue their higher education. With its headquarters in Paris, its first administrative committee included, in addition to the two names mentioned above, Ahmad Qadri, Rafiq al-Tamimi, Muhammad Mih-masani, 'Abd al-Ghani al-'Uraysi, Sabri al-Khawja and Tawfiq al-Natur.

Ahmad Qadri claims that although their written programme did not spell out the idea of Arab independence, it was one of their secret aims. It continued to operate as a clandestine organization under its collective leadership until 1920. Its most important contribution to the Arab cause was the initiative it took in 1913 to organize the Paris Congress (see below). Moreover, one of its most potent instruments of propaganda was the newspaper *al-Mufid*, with one of its members, al-'Uraysi, acting as its editor. Its methodical and cautious approach to recruitment turned it into a highly élitist instrument of political struggle. Those who joined it hailed in the main from Greater Syria, with a few members from Iraq. After the conclusion of the Paris Congress in June 1913, it moved its centre of operations to Beirut and established a branch in Damascus.

The entry of the Ottoman Empire into the war prompted al-Fatat to establish its headquarters in Damascus. This move was accompanied by the decision of its administrative committee to throw in its lot with the Ottoman state in order to foil European designs in Arab Asia. When Amir Faysal, Sharif Husayn's son, visited Damascus in March, 1915, it succeeded in recruiting him into its ranks. In the meantime, Sharif Husayn had entered into negotiations with British officials in Cairo to declare Arab independence. One month earlier, British forces had repulsed an attack on the Suez Canal, launched by the Ottoman representative of the CUP in Syria, Jamal Pasha. Following the Ottoman failure to 'liberate' Egypt, Jamal Pasha's regime became increasingly repressive, culminating in the execution of the first batch of 'Arab martyrs' on 21 August 1915 (ten Muslims and one Christian).[38]

These executions, together with a policy of deportation and transferring of Arab officers, convinced al-Fatat and another secret organization, al-'Ahd, to work with Sharif Husayn for Arab independence.
5   On 28 October 1913, and following the failure of the Paris Congress to convince the Ottoman authorities to implement its programme of reform, in addition to the disastrous Balkan war, and the loss of Ottoman Libya to Italy, some fifty officers in the Ottoman army decided to set up a secret military organization to work for 'a federal state', based on the autonomous equality of all its ethnic communities.[39] However, it had a preponderance of Iraqi officers led by Taha al-Hashimi (1888–1961). The secret military society, al-'Ahd, had at its head Aziz Ali al-Misri (1879–1965) who had originally belonged to the now defunct al-Qahtaniyya organization. Its officers led the regular Arab army in the Arab revolt and its Iraqi wing, which emerged in 1919, was largely instrumental in creating and managing modern Iraq after 1920.

Political Arabism, 1900–1945

Thus as Arabism entered its second phase, it acquired an eminently political character. In this phase the concept of the fatherland became associated with self-determination, independence and the active participation of indigenous elites in deciding its general well-being.

The Ottoman empire as a supranational entity and state collapsed at the end of World War I. Total Ottoman collapse was followed by the failure of various local Arab movements to achieve full independence, or devise viable political systems and sustainable economic growth. Indeed, in one single decade (1920–30), one Arab rebellion after another, all directed against European colonialism, was either utterly defeated or achieved partial and ephemeral success. This was the case in Syria, Iraq, Egypt, the Sudan, Libya, Tunisia and Morocco. Additionally, the question of Palestine, particularly the failure of the Palestinian Revolt in 1936 against British occupation and Zionist settlement, served to sharpen the need for solidarity among Arabs throughout the region.

It was in this period that notions of Arabism and the Arab nation were elaborated in more rigorous terms. Although patriotism, confined to a particular Arab country, remained a powerful force, it began to be increasingly supplanted, and often submerged, by the drive for a wider Arab unity. It was often argued, particularly in the 1930s, that the overwhelming domination of European powers could only be encountered by a pan-Arab, well-organised movement. Political parties, with hierarchical structures, were consequently formed in a number of Arab countries.

Articulation of Pan-Arabism

One of the first Arab civil servants and member of the intelligentsia to postulate a national existence of the Arabs, with a corresponding right to separate political institutions, was the Syrian religious scholar 'Abd al-Rahman al-Kawakibi (1849–1902). He did so by calling for the restoration of the Arab Caliphate as an authentic representative of the nation.

In a book published in 1900 (*Characteristics of Tyranny*),[40] he articulated a new concept of the nation in Arab political theory, basing his premises on the active participation of the people as free individuals and citizens. Some of his ideas on the nature of political oppression, initially directed against the rule of Sultan 'Abdülhamid, have been traced by a number of scholars to a Turkish translation of Vittorio Alfieri's *Della Tirannide*, which was first published in 1800.[41]

Two noteworthy contributions were made by al-Kawakibi, and irrespective of his ultimate sources: (1) he spoke of an Arab nation bound together by ties of patriotism, and (2) he made the Arabs themselves responsible for their future, rather than their Sultan, Caliph or any other. Thus, democracy, accountability and the necessity of a new type of organization were introduced as part of a pan-Arabist vocabulary.

What is noteworthy in al-Kawakibi's contribution is his emphatic emphasis on the political aspects of national regeneration. He thus represented an important link in the transition from cultural to political Arabism. And his new approach formed a fundamental ingredient in the ideological development of the Junior Circle of Damascus (see above) and subsequently of the Arab Renaissance Society.[42] Indeed, al-Kawakibi's introduction to his *Characteristics of Tyranny* is meant to highlight the need of a new science of politics capable of expressing the ambitions and interests of Arab youth who are said to be the hope of the nation. From the beginning, al-Kawakibi does not hide the fact that what he had to say was either the result of his own effort and observation or borrowed from European sources (p. 2).

To him, politics was a vast field subdivided into various branches which are not easily mastered by one single individual. Moreover, it was a new science in the sense that in the past political discourse entered the field of discussion as a subsidiary of either historical accounts and treatises on ethics or as part of literary and legal expositions. This was true of both European and Islamic civilizations, with the exception of some 'Republican Roman' writers. It was thus only in the modern period that a separate science of politics emerged in Europe. Although some Arab writers did begin to broach the subject,[43] al-Kawakibi continues, they had not yet dealt with 'the most important political subject' of the day, namely tyranny and how to replace it with a better system (pp. 3–5).

Writing at a time when Sultan Abdülhamid ruled his empire with an iron hand, and was wrestling with constant rumours of foreign and local plots to set up a rival Arab caliphate,[44] al-Kawakibi's treatise had an unmistakable relevance to the Arab nascent movement and its political future. Hence, analysis of tyranny mingles with an earnest attempt to arrive at a modern definition of Arabism. In other words, by situating politics and its ultimate purpose at the heart of Arabism, the transition to a higher political stage was underlined and made an integral feature of things to come. Moreover, there was no hesitation on his part to spell out the stark choice between regression and progress, stagnation and dynamism, the political will to overthrow tyranny and the assertion of nationalism as the midwife of a new dawn. By doing so, he operated a clear rupture between the past and the present, transforming political debate to a different level of national emancipation.

By a process of elimination, al-Kawakibi demonstrated the impossibility of overthrowing tyranny by partial reform or pleas for justice from downtrodden subjects. In order for tyranny to be completely eliminated, he asserts, the executive branch of government had to be accountable to a legislative assembly which is, in turn, 'accountable to the nation' which knows how to exercise its power of supervision and holds its representatives to account (p. 8). Moreover, all heads of state, be they monarchs or presidents, were prone to tyranny, unless curbed by strict supervision and the direct participation of their subjects in government. Were it not for the alertness of her English subjects, even Queen Victoria would not hesitate to avail herself of tyrannical powers (p. 9).

According to al-Kawakibi, religion was used in the past to buttress the divine rights of kings. The king's subjects were considered like a flock of sheep. The church itself endowed its popes with infallibility and God's vicarshisp until the advent of protestantism. As for Islam, it introduced a political system 'halfway between democracy and aristocracy'. It was democratic by its espousal of the equality of all its subjects, be they rich or poor, and aristocratic by instituting consultation of its prominent notables in political deliberations. This was particularly the case in the formative period under the rule of the four rightly-guided caliphs (pp. 13–20).

At this point, al-Kawakibi chooses to criticize Sufi practices and superstitious beliefs as being alien innovations, imported into Islam to perpetuate popular ignorance and prop up tyrannical rule. Moreover, he warmly welcomes all the latest scientific theories in biology, astronomy, chemistry, physics and medicine by citing a selective array of Quranic verses (pp. 22–7).

To be free is to become aware of one's rights and learn to rely on rational judgements, arrived at by independent means of inquiry. To achieve glorious deeds and leave one's mark in society has nothing to do with birth or ascribed status. On the contrary, most 'noble families' cling to tyranny and its nefarious pursuits. Hence, al-Kawakibi explains, tyranny may originate as the relentless ambition of an individual, but it does not endure unless it penetrates society. It does so by creating an army of sycophants and corrupt followers, who in their turn, duplicate the acts and practices of their master. This army of followers, from the Grand Vezir to the doorman, collude in spreading ignorance and fear as the most effective weapons of averting political change (pp. 34–48).

No one should be deceived into thinking that justice could be expected from a group of followers, who while continuing to serve their tyrannical master, pretend to be working for a better system of government (p. 49).

Al-Kawakibi was convinced that to change society one had to begin with the individual. By being self-sufficient, investing his efforts in earning his own living, and becoming fully aware of his merits as a human being, an individual takes the first step towards effecting permanent and enduring change. Progress depends on a dynamic force of constant endeavour, exemplified in the will to survive. Survival in the modern world is the prerogative of nations whose individuals have become aware of their identity (pp. 98–9). But a nation does not deserve to be strong and prosperous unless all of its individuals are seen to be working towards the same end (pp. 99–102).

Muslim, Christian and Jewish Arabs,[45] should learn from their religions and the example of countries such as Australia and the United States of America to find means of creating a firm national unity to the exclusion of religious or sectarian ties. Moreover, religions should be left to govern life after death, while life on earth is regulated on the basis of national solidarity (pp. 109–11). Hence, for a nation to come into being and occupy its rightful place in the world, it has to take its future into its own hands and establish a democratic system of government. Democracy is a system whereby the community at large exercises political authority and has an inherent right to depose those who violate its laws or fail to perform their assigned duties (pp. 121–2).

Democracy is thus the highest stage of social development as well as the first step on the ladder of human progress. For progress is infinite, constant and an intrinsic quality of life (p. 122).

However, al-Kawakibi was convinced that the best way to resist tyranny, and pave the way for its eventual collapse, is to create an enlightened public opinion in a gradual and peaceful manner. Tyranny, supported by armed force, financial power, religious authorities and foreign collaborators, could not be expected to be swept away overnight. More importantly, one has to decide beforehand what kind of system would be best suited to replace a tyrannical regime. An alternative system has to be worked out in detail and should receive the tacit or explicit approval of the community.[46] Such a plan of action, al-Kawakibi points out, may take years to come to fruition. More intriguingly, he put forward the idea that after the nation had become fully mobilized behind the new programme, it could ask 'the tyrant' to introduce, either willingly or forcibly, a democratic system, thereby avoiding violence and bloodshed (pp. 134–6).

In 1908, but under different conditions, 'Abdulhamid was forced to reinstate a constitutional government.

'Abd al-Rahman al-Kawakibi was born in Aleppo and received a traditional education in Islamic studies, Arabic and Turkish. He worked as an Ottoman official in his native city and edited a number of newspapers. The cosmopolitan atmosphere of Aleppo brought him into contact with European traders, missionaries and consuls.

The rivalry between his family and that of Huda al-Sayyadi for the deanship of the descendants of the Prophet (Niqabat al-Ashraf), a prestigious and lucrative post, embittered his relations with the Ottoman authorities and drove him to migrate to Cairo in 1898. Abu al-Huda al-Sayyadi (1849–1909) was a member of a Sufi order who claimed descent from the Prophet and succeeded in gaining Ottoman approval of his appointment as dean of the Prophet's descendants in Aleppo when he was twenty-five years old. After the suspension of the Ottoman Constitution in 1878, he became a close adviser to Sultan 'Abdülhamid. His main function was to promote 'Abdülhamid's image as the Caliph of all Muslims and the symbol of Islamic unity. His highly conservative and traditionalist interpretation of religion, considering the Sultan God's shadow on earth, created a rift within the ranks of Muslim 'ulama and served to turn Islamic reformism into a political movement. 'Abd al-Rahman al-Kawakibi was one of those who espoused the cause of reform and suffered as a result harassment and persecution. His decision to settle in Cairo fell in line with a growing tendency on the part of Arab Ottoman reformers to seek the relative security and freedom of British-occupied Egypt. Rashid Rida (1865–1935), who originally hailed from a village near Tripoli in North Lebanon, left his home town for Cairo in 1897, and launched there in cooperation with Muhammad 'Abduh his periodical *al-Manar*, one of the most influential instruments of Islamic reformism in the first three decades of the twentieth century. 'Abd al-Hamid al-Zahrawi (1871–1916) did the same in 1902, following his publication of articles questioning the validity of 'Abdulhamid's claim to the caliphate and throwing doubt on the compatability of traditional Islamic legal schools with modern life. He also attacked Sufism as an obscurantist movement preaching 'asceticism as a pretext for laziness and social parasitism'.[47] He remained in Cairo, where he continued to publish articles and books on Islamic reform, until the 1908 revolution.[48] Finally, Tahir al-Jaza'iri, the spiritual founder of Islamic reform and Arabism in Damascus, headed for Egypt in 1907 and remained there until 1920.

All these reformers, and many others, shared a common worldview centred on the need to modernize Islam by restating its original message and precepts according to the spirit of the age and its rationalist ethos. Another strand in their thought was the special role they assigned to the Arabs in reforming Islam. In a text[49] published shortly before his death, al-Kawakibi expressed this approach most forcefully. Moreover, he underlined the necessity of setting up clandestine and public organisations and associations to promote the idea of reform.

Whereas al-Kawakibi's concept of a separate national existence remained submerged for the time being, his secular and democratic principles coincided with those enshrined by the Young Turk Revolution of 1908. This revolution forced Sultan 'Abdülhamid to restore a constitutional form of government, leading one year later to his abdication in favour of a more pliant sultan.

However, between 1908 and 1913 the Ottoman state lost virtually all its European dominions, while ceding in the same period the Arab province of Libya to Italy. This led the Committee of Union and Progress (CUP), an umbrella organization dominated by the army, to seek tighter central rule, together with an emphasis on Turkish as the medium of communication and government.

As a reaction, a number of Arab organizations, consisting mainly of students, military officers and civil servants, came into being. These organizations, while not espousing independence or separation, redefined Ottomanism so as to become a partnership between two equal communities: the Turks and the Arabs. In North Africa, Moroccans, Algerians and Tunisians were arguing at the same time for greater equality between Arabs and French settlers, while Egyptians were divided into two camps: one calling for a better deal from Great Britain, and the other insisting on complete independence.

These demands laid the foundations of an ever-widening dichotomy between two ethnic communities in the Arab provinces of the Ottoman Empire. In Egypt and North Africa, while Islamic or local overtones became more pronounced, there emerged an underlying principle based on a broad Arab culture. It was, however, in the Levant that Arabism was first articulated as a modern political ideology.

By 1911, two political trends had emerged in the new constitutional era of the Ottoman Empire: assimilationist and decentralist. The assimilationist trend wss represented by the CUP which envisaged an integrated society sculpted out of its disparate ethnic communities and marshalled to embody a single Ottoman identity. This vision went beyond the earlier programme of the Tanzimat period which aspired to reform the state without undue disturbance to the traditional communal and ethnic identities. Ottomanism was now considered a nationalist creed and a policy of radical social transformation. Using Turkish as an official language of government and instruction, for example, took on new connotations, denoting adherence to a new ideology of national regeneration. It, moreover, gave its adherents a legitimate air of authority based on embodying the state in its administrative and military institutions. By purging the upper echelons of former officials and bureaucrats and who hailed from varied ethnic origins, the CUP lent credence to its opponent's charges of being motivated by narrow Turkish interests. In the wake of dismissing 'Abdulhamid's Arab advisers, for example, the CUP encouraged a chorus of anti-Arab press reports which seemed to engulf the whole community in its critical attitude (see above).

The decentralist trend was on the whole an opposition movement which included former elements of the Hamidian era, representatives of ethnic communities, such as Albanians, Armenians and Arabs, and entrepreneurial groups who preached the gospel of self-reliance and a liberal economy. Moreover, it was a trend which sought the salvation of the empire in a decentralized system of government in which all ethnic and religious communities would be represented on an equal footing.

However, the social composition of these two trends, while largely true of the Turkish hinterland, began to shift in new directions, following the deposition of 'Abdulhamid in 1909. While Arab reformists in the Ottoman empire welcomed the 1908 revolution and went out of their way to cement a new alliance with CUP leaders, this political agenda remained on the whole decentralist in its approach. On the other hand, old-style Arab Ottomanists revealed their hostility to the new order by pinning their hopes on 'Abdulhamid. His disappearance from the scene reshuffled the cards, leading to a new alliance between the old guard in Ottoman Syria and Iraq and the CUP. Sharif Husayn and other Arabian chiefs did not conform to the new political reconfigurations, as they had opposed the revolution since its inception.[50]

Consequently, most Arab reformers after 1909 began to reassess their political stance and to distance themselves from CUP policies. This explains their alliance with Sharif Husayn in 1916, although each camp had joined the opposition for different reasons. The emergence of a new Ottoman political party in 1911, the Entente Libérale, with its programme for administrative decentralisation, looked as if all disaffected elements in the empire could find a voice to articulate their grievances within a more tolerant state. Between 10 July 1912 and 23 January 1913 the Entente Libérale replaced the CUP as the effective government of the empire. Preoccupied with the Balkan wars, and the repercussions of the loss of Libya and the rivalry of the Great European powers, it lost its short rule to a coup d'état staged by the CUP triumvirate, Enver, Tal'at and Jamal. However, this brief ascendency of the decentralists encouraged various local Arab groups and associations to articulate their political demands more often than not, in direct response to the policies of the Ottoman government.[51] This period also coincided with renewed French interest in the fate of Syria, while Britain was expanding its economic interests in Iraq. The new Arab Reform Societies which emerged in 1912–13, were all geared towards one single aim: administrative decentralization. The first society to come into existence was set up by a group of Syrian émigrés in Egypt by the end of 1912. It simply called itself the Ottoman Party for Administrative Decentralisation. Its supreme committee composed of twenty members, elected Rafiq al-'Azm, a notable of Damascus, President, and Iskandar 'Ammun, a lawyer of Mount Lebanon, Vice-President. Another association, the Reform Society of Beirut was formed in January 1913, shortly before the collapse of the Liberal government in Istanbul. At the time, the *wilayat* of Beirut extended from Latakia in northern Syria down to Acre and Nablus in northern Palestine, with Beirut as its capital. The constituent Assembly of the Society included an equal number of Muslim and Christian delegates (84) and two Jewish delegates. Its leading member, Salim 'Ali Salam (1868–1938), a prominent Muslim notable, was initially prompted to organize such a reform movement in order to ward off French occupation or annexation to another foreign-occupied Arab country, such as Egypt. Salam, together with Ahmad Mukhtar Bayhum (1878–1922), another Beiruti notable, formulated its first list of reforms and were later to represent Beirut in the 1913 Paris Congress. These two were the best organized societies and their members exerted a direct influence on the direction of the Arab nationalist movement in the years to come. Moreover, a less well-known society was set up in Iraq under the leadership of Sayyid Talib al-Naqib (d. 1929), named after his home town and centre of activity, the Reform Society of Basra on 28 February 1913. Talib al-Naqib, a prominent Iraqi notable, represented his city in the Ottoman parliament and stood as a fierce opponent of CUP policies in the Arab provinces. He joined the Party of Entente Libérale upon its foundation, but the return to power of the CUP in January 1913 convinced him to rely on his own resources and set up his own organization. Unlike other reformist leaders, Talib was more of a local chieftain, with a wide popular base and prone to exact his own revenge. His opposition was based on an alliance with local tribal chiefs and a wide network of contacts in the Arabian peninsula. However, his aggressive attitude often antagonized his closest allies and served to turn them against his erratic policies. He, moreover, combined his opposition to the Ottoman establishment with an equally determined stand against foreign interests in Iraq. His untenable position of pledging support to the Ottoman Sultanate, while working for full autonomy in his province, ended with the outbreak of the war.[52]

In June 1913, an Arab Congress was convened in Paris to draw up a list of demands based on decentralization and administrative reforms within the Ottoman empire. It was organized by the moderate Ottoman Administrative Decentralisation Party and Beirut Reform Committee, as well as the secret and radical party al-Fatat (The Young Arab Society). The Congress was dominated by Syrian representatives, particularly those resident in Beirut, Damascus and Cairo. All in all, 23 delegates attended, divided into eleven Muslims, eleven Christians and one Iraqi Jew.

It was at this Congress that the concept of pan-Arabism became less vague and acquired theoretical rigorousness, whereas its geographic limits were confined, for political and international reasons, to the Arabian Peninsula and the Fertile Crescent.

A Beiruti editor and publisher, and a member of al-Fatat organisation, 'Abd al-Ghani al-'Uraysi (1890–1916), argued that theoretically the Arabs constituted a political community and a nation on the basis of five interrelated factors: language, race, history, customs and political aspirations. Geographically, the Syrian chairman of the Congress, 'Abd al-Hamid al-Zahrawi (1855–1916) conceded to an Egyptian, attending as auditor, that Egypt was indeed an Ottoman Arab province, but its particular grievances (British occupation) fell outside the remit of the Congress.[53] It is in this context that pan-Arabism in its Asian background is to be understood as largely a movement of Ottoman Arabs struggling against policies of turkification. Their hopes were, moreover, pinned on British or French assistance. However, no concrete results were achieved.

This movement culminated in the Arab Revolt of 1916. It was led by the spiritual leader of Western Arabia and a descendant of the Prophet, al-Sharif Husayn, and in association with Syrian and Iraqi army officers. To the Entente powers (Britain and France), the Revolt formed part of their military efforts to destroy the Ottoman State after its entry into World War I on the side of Germany.

Although independence was promised as a reward to Arab forces for participating in the war, Britain and France established themselves, following the Paris Peace Conference in 1919, as mandatory powers in the Fertile Crescent. In Arabia, Sharif Husayn lost his newly established authority as King to the advancing forces of the Wahhabites, led by 'Abd al-'Aziz Al-Sa'ud. In 1932 the Kingdom of Saudi Arabia came into existence. This was the only Arab state, together with North Yemen, to achieve a semblance of independence and escape direct European occupation. Both countries were ruled along traditional lines with minimal state authority.

Political Parties

Following the failure of various Arab revolts against European colonialism and mandatory systems between 1919 and 1932, the stage was
set for the emergence of new political forces led by an educated young
generation. The fact that certain Arab countries gained relative political independence – Saudi Arabia, North Yemen, Iraq and Egypt –
encouraged these new parties to put forward programmes of action,
deemed relevant to the Arab world as a whole.

The first public glimmerings of such an approach emerged in 1931
during the convention of a pan-Islamic congress in Jerusalem. As its
name indicates, this was an Islamic gathering convened to highlight
Muslim fears pertaining to the future of Palestine, particularly the
aggressive policies of Zionism. Almost all Arab countries sent delegates
to attend. It was the first time that Arab delegates from the Maghreb,
Egypt, the Arabian Peninsula and the Fertile Crescent had come
together under one roof. They thus held a separate meeting to discuss
purely Arab matters, and proclaimed a new pan-Arab covenant composed of three principal articles. These were:

1. The Arab countries form an integral and indivisible whole. Hence,
    the Arab nation does not accept or recognize the divisions of
    whatever nature to which it has been subjected.
2. All efforts in every Arab country are to be directed towards the
    achievement of total independence within one single unity; it
    being understood that every endeavour which aimed at confining
    political activities to local and regional issues is to be fought
    against.
3. Since colonialism is, in all its forms and manifestations, incompat-
    ible with the dignity and paramount aims of the Arab nation, the
    Arab nation rejects it and will resist it with all the means at its
    disposal.

The delegates decided to convene at an unspecified future date a
general congress to be attended by all pan-Arab organizations, and
prominent leaders. Furthermore, the delegates believed that King
Faysal of Iraq would act as the Patron of their new programme and
lend it his moral and material support. However, the British opposition to the idea of the congress as well as the unexpected death of
Faysal in September 1933, rendered the whole plan almost
impractical.[54]

Nevertheless, the first pan-Arab political party to be organized after the introduction of the Mandate system was the direct result of the Jerusalem Congress. This was the Arab Independence Party (AIP), founded on 13 August 1932 by Palestinian activists who had formerly belonged to al-Fatat Society and its short-lived frontal organization, the Independence Party.[55]

The AIP, while confined in its practical activities to the Palestinian political field, it aspired to work for Arab unity and solidarity so as to strengthen its position in the face of the British Mandate and Jewish Settlement. It declared its principles to be the complete independence of the Arab lands, their indivisible unity, and the Arab character of Palestine 'as an integral part of Syria'. Its immediate plan of action called for the abrogation of the British Mandate and the Balfour Declaration, in addition to the foundation of an Arab parliamentary system of goverment in Palestine.[56]

In August 1933, another pan-Arab political party, the League of Nationalist Action (LNA) was founded at a meeting in a Lebanese town. Its founding members, drawn from Greater Syria and Iraq, belonged to Western-educated professional groups – lawyers, teachers, medical doctors, editors and journalists. Its constituent assembly, composed of over thirty representatives whose age span ranged between 24 and 34, issued a statement which expanded themes briefly discussed by the pan-Arab covenant of 1931. Thus, the statement dwelt at length on the characteristics of colonialism and its nefarious schemes to combat Arab nationalism, turn Palestine into a Zionist entity, and create in the process a class of Arab collaborators and agents.[57]

The League of Nationalist Action defined its two principal objectives as being: (i) the absolute sovereignty and independence of the Arabs; and (ii) comprehensive Arab unity. It also stressed the necessity of carrying out a radical programme of socio-economic and moral reform. Although it left open the specific nature of the political or economic system it aspired to implement, it called for non-cooperation with all western colonial powers and asserted the need to boycott goods and commodities sold or produced by foreign companies. It demanded the removal of customs barriers between all Arab countries, the formation of a common Arab market and the establishment of a strong industrial base.

In an Arab world which witnessed in the preceding forty years or so the emergence of a new class of absentee landowners, edging their way towards the highest summit of local politics as the only viable medium of negotiation with colonial powers, the League wished to deprive them of their material underpinnings. It therefore proposed to introduce agrarian reforms by abolishing 'feudalism' and limiting landownership in such a way as to 'promote growth' and encourage new investments in rural areas. In the cultural and social fields, it stressed the necessity of nurturing 'Arab national consciousness' as opposed to family, sectarian and provincial affiliations. It also highlighted the need for new policies designed to improve the status of women and the living standard of peasants, workers and Bedouin.

What is perhaps noteworthy in this document is the moral tone that pervades all its pronouncements and judgements. Apart from its exhortations for selflessness, self-sacrifice, uprightness and abstention from collaborating with the mandatory system, it singled out gambling, alcohol consumption and dissolute conduct as morally reprehensible and contrary to the values of a reborn Arab nation. To that end, it lifted the use of literary and spoken Arabic in daily life to a higher plane of authentic citizenship. The bond of language was thus the moral glue of Arab unity.

This party gained a certain popularity throughout the 1930s, and its leader, the Syrian lawyer 'Abd al-Razzaq al-Dandashi, enjoyed a brief ascendancy until his sudden death in 1935. However, it remained an elitist organization, confined to the Fertile Crescent as its main theatre of operations. As an organisation, it did not survive beyond 1940. Its critics accused it of succumbing to the lure of governmental posts offered by the leaders of its local rival, the National Bloc.

During the same period, there emerged two other similar, but secret, societies. These were the Arab Liberation Society (ALS), and another, most commonly called the Arab Nationalist Party (ANP).[58] The ALS was the brainchild of the western-educated Lebanese lawyer, Farid Zayn al-Din (b. 1907), who teamed up with the Palestinian schoolteacher and historian Darwish al-Miqdadi[59] and Nafi' Shalabi, a Syrian from Aleppo and a graduate of German schools. They were joined in the early 1930s by like-minded nationalists in Syria, Lebanon, Iraq and Palestine. The Party was organized on the basis of small cells, with each cell directly linked to an Executive Committee, which included in addition to the original founders, the Iraqi army officer, Mahmud al-Hindi, and the Palestinian writer, Wasif Kamal. The structure and mode of operation of the ALS were to a large extent based on the now defunct al-Fatat Party, which in 1920, while keeping its clandestine nature, set up a frontal organization to deal with the immediate political issues of the Syrian state under Faysal. The ALS widened this organisational aspect to embrace as many Arab countries as possible. It, moreover, developed another tactic designed to infiltrate recently established societies and clubs which had pan-Arabist programmes. It was, thus, instrumental in the founding of the League of Nationalist Action in 1933, and the birth of the Baghdad Club,

Nadi al-Muthanna, in 1935. The Muthanna Club brought together committed Arab nationalists from Iraq and other Arab countries.

Moreover, it devised for its members a programme of ideological instruction in the form of a number of booklets and pamphlets. Its most famous booklet of instruction was referred to as 'The Red Book', because of the colour of its cover. The Red Book was composed as a collective effort and meant to express the most definite statement of an Arab nationalist programme. After a long silence, Qustantin Zurayq alluded in the course of listing his life's achievements to the contribution he personally made, together with 'other Arab nationalist activities, to the Red Book which became 'the constitution of a nationalist current in a number of Arab countries, with its leading believers (propagators) and soldiers meeting their death in the fields of struggle, and others keeping their faith in its principles . . .'.[60]

It seems that after the foundation of the League of Nationalist Action, the ALS[61] merged, or coordinated its activities, with another clandestine pan-Arab organization, established most probably in 1934. This organization had no specific name, but was known as 'the Red Book Group', which was the same one mentioned above. However, it has been dubbed by its former adherents as the Arab Nationalist Party (ANP). Its social composition and the age-span of its membership were similar to those of the LNA and the ALS. Moreover, their theatre of operation remained in the main confined to Arab Asia, although some North African intellectuals and personalities joined their ranks. Their outlook was secular and modernist whereby 'the Creed of Arabism' took priority over all other affiliations, including religion. Moreover, they all pinned their hopes on Iraq to lead the Arab Nationalist Movement and offer its organized societies moral and financial support. In this sense, the two secret parties were designed to infiltrate other associations, influence events and leaders rather than generate a popular current at a large scale. Their ideologues and cadres drifted in and out of established state institutions and had to compromise their initial political purity by accommodating themselves to the programmes of local personalities and provincial policies. The League of Nationalist Action, as we have seen, lost its credibility after its leaders allowed themselves to be used for the short-term calculations of Syrian notables, such as Shukri al-Quwwatly. The ALS seems to have suffered the same fate, whereas the ANP, led at different stages by Kazim al-Sulh of Lebanon, Younis Sab'awi of Iraq and Qustantin Zurayq of Syria, seems to have fared better than the other two, until it met its spectacular end in the Iraqi uprising of 1941. This uprising had initially a purely Iraqi dimension centred on the grievances of four army officers[62] against British policies. Dubbed the Golden Square, these army officers had originally formed an alliance with Faysal's successor, King Ghazi, who was reputed for his Arab nationalist tendencies. However, Ghazi was accidentally killed while driving his car at high speed on 4 April 1939. His sudden death led to accusations of a British plot to liquidate a young monarch who wished to build a strong army and was actively involved in enticing Kuwaiti opposition leaders and merchants to demand the annexation of their statelet or Shaykhdom to Iraq. The fact that some Kuwaiti personalities and political organizations did harbour such an idea is borne out by a statement issued in 1938 to that effect.[63] In its pre-war era, Kuwait was ruled by its local dynasty, al-Sabah family, in partnership with an elite of merchants who derived their wealth from pearling, trading and smuggling. But by 1938 oil had been discovered and the prospect of a new source of wealth controlled by the state, drove the merchants to demand representation and a proper parliamentary system. Although this movement for reform antedated the discovery of oil, it began to gather momentum in 1938, culminating in the election by the merchants of a Legislative Assembly which the ruler of the day was forced to accept. The Assembly was largely dominated by the National Bloc, a party representing Kuwaiti merchants and intellectuals. The Assembly drafted a basic law which empowered its members to exercise full control over budget affairs, public security and education. It thus asserted that 'the nation' rather than the ruling family was the ultimate source of authority. Six months later, on 17 December 1938, the Assembly was dissolved and new elections were held on 24 December. Contrary to the ruler's expectations, the National Bloc won a resounding victory, leading to the dissolution of the Second Assembly in March 1939,[64] shortly before the death of King Ghazi of Iraq. Leading Assembly representatives, namely 'Abdallah Hamad al-Saqr, Sulayman al-'Adsani and 'Abd al-Latif al-Ghanim had been recruited into the ranks of the Arab Nationalist Party during the sojourn of the first two in Syria and Iraq. They were particularly impressed with the cultural activities of the Arab Club in Damascus and al-Muthanna Club in Baghdad, two frontal societies of the above clandestine pan-Arab parties.[65]

Upon the dissolution of the Assembly by the Kuwaiti ruler Ahmad al-Jabir (1921–50), its members refused to comply with his wishes. Sulayman al-'Adsani, an ANP activist, went a step further by circulating a petition to be signed by Assembly members calling on King Ghazi of Iraq to annex Kuwait to his country. al-'Adsani was apprehended and thrown into prison, prompting his colleague 'Abdallah al-Saqr to flee to Iraq. Other Kuwaiti dissidents joined him in Iraq and were welcomed into the ranks of Rashid 'Ali al-Kaylani's uprising in 1941.

Although Iraq did not offer more than verbal support to the Kuwaiti dissidents[66] and merchants, its political influence and claims continued to overshadow Kuwaiti affairs for the rest of the twentieth century. As for the Legislative Assembly, it set a precedent for others to follow in Kuwait and the Gulf and gave birth to the first modern pan-Arab organization in the small Shaykhdom. Thus shortly after the establishment of the Assembly, some of its members set up the National Youth Society (Kutlat al-Shabab al-Watani) with principles and aims recapitulating those of the LNA and the other two secret parties. It, moreover, adopted the cause of Palestine as an internal Kuwaiti problem and the fact that both Palestine and Kuwait formed an integral part of an 'indivisible Arab nation'.[67]

As for Iraq and the role of the Arab Nationalist Party, political events were more complicated as Iraq, unlike Kuwait, was nominally independent with a parliamentary system already in place and a more vigorous configuration of party politics. After the death of King Ghazi, Iraq came under the control of the regent to the heir to the throne, 'Abd al-Illah and the veteran former Ottoman officer, Nuri al-Sa'id, who was then prime minister. The four army officers mentioned above had been close allies of Ghazi and his sudden death fuelled their suspicions of British policies in Iraq and the Arab world. Nuri al-Sa'id and the regent revealed their British sympathies by invoking their obligation under the 1930 Anglo-Iraqi Treaty to join Britain in its war with Germany. The arrival of Hajj Amin al-Husayni, the Palestinian leader, in Baghdad on 16 October 1939, after his escape from Lebanon, injected a new Arab dimension into local Iraqi politics. Hajj Amin (1895–1974) had become by then a legendary figure who, as the religious leader of the Supreme Muslim Council and head of the Higher Arab Committee in Palestine, represented the symbol of Palestinian resistance to British and Zionist policies. Following the 1936 revolt in Palestine, the Arab Higher Committee was dissolved by the British authorities, and Hajj Amin fled to Lebanon in October 1937. By that time, he had been instrumental in organizing an all-Arab conference in Bludan, Syria. The Bludan Conference, held on 8–9 September 1937, brought together delegates from all over the Arab world. Its sole purpose was to discuss ways and means of saving Palestine from falling prey to 'British-supported expansionist Zionism.'[68]

Those who attended the conference represented various shades of pan-Arabist opinions, but all agreed that Palestine was an integral part of the Arab nation and should be granted its independence. It was attended by 524 official and unofficial delegates under the chairmanship of a former Iraqi prime minister, Naji al-Suwaydi, while Hajj

Amin was elected honorary President of the conference in his absence. Next to the 1931 Jerusalem Congress (see above), this conference represented the largest gathering of pan-Arabists, who found in the Palestine question a strong motive to unify their efforts irrespective of local difference and provincial problems. While Hajj Amin had organized the Islamic Congress of 1931 in Jerusalem, he was not represented in the deliberations of the Arab delegates who held in the same year a separate congress of their own. In this sense, it would not be accurate to style the Palestinian leader as an Arab nationalist. His ideological commitments were primarily motivated by the plight of the Palestinian people, tinged with an Islamist tendency which sometimes took on an Arabist colouring. He thus had more affinity with figures such as Shakib Arslan (1869–1946), a Lebanese notable and a former Ottomanist and Rashid Rida (1865–1935), whose journal *al-Manar* had become by 1930 an advocate of a strict Islamist worldview.

Nevertheless, upon his arrival in Iraq in 1939, Hajj Amin was received as a hero of Arab resistance to British occupation and Zionist policies. Although he had undertaken to abstain from political activity while on Iraqi territory, he almost immediately became involved in the internal struggle of power between Rashid 'Ali al-Kaylani (b. 1892) and the regent. Hajj Amin persuaded the four army officers to support al-Kaylani, who, together with the Palestinian leader, saw an opportunity to enlist German support on their side. On 1 April 1941, Iraq came under the direct rule of the army, with al-Kaylani acting as prime minister. However, no German support reached them; the British reoccupied Iraq by a relief force, which was assembled in Palestine and crossed the desert into Iraq in early May. And the debate over the right of the British army to pass through Iraq became irrelevant.

The Arab Nationalist Party played a minor but significant role in the events leading to the second British occupation of Iraq. In 1939, its president was the Iraqi lawyer, Younis al-Sab'awi (1910–42), who emerged as a leading member of the uprising, and was appointed Minister of Economy during the short-lived government of May 1941. Moreover, whereas Hajj Amin and al-Kaylani sought German assistance and took refuge in Germany after their failure, al-Sab'awi tried to convince the Soviet government to support the Arab nationalist cause. His efforts failed as a result of the realignment of the Soviet Union on the side of the Allies in their war against Germany. He and the four colonels were captured, put on trial and executed in 1942.

The Iraqi episode aroused anger and frustration throughout the Arab world and was perceived as an expression of a growing Arab nationalist current. On 29 May 1941, the British Foreign Secretary, Anthony Eden, made the following statement:

> This country has a long tradition of friendship with the Arabs, a friendship that has been proved by deeds, not words alone ... The Arab world has made great strides since the settlement reached at the end of the last war, and many Arab thinkers desire for the Arab peoples a greater degree of unity than they now enjoy. In reaching out towards this unity they hope for our support. No such appeal from our friends should go unanswered. It seems to me both natural and right that the cultural and economic ties between the Arab countries, and the political ties too, should be strengthened. His Majesty's Government for their part will give their full support to any scheme that commands general approval.[69]

According to Wm. Roger Louis, this statement was made against the background of British military defeats in the Western Desert of North Africa and 'the possibility of a German breakthrough into the Fertile Crescent that would mean the loss of the oil in Iraq'.[70]

From the mid-1920s onwards, the drive for Arab unity became entangled with the question of reinstating the Islamic Caliphate after its abolition by Atatürk in 1924. This question loomed larger than its practical importance in the rivalries of three Arab countries, each trying to assert a certain regional role. These countries were Iraq, Saudi Arabia and Egypt. By the early 1930s the issue of the Islamic Caliphate began to fade into the background[71] and was to be super-seded as the decade wore on by various schemes designed to strengthen inter-Arab ties. These schemes ranged from a political alliance of independent Arab states to a more durable Arab federation. It was during this period that Egyptian writers, politicians and jour-nalists began to adopt a more positive attitude towards Arab national-ism. Moreover, as demands for independence were being increasingly voiced in North African countries, Egypt became a meeting place for Maghrebi leaders, either fleeing persecution or seeking to mobilise Arab opinion in their favour. By the end of World War II, Egypt had emerged as the leader of an Arab world that was teeming with proposals and ideas for unity or solidarity, both at the official and unofficial levels.

At the official level, this movement culminated in the foundation of the League of Arab States on 22 March 1945. Its seven founder members were all considered to be independent players in the inter-national arena. These were Egypt, Saudi Arabia, Iraq, Syria, Lebanon, Yemen and Transjordan (later the Hashemite Kingdom of Jordan). Between 1951, the date of Libya's independence, and 1977, a further fourteen independent Arab states had joined the League. Palestine is represented by the Palestine Liberation Organization and considered an independent state. Some countries which were not entirely Arab, such as Somalia and Djibouti, were admitted upon their request in 1974 and 1977 respectively. The League was conceived as an umbrella organization whose principal objective was to promote the economic, cultural and political co-operation of its member states. Thus, its covenant reaffirmed the sovereignty and territorial integrity of each Arab state, while at the same time leaving the door open for further cooperation.

The Arab League represented the optimum degree of Arab coordination as envisaged by official states, each with a different set of priorities and policies. It also indicated, particularly at its inception, the maximum extent colonial powers such as Great Britain, could approve or tolerate. Although Britain was not officially a party to the deliberations of the seven founder members, British diplomats based in Cairo, were much interested in steering these discussions towards a watered-down version of Arab unity.[72] Britain, after all, was still the Mandatory power in Palestine. Moreover, two key founder members, Egypt and Iraq, in addition to TransJordan, were bound to Britain by Treaties of Alliance. British military installations and troops were everywhere to be seen, covering a strategic area that included the Sudan, Egypt, Palestine, Jordan, Iraq and Libya, not to mention the Gulf region extending all the way from Aden to Kuwait. Saudi Arabia was still receiving a British subsidy to make up for the loss of its pilgrimage revenues because of the war. However, the subsidy amounting to £4 million a year was half-paid by the United States whose oil companies were on the verge of turning the desert Kingdom into the richest state in the Arab world. Thus Arab rivalries and British imperial interests formed the background to the deliberations which produced the Arab League in its present form. However, its mere foundation set the scene for two influential trends which were to dominate Arab politics in the next decades: Egypt's central role in the future of Arab nationalism and the drive for unity across the Arab world.

4

Educating the Nation:
Sati' al-Husri

Perhaps more than any other Arab nationalist thinker, Sati' al-Husri (1879–1968) has been the subject of intensive scholarly scrutiny and intellectual controversies. Studies published on his career and works, both in the west and the Arab world, testify to his central role in encapsulating the political phase of Arab nationalism and its transformation into a more widely-based social movement.[1] William L. Cleveland justifies devoting a book-length study to this subject by stating that, as 'educator, ideologue, prolific author, lecturer and confidant of King Faysal', al-Husri 'exerted considerable influence on educated Arab opinion in the decades following the end of the First World War'.[2] Bassam Tibi, even goes further by attributing to his thought wider implications by claiming that al-Husri's writings 'had a considerable impact on political developments in the Middle East'.[3]

Sati' al-Husri was born in San'a', the capital of Yemen, in 1879. His father Muhammad Hilal hailed originally from the city of Aleppo in northern Syria. At the time of his son's birth he was a distinguished judge in the Ottoman civil service. After a short stint in Yemen, he served in a number of other Ottoman provinces, including Tripoli in Libya. In 1900, Sati' al-Husri graduated from the Ottoman Mülkiye College in Istanbul, after a seven-year period of secondary and higher education. The college was a secular institution which offered a broad programme of education designed for preparing students to join the civil service. Consequently, al-Husri studied history, French, mathematics and natural science,[4] However, instead of joining the civil service, al-Husri chose to spend the next five years after his graduation as a secondary schoolteacher of natural science. During the same period, he published textbooks on zoology, agriculture and botany which were adopted by schools throughout the Empire. Between

1905 and 1908, he joined the Ottoman civil service as an administrator in the Balkan district of Kosovo. The corrupt and inefficient nature of the Ottoman administrative machinery which he experienced first-hand brought him into closer contact with members of the secret organization, the Committee of Union and Progress. When the CUP ushered in the 1908 revolution, al-Husri returned to Istanbul to launch a new career by publishing journals expounding modern theories of pedagogy and the need to overhaul the Ottoman educational system. His modernist views secured him the post of Director of the Teacher's Training College in Istanbul, a post which he held until 1912. It was in this period that he decided to visit Paris, Switzerland and Belgium in order to acquaint himself with the latest methods of teacher training. Despite the emergence of a number of Arab societies in the Ottoman capital, he remained steadfastly loyal to the Empire and its overarching Ottoman identity.[5] His closest associate in this period was the liberal Ottomanist writer Tevik Fikret (1867–1915). By 1911, al-Husri had emerged as one of the foremost modernist educators throughout the Ottoman territories. His influence as 'a liberal Ottomanist' was demonstrated in a widely publicized controversy which erupted in the debating clubs and in the press between him and the future spiritual founder of Turkish nationalism, Ziya Gökalp (1876–1924). Gökalp posited the idea of Turkism as a more effective doctrine than either liberal Ottomanism or Islamism in the new era of Ottoman resurgency. The concept of Turkism stressed the glorious past of the Turks in their pre-Islamic days, thereby delineating a separate Turkish national identity as opposed to their more recent Islamic one or the bewildering amalgam of Ottoman loyalties. By contrast, al-Husri rejected such nationalistic notions as a result of his belief in a liberal education geared towards nurturing the qualities of the individual within an Ottoman empire composed of different communities. By this time, al-Husri could have become a supporter of the Party of Liberty and Union and its espousal of decentralization. However, he went a step further by stressing the belief that once the process of modernization was set in motion, it had to be thorough, consistent, and executed with an unflinching determination.[6] Almost forty years later, when he delivered a series of lectures at the Egyptian Geographical Society in 1948 on 'the genesis of the nationalist idea', he devoted a whole lecture to the post-Hamidian period and the rise of Turkish nationalism. Hence, his exposition represents the views of an eye-witness and participant in the events and intellectual debates which culminated in the collapse of one of the most enduring imperial structures in the history of the world. According to him, the political currents prevalent amongst the new Ottoman ruling elite fell into three categories: Ottomanism, Islamism and Turkism. He linked each current with the names of Tal'at, Enver and Jamal respectively.[7] These three formed what came to be known as the CUP triumvirate. It would not thus be far-fetched to assume that Ottomanism as represented by Tal'at Pasha (1874–1921), which large sections of the Arab educated elite supported until the demise of the Empire, was the category most favoured by al-Husri. On the other hand, another prominent Ottoman Arab leader, Shakib Arslan, who advocated pan-Islamism, became at this juncture a close friend of Enver Pasha.[8] Hence, whereas al-Husri went on to adopt nationalism as a full-fledged modernist doctrine, Arslan clung to a more traditional notion of Islamism tinged with an Arabist dimension in the 1920s and 1930s.[9]

With the defeat of the Ottoman Empire, and the occupation of its capital by British, French, Italian and Greek forces (November 1918), Arabs and other minorities began to stream out of Istanbul. In June 1919, al-Husri joined the exodus and headed for Damascus which had been liberated in October 1918 by a combination of Arab and British forces. One month later, al-Husri was appointed by Faysal's provincial government first as Director of General Education and then Minister of Education. It was in his last capacity that he was despatched by the Syrian government to negotiate with the French General, Gouraud, regarding his ultimatum to Faysal. His mission failed, and the French army proceeded to dismantle the nascent Arab government in Damascus.

In the few months he spent in Damascus, al-Husri devoted his energies to the cause of setting up a modern education system and the propagation of a secular notion of Arabism. The close friendship which had developed between him and Faysal, was further cemented during their joint exile after the collapse of the first Arab independent government in Syria. Before joining Faysal as King of Iraq, he journeyed to Rome and visited Egypt to observe its education system. Having visited Egypt on a previous occasion, when the 1919 Egyptian revolt was in full swing, he was now confirmed in his belief that Egypt was destined to become the centre of the Arab Movement for unity and modernity.

In Iraq, with Faysal installed as the King of a newly-created state and the British firmly established as the Mandatory authority, al-Husri was afforded the opportunity, as Director General of Education (1923–7), to overhaul the entire system of elementary and secondary education.[10] His tireless energy, tenacity and wide expertise helped him to overcome many obstacles of bureaucratic lethargy, sectarian divisions and personal jealousies. His close friendship with King Faysal was furthermore an asset which he nurtured to push through his reforms and neutralize as much as possible British supervision and intervention.[11] It was during those years that the Iraqi system of education was modernized, run according to strict rules and regulations and made an instrument of national regeneration. Arabic was made the language of instruction in all elementary schools, and English was only taught as a foreign language at the higher levels. He went out of his way to raise standards in all subjects and recruited for that purpose the best qualified teachers. Hence, his recruitment in 1924–5 of Darwish al-Miqdadi (see chapter 2), Anis al-Nusuli, 'Abdallah al-Mashnuq and Jalal Zurayq, all graduates of the American University of Beirut, to teach history, mathematics and methods of education in the secondary schools and the teachers' training college.[12] He, moreover, tried to bridge the gap between the Shi'ite and Sunnite communities of Iraq by adopting a flexible approach to their divergent interpretations of certain Islamic legal rules. He did so by devising a single textbook which highlighted the numerous similarities between Shi'ite and Sunnite legal injunctions.[13]

In this sense, al-Husri enjoyed a wide margin of independence as Director General of Education and knew how to widen this margin to introduce a modern system of instruction, while at the same time endeavouring to make Arab nationalism an integral part of the elementary and secondary school curricula.

However, his Ottoman and Syrian background was used by his detractors and conservative elements in Iraq to undermine his position. His constant demands for high standards, scrupulous attention to detail in dealing with Iraqi and British officials, and his insistence on merit and proper qualifications in the appointment of new teachers, did not go down well with a large section of vested interests. In 1927, he decided to resign his post and devote his efforts to his original profession, and for the next four years taught at the teachers' training college.[14] During the same period he founded and edited the Journal of Education. His continuing influence and high reputation were reflected in the constant requests he received from government ministers on educational matters, leading to his brief appointment as Inspector General of Education in 1931. Between 1932 and 1935 he served as Dean of the Law College, which he turned into an efficient institution run along professional lines.[15] He then assumed the position of Director of Antiquities until his deportation from Iraq in 1941 (see below).

It was during this period that he came into direct conflict with the American-educated Sami Shawkat who served as Director General of Education and was the driving force behind setting up the paramilitary youth organization, the Futuwwah, in 1935. Sami Shawkat was a flamboyant figure best remembered for a speech he made in 1933, under the title 'The profession of death'.[16] Shawkat's address was meant to explain to secondary school students the importance of military studies and training in a country, such as Iraq, striving to strengthen its independence and achieve Arab unity. He therefore cited the example of Prussia in uniting Germany as being equivalent to 'Iraqi dreams' of uniting all the Arab world. His idea of 'the profession of death' was in this context meant to entice the new generation to combine 'knowledge' with 'strength' in order to spare their country the humiliation of falling under the boots of foreign armies. To al-Husri, Shawkat's unfortunate use of words was regrettable. Taking into account his laudable endeavours to introduce military conscription, which was finally achieved in 1934, he thought that the extreme connotations of Shawkat's phrase, 'the profession of death', could have been substituted by the term 'self-sacrifice' without losing its original meaning. However, Shawkat was not satisfied with exhorting Iraqi youth to die for the honour of their country. He began to question the wisdom of exhibiting a neutral pedagogic attitude towards some classical Arab historians whose works contained disparaging remarks towards the Arabs as state builders. Shawkat singled out Ibn Khaldun's celebrated *Prolegomenon* in a vituperative harangue. Ibn Khaldun (1332–1406) was one of al-Husri's favourite Arab historians. His theory which posits the notion of 'group solidarity' (*'asabiyya*) as the most potent bond in the initial stages of state-building, was considered by a number of scholars, including al-Husri, to be a useful sociological concept, far more adequate than postulating 'the religious bond' as the main factor in the rise of nations. In this sense, Ibn Khaldun took the social bond of group solidarity as a precondition of turning religion into a political movement or a dominant ideology.[17] More importantly, Ibn Khaldun's work, written at the height of Arab decline, uses the generic term 'the Arabs' or *al-'arab* to designate all nomadic and Bedouin communities, such as Kurds, Turkoman and Berbers. The context of Ibn Khaldun's references to the Arabs as bedouin nomads prone to factionalism and incapable of building state structures unless subordinated to an external force, such as a Prophet's religious message, leaves no doubt that he did not include 'urban Arabs' in his negative appreciation of their social qualities. Shawkat thought otherwise. He called upon all true patriots 'to excavate Ibn Khaldun's grave and burn his books.' This extravagant nationalism was branded by al-Husri as 'blind enthusiasm', which should not go unanswered. He reasoned that 'harmful ideas' could not be refuted by excavating graves and burning books, but through an objective and convincing criticism of their premises. Furthermore, Shawkat had, in his blind 'enthusiasm', misinterpreted Ibn Khaldun's references to the Arabs and missed their sociological nuances. Only 'an intellectual charlatan' could think of desecrating the name of such an internationally renowned thinker,[18] and the pride of all Arab countries. After his departure from Iraq, al-Husri published in 1943 and 1944 a two-volume study on Ibn Khaldun and his thoughts, which were later expanded and republished in 1961.[19]

Along with a number of other Arab nationalist activists, Sati' al-Husri was deported from Iraq upon its reoccupation by Britain in 1941. He was, moreover, stripped of his Iraqi citizenship which he had acquired as a close confidant of King Faysal. However, in 1952, the Iraqi parliament restored his citizenship in recognition of his services to education and the new generation.

In his Iraqi episode, al-Husri did not confine himself to official and administrative activities. He gave public lectures, participated in founding cultural societies, visited Spain, Egypt and North Africa, and corresponded with prominent Arab writers. He published a number of articles in Iraqi and Egyptian newspapers and journals and made use of the newly-installed Iraqi Radio Station to put across his ideas on Arab unity and national regeneration. Apart from his book on Ibn Khaldun, in 1944 he published an anthology of articles and addresses written or delivered in the 1920s and 1930s,[20] followed in the same year by a collection of articles on education and society, and a third volume consisting of six lectures he delivered in 1948 on the genesis of nationalism. These three works, and others published in the same period or in the 1950s and '60s, established his reputation as one of the most articulate and consistent exponents of Arab nationalism.

His Iraqi experiment in rebuilding an entire national system of education was, albeit on a smaller scale, repeated in Syria in 1944. Unfettered by treaties or mutual defence pacts, as was the case in Iraq and Egypt, the government of a newly independent Syria invited al-Husri to offer his advice on the best ways to restructure its educational system at all levels. He immediately welcomed the opportunity, and produced within a few months sixteen reports setting out his vision for reforming a largely French-inspired system. What he had in mind, apart from raising standards and applying rigorous and unified examinations conventions, was the achievement of 'cultural independence' in order to buttress Syria's political emancipation from its former colonial power. He thus insisted on full Arabization of all taught subjects and the postponement of studying foreign languages until the secondary stage. Religious education was to be refocused so as to bring out its moral dimensions and humanitarian aspects. Although there were objections to his reforms from powerful religious and political quarters, as well as graduates of French schools, the Syrian Parliament passed his recommendations in their entirety.[21]

The Arab League

In 1945, the League of Arab States was founded to coordinate the policies of its newly-independent members and preserve their sovereignty, territorial integrity and systems of government. The permanent headquarters of the Arab League were to be established in Cairo, headed by a secretary-general. The League was to be governed in the execution of its agreed policies by a council representing all Arab states, and a number of commissions charged with putting into effect measures of close cooperation in the economic, social, cultural and other fields of common interest. The foundation of the League was the result of protracted negotiations initiated by the Egyptian Prime Minister, Mustafa al-Nahhas, in 1943. Representatives of seven states – Syria, Lebanon, Jordan, Yemen, Saudi Arabia, Iraq and Egypt – attended these preliminary discussions and then agreed to meet in Alexandria in September 1944. The seven founding members, in addition to a Palestinian representative, issued at the end of their Alexandria preparatory conference a 'protocol' which envisaged the establishment of a League of Arab States presided over by a council, representing all members and enjoying the authority to ensure the implementation of common policies, particularly in the field of foreign affairs. The fact that the protocol singled out Lebanon as a state whose 'sovereignty and independence' would be respected and strengthened, meant that other Arab states saw the League as a preliminary step towards a higher level of unification. However, the final pact agreed on 22 March 1945 generalized its special decision on Lebanon to apply to all Arab states.

More importantly, the foundation of the League was to a large extent an official response to a growing public opinion calling for Arab unity or solidarity. This was particularly noticeable in the various pan-Arab conferences and congresses convened by professional, political and trade union organisations. Beginning with the 1931 Jerusalem conference, and the 1937 Bludan conference in Syria,[22] which were non-governmental and largely motivated by the Palestine question, official congresses were soon to follow. Whereas in Jerusalem and Bludan the Syrian dimension in pan-Arab politics was clearly visible, after 1938 it was the new Egyptian factor which began to make itself felt. In October 1938, Egypt hosted the 'World Parliamentary Congress of Arab and Muslim Countries for the Defense of Palestine', and the Arab Doctors' Conference in January 1939. By this time, the Egyptian Women's Union, under the energetic leadership of Huda Sha'rawi (d. 1947), had organized a 'Conference of Eastern Women for the Defence of Palestine' in October 1938.[23] In early 1939, official delegations from Egypt, Iraq, Transjordan, Yemen, Saudi Arabia and Palestine were invited by the British government to attend a conference in London to discuss the future of Palestine. This conference was preceded by joint meetings of Arab delegates aimed at formulating a common policy. Such meetings, hosted by the Egyptian government in Cairo, represented the emergence of a trend which was to gather momentum in the years to come. Although the London Conference, convened in February and March, failed to break the deadlock over the Palestinian issue between the Jewish and Arab approaches, it signalled the first official pan-Arab involvement in an issue that was to trouble the region for the rest of the century.

Furthermore, the foundation of the League of Arab States came in the wake of a number of official Arab proposals to achieve a concrete form of unity. The foremost of these was the Fertile Crescent Plan, presented to the British government by the Prime Minister of Iraq, Nuri al-Sa'id, in January 1943.[24] The Iraqi Plan, although initially confined to Greater Syria and Iraq, envisaged an Arab 'federation' or 'League'.

In a letter addressed to the British Foreign Office, Nuri al-Sa'id rehearsed the development of the Arab Movement for Independence since the early twentieth century and the various obstacles it encountered, including unkept promises by Britain and France. He included in his general survey the Arabs of North Africa and those of Asia. He also dwelt at length on the Palestinian question, pointing out that the invitation extended to five Arab states to attend the 1939 London Conference on Palestine 'marked a return by Great Britain to the spirit of her old pledges to King Husain which regarded all Arabs in the old Ottoman Empire as one community united by one ideal'.[25] He, therefore, proposed:

1. That Syria, Lebanon, Palestine and Transjordan shall be reunited into one state.
2. That the form of government of this state . . . shall be decided by the peoples of this country themselves.
3. That there shall be created an Arab League to which Iraq and Syria will adhere at once and which can be joined by the other Arab States at will.
4. That this Arab League shall have a permanent (council) nominated

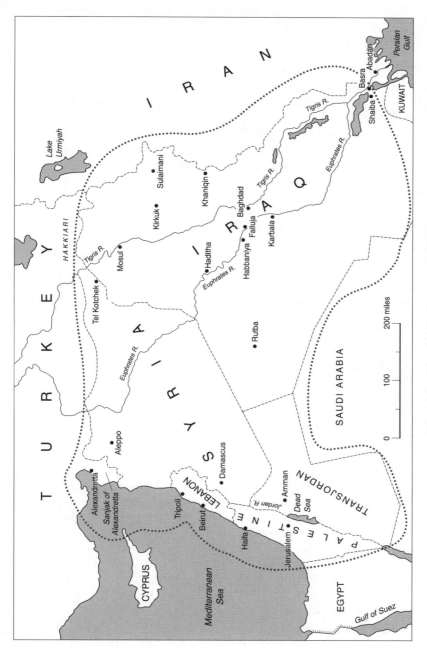

Map 4.1 The Fertile Crescent in 1945

by the member states, and presided over by one of the rulers of the states, who shall be chosen in a manner acceptable to the states concerned.

The proposal conceived the responsibilities of the Arab League Council along the lines of a federal structure whereby foreign affairs, defence, currency, communications, customs and minority rights would be placed under its jurisdiction. The Jews in Palestine would be given 'semi-autonomy' within the Syrian Union and the Maronites of Lebanon would be granted 'a privileged regime' similar to the one they had enjoyed between 1861 and 1914.[26]

The Iraqi proposal did not receive the official endorsement of the British government. Nor was it favourably viewed in either Egypt or Saudi Arabia which saw the proposal as an expression of Hashemite ambitions to re-establish the credentials of Iraq and Transjordan as the legitimate leaders of a new Arab alliance. Moreover, in 1941 the ruler of Transjordan, 'Abdullah,[27] had put forward his 'Greater Syria' project, hoping to gain British support. While the British response to 'Abdullah's project was lukewarm, Saudi Arabia, Syria and Egypt opposed it for various reasons related to inter-Arab rivalries. So it was that the idea of an Arab League formed to coordinate official policies rather than amalgamate all Arab states into a federal structure began to gain ground.

The first agreement to be signed by the founding members of the League shortly after its establishment, and embodying their willingness of coordination, was in the fields of culture, education and sports. It was not until 1950 that a similar common agreement was reached on economic and military coordination. Realizing the importance of the radio as a new instrument capable of reaching wide audiences throughout the Arab world, the same members, in addition to the newly independent Libya, concluded a third agreement to coordinate and encourage areas of cooperation of Arab broadcasting stations 'so as to strengthen the spirit of Arab brotherhood, and nurture an enlightened Arab generation fully proud of its Arab nationalism'.[28]

In 1947, al-Husri assumed the post of adviser to the Cultural Committee of the League. However, his background as educationist, schoolteacher and university lecturer prompted him to propose the creation of an institution that would be more suitable to his talents and experience. Thus, in 1953 the League set up the Institute of Higher Arab Studies and appointed al-Husri as its first director. Apart from running programmes of study and research connected with the history, geography, economy, literature and legal systems of the Arab world, the Institute was intended to make Arab nationalism an object of proper scholarly studies and 'adapt the principles of Arab culture in order to benefit from the progress of modern civilisation'.[29]

Although the Institute was at first highly effective in carrying out a number of activities, ranging from organizing public lectures on Arab nationalism to publishing monographs on various topics, al-Husri began to entertain certain doubts about its performance. This was particularly the case with the way its students were being taught, and in a way which stifled their own creativity and independent intellectual development.[30] In addition to the post of director, al-Husri held a professorship at the same Institute. He resigned both posts in 1956 and 1957 respectively. By now, al-Husri, at the age of 78, had established himself as the most revered and respected member of the Arab intelligentsia. After spending a few years in Cairo, he moved to Beirut and then to Baghdad where he died in 1968. This political and intellectual legacy has on the whole stood the test of time. It is true that in the 1960s and '70s, his writings were subject to sustained and withering criticisms by a number of left-wing Marxist-oriented writers who questioned the validity of his pure nationalist approach which seemed at times to ignore economic issues and the close connection between the rise of nationalism in Europe and the concomitant imperialist drive. Bassam Tibi's *Arab Nationalism*, referred to above, is a typical example of such an indictment. Others, who belonged to a younger generation of Arab nationalists and members of ideological parties, such as the Iraqi Ba'thist Sa'dun Hammadah, blamed al-Husri for his 'abstract notion' of nationalism which seemed to treat Arabism as a sub-species with no authentic characteristics of its own. Some of these criticisms were rebutted by al-Husri while he was still alive, constituting to a large extent a dialogue between one trend which had matured during the political phase of Arab nationalism, and another, formulated in its social phase.[31] Hence, al-Husri's contribution is here treated in its historical context and close association with the Arab movements of the first half of the twentieth century.[32]

What is Nationalism?

To al-Husri, the most important question that he had to tackle throughout his career was the emergence of nationalism as a world-wide movement. In a sense, education did figure for him as another subject of enormous consequences. But it was almost invariably conceived as the most effective instrument that was to be put at the service of the lofty aim of national regeneration. It was thus subordinated to nationalism and made to speak its language, literally and metaphorically. In one of his early articles (1928), he characterized modern social life as being slowly dominated by three new factors: universal military conscription, universal suffrage and universal education.[33] Although he very rarely expounded his views on universal suffrage, and did not make military conscription a subject of detailed study, he compared the function of 'the military barracks' to an institution of education, and encouraged the development of both.[34]

Hence, those three universal pillars of modern life constituted for al-Husri the hallmark of nationalism and the direct result of its emergence. In a series of lectures he delivered at Cairo University in 1948, his opening remarks reveal his concept of nationalism as a modern movement which became firmly established as a dominant political force in the nineteenth century. It was thus in that century, and more precisely between 1821 and 1921, that the map of Europe was radically changed, whereby numerous new states were born and a number of old ones, including the Habsburg and Ottoman empires, completely disappeared. Movements striving for separatism or unification dominated continental Europe, leading to the disintegration of artificial states and the birth of nations as natural entities, having language and history as their underlying components. A common language and a broadly shared history were the stuff nations are made of and the cause of so much agitation and readjustments, until the world finally recognized that nationalism and congruence between nation and state were the signs of the time. This scheme of things, al-Husri asserts, was a recent development, so recent that some communities had just begun to grapple with it. In order to show that language and history constitute the most important factors in shaping a nation's cultural and political identity, he chooses a number of case studies to prove his point. These include Germany, Greece, Bulgaria, Rumania, Yugoslavia and Albania. In all these cases, the revival of vernaculars and the recovery of history, as a shared memory of glorious deeds, are shown to be the most salient characteristics which lent nationalism its driving force and determined the final outcome in the struggle to build new nation-states. He finally turns his attention to Turkish and Arab nationalisms which are shown to obey the same laws prescribed by the determinant functions of language and history.[35]

Why should these two factors, and not so many others, cherished and expounded by countless nationalist writers and activists, be singled out as the crucial ones in delimiting nations and underlying national identification? In a lecture he delivered in 1923 at the Higher Teachers' Training College in Baghdad, al-Husri attempted for the first time in the Arab phase of his career to define the nation in conceptual terms which were to constitute a recurring theme in most of his speeches and writings. The lecture was entitled 'Patriotism and Nationalism' (*al-wataniyya wa al-qawmiyya*). Simply stated, patriotism means loyalty to the fatherland (*al-Watan*) as a territorial entity, whereas nationalism indicates allegiance to the nation as a group of people. Hence, both patriotism and nationalism could be considered alternative terms denoting the same feeling of love, whereby love of the fatherland implies love of the nation and *vice versa*. Whereas the fatherland constitutes a territorial unit and the nation a human community, the state forms a sovereign independent political association conjoining a group of people to a common, well-defined land. However, nation and state may or may not coincide in the cultural or political realm of human association. If they do coincide, such as in Sweden at the present time, it could be said that the nation and the state are one and the same. By contrast, a nation could be divided into several states, each professing a creed of local patriotism. Under these circumstances, nationalism becomes an earnest endeavour to unify these various states into one single state and generate a new overarching patriotism that subsumes all the provincial loyalties. In this case, the concept of 'an ideal fatherland' establishes itself as the motive force for turning the ideal into a concrete reality. Both Italy and Germany in their historical movements of unification illustrate this tense interaction between local and general patriotism.[36]

If, on the other hand, a nation is deprived of its own state and subjected to the rule of a foreign power with its own patriotism, which it attempts to impose on all the subjugated nations within its borders, a new type of nationalism is bound to emerge. Instead of seeking unification, the nation would strive for independence and separation. Bulgaria was such a nation during its subjugation to the Ottoman Empire. A fourth category is exemplified by a nation that has lost its independence and is at the same time divided and partitioned into a number of provinces ruled by different foreign powers. The divided and foreign-subjugated nation would naturally reject both its subjugation and partitions by attempting to wrest its independence and establish a new national state unifying the fatherland and its inhabitants. Poland was such a nation until World War I.[37]

All these categories of nationalism, al-Husri points out, were the product of a chain of events which began to unfold at the turn of the nineteenth century. In the Middle Ages and the preceding two centuries, he explains, the concepts of state and fatherland in Europe were not clearly differentiated. Moreover, patriotism simply meant allegiance to the monarch and the monarchy. Monarchs could annex territories, dispose of them or barter away their subjects. To acquire or exchange one piece of land for another was deemed to be the inherent right of the chief landlord of the Kingdom. Thus, either through marriage, conquest or mutual agreements, subjects were mere chattels with no right or identity of their own. The underlying principle of such conceptions and practices was the belief in the divine right of monarchs. Once this belief had been undermined and overturned,[38] a totally new scheme of things was born, whereby nationality imposed itself as the ultimate criterion of political loyalties. Consequently, empires began to disintegrate and new nations were formed. Thus, the nineteenth century was the age of nationalism *par excellence*. It was then that to love one's fatherland and cherish one's nation became powerful 'moral bonds' overriding all other ties, be they local or cosmopolitan. Hence, nationalism ushered in a novel form of social solidarity which, in its turn, determined the formation of political associations based on the unity of language and history.[39]

In this early period, the idea of the fatherland embracing a well-defined territory and of the nation as the inhabitants of that territory is stated in unequivocal clarity. It is thus, somewhat ironic that al-Husri was to devote at a later stage a great deal of his intellectual energy to refute such a connection.[40] However, what he had in mind was the manner in which language and history moulded the character of the nation as a human community rather than its geography. It is for this reason he dwelt at length in his 1948 Cairo lectures on the divine right of Kings and its close association with religious notions of obedience and the will of God. Hence, since the monarch was believed to represent God on earth, the peoples of Europe figured as mere subjects and creatures of both. This all changed with the advent of new philosophies based on the idea of the social contract and the natural rights of human beings. In this sense, it was the people and not the King who was assumed to have ultimate authority. By the end of the eighteenth century this idea became so widespread and deeply rooted that one could not but conclude that the French Revolution was the direct result of such a popular mood. The principle of the right of the people to determine and control political authority contained within it a far more significant implication: it adumbrated 'the rights of nationalities'. This was, al-Husri explains, all the more natural, since, one had to ask: 'What is a people? What are its constituent elements? How does a people manifest its will? And in what particular manner does it exercise its sovereignty and authority?'.[41]

With these questions being asked, and given the fact that all members of society had the opportunity to enquire further and formulate their own answers, peoples developed a sense of their national differences. Although some communities happened to belong to a single unitary state, the question of being a 'minority' or a 'majority', and the existence of 'ruling' and 'ruled' nations, became pertinent and hard to ignore. The inevitability of 'the rights of nationalities' thus decreed that each nation had the right to form its own state and invest it with ultimate authority in order to ensure its sovereignty and independence.[42]

However, this was the story of European nationalisms, and which could be narrated as a succession of episodes, relentlessly sweeping forward and engulfing one country after another. Although it had its opponents and was met with vehement resistance in some quarters, it continued its inexorable march and re-established the states of Europe on completely new foundations. This historical achievement, al-Husri reminds us, took different forms and was reached from various directions, depending on the political circumstances and social levels of development in each European nation. Thus, despite its division into numerous states and statelets, Germany had a highly developed culture which made it easier for it to concentrate exclusively on the question of political unification.[43]

Accordingly, the examples of the genesis of German, Italian, Greek, Bulgarian and Turkish nationalisms are briefly discussed to illustrate their divergent pathways. Nevertheless, a common thread was detected to run through all these movements: the underlying unity of language and history. These two factors distinguish one nation from another and serve to preserve the integrity of the community as a social organism. It may well be, al-Husri continues, that nationalism has reached its maximum point of development in most European countries, a fact which lends credibility to the idea that the world has entered the era of supranational organization. However, in the Eastern countries as opposed to the Western, such an era is far from being a possibility. This is all the more so in the Arab lands, where the idea of nationalism did not take root until much later than in Europe. It is still a nascent movement which could hardly be expected to become effective before the Arab world is radically transformed in moral and political fields. Moreover, supranational blocs are built out of fully-constituted nation-states which keep their identities intact while trying to form alliances in the international arena. The nationalist idea will one day 'reach its end' in the Arab world, but that day belongs to the future, not the past or the present.[44]

In this sense, al-Husri took upon himself the task of formulating a consistent and systematic theory of nationalism, and to propagate it by all available means. His prominent and direct role in various educational institutions in the Arab world furnished him with unrivalled opportunities and stamped his reports, articles and lectures with an aura of authority. The fact that he propounded a set of ideas according to a regular pattern of style and chain of reasoning made his arguments both accessible and credible. Moreover, his theorization of the nation lifted it out of its local narrow context and turned Arab nationalism into an integral part of modernity and the universal march of culture, all aiming to reach the same summit, from different directions and at a pace suited to their historical background or the degree of their political maturity.

His universal categories which were meant to apply to all nations can also be seen as the product of a humanist trend which, while clinging to its national heritage, was genuinely seeking to join a global culture, not as a fellow traveller, but as a participant who has something to contribute and exchange.

Seen in this light, the contention that what he borrowed from Herder, or Fichte's *Addresses to the German Nation*, determined the direction of his thought, misses the essential ingredients of his approach. After all, Herder was cosmopolitan and parochial at the same time. His rhapsodic accounts of village cultures, folkloric customs, popular songs and old tales combined with and intruded into his belief in a cosmopolitan society. His mystical juxtaposition of language and nationality was a purely cultural construct that had no meaningful political significance. His adulation of spoken as opposed to written languages could hardly be expected to appeal to someone imbued with the beauty of a common standard language of literary Arabic. Furthermore, Herder's nightmare, 'the accursed state', condemned by him as an 'artificial contrivance', stifling immediate family and kinship life, stands a world apart from al-Husri's distinct political agenda.[45] The fact that al-Husri quotes Herder on the crucial role of language in determining patterns of thought and establishing networks of mutual communication, while his entire philosophical system of which the use of language forms a part is neglected, hardly qualifies as a Herderian view of culture.[46]

As for Fichte, al-Husri chooses again to select passages from his *Addresses* which highlight the specific role of language in nation-formation, almost to the exclusion of other philosophical and political ideas. Furthermore, he distances himself from Fichte in his non-linguistic pronouncements by stating:

> The above mentioned *Addresses* contain a long series of recommendations dealing with moral, cultural, social and political reform . . . All of this is placed within a framework of philosophical opinions and instigatory remarks. There is no need or space for our purposes to survey and criticise the various ideas expressed by Fichte in these addresses so as to

sort the good apples from the bad. My sole purpose is to summarize what they say on the relation of language to nationalism.[47]

Then he goes on to quote a selection of appropriate passages.

He recognized that nationalism originated in Europe and was slowly making inroads into 'Eastern nations', including the Arab world. This recognition was, however, hedged by a significant qualification. Nationalism was not a European gift presented on a silver platter, but an inherent right of all nationalities throughout the world. This is all the more so, since European statesmen and a large army of their intelligentsia exerted enormous effort to prove otherwise. They formulated theories and pursued practical policies to deny oppressed nationalities their right to self-determination and nationhood. In this respect, al-Husri turns European nationalism against its own masters, revealing the deep wounds it inflicts on other human beings because they happened to live in a different part of the world, belong to another colour in the scale of concocted racial theories or adhere to one religion rather than another.

Although al-Husri was initially vehemently opposed to the theory which linked the rise of nationalism with European imperialism, arguing that the latter predated the former by at least two centuries,[48] he began to soften this vehemence in the early 1960s. Whereas in the 1930s and 1940s he discussed the emergence of nationalism in Europe as a liberal movement closely associated with 'the Rights of Man' and Nationalities, later on, when political debates in the Arab world became almost solely focused on imperialism and its perpetuation of underdevelopment in the Third World, his view of things nationalist widened in scope. He now saw the nineteenth century as being dominated by three interlinked movements or major developments: 'the spread of the principle of nationality, the onset of the Industrial Revolution owing to the invention of new tools and machines, and the rampant growth of European imperialism'. He went on to stress that European imperialism was the direct result of the first two factors. For the principle of nationality and its practical consequences left no room for the new states to expand within the European continent, and the invention of machines led to an enormous increase in industrial productivity. As a result, European states embarked on an expansionist drive outside their continent and were impelled to search for new markets to sell their industrial commodities, on the one hand, and acquire raw materials for their manufacturing factories, on the other. Imperialism, or more accurately colonialism, al-Husri continues, 'was the shortest and most efficient method to achieve these two ends: the state was in a position to impose on its colonies whatever economic conditions suited it best, and monopolize for itself all their resources and markets.[49]

Moreover, in this new age of imperialism, former colonial practices (whereby entire native populations were wiped out, and African slaves were hunted down like savage beasts), gave way to more refined and subtle ways to assuage guilty consciences and justify policies of exploitation. Human beings were therefore divided into different races, and each race was assigned certain ingrained traits and characteristics. Thus was born the theory of non-white inferior races incapable of progress and destined to be ruled by a superior white race for the benefit of humanity. Colonialism was, however, destined to be a mere phase in the history of mankind, so that by the end of World War I and the emergence of Japan as an advanced eastern nation, it began to crumble, along with its theoretical premises. In their rivalries and competition for colonies, European powers often engaged in propaganda campaigns against each other, a fact which only served to undermine their moral authority. Furthermore, by resorting to the recruitment of native soldiers in their wars, they unwittingly brought forth a new breed of men, no longer to be intimidated by cannon fire and bomb explosion. The devastating effects of these factors were further reinforced by the rising tide of cultural and national awareness, leading in due course to organized passive resistance in some colonized countries, and to revolutionary armed struggle, in others.[50]

This gradual shift of emphasis in interpreting the genesis of nationalism can also be seen in al-Husri's view of language as a founding element of nationhood.

Over the years, al-Husri refined his understanding of the role of language until it became a practical instrument forged to create effective modes of communication and carry out practical tasks related to the welfare of the individual in a state which treated all its citizens on an equal footing. In the early part of his career, language was referred to in an almost romantic fashion and treated as a precious gift designed to buttress feelings of solidarity between its speakers. Its function was to mould the person in its own image and reproduce him or her as a representative of a group that was governed by the same laws of linguistic determination. Thus, national identity was itself dependent on its language and whatever particular characteristics that language already had in store as the treasury of emotions, feelings and spontaneous reactions to sorrow or happiness. This shared pattern of inner thoughts expressed in words, which are themselves indicative of an underlying unity of significance and ways of seeing things and interpreting their meaning, tied the users of a particular language to a symmetrical grid of homogeneous and identifiable characteristics that reproduced individuals as almost exact copies of each other.[51]

In the late 1950s, al-Husri began to see connections which his sociological theory of education implied and then became irresistible to ignore. For if the age of nationalism ushered in the three universal pillars of modern life – education, suffrage and military conscription – then it made sense to conclude that such standardized instruments of modern life required a universal medium that was understood by everyone and made accessible to the citizenry of an egalitarian society. Thus, language was now seen to serve a more tangible function which the political system of a democratic society had to use in order to carry out its multifaceted functions in a complex social environment.

Before the age of nationalism, the management of society was a primitive and simplified set of well-rehearsed measures. Ruler and ruled lived in two different worlds and barely felt the need or had the opportunity to communicate with each other. Not only did they lead separate lives and conduct their affairs independently of each other, they often used two different languages, one for the court or aristocracy and another for the common people. All this changed when societies began to develop varied institutions and social structures which made differentiation into more specialized economic and professional groups, and the proliferation of complex functions of state officials, appear to favour horizontal rather than perpendicular means of interaction and communication. Thus, instead of discontinuous social and political networks, each operating in enclosed enclaves and regional compartments, continuous surfaces spread horizontally, across a reconstituted national territory, thereby establishing themselves as a permanent feature of life in a modern society. In order for government to apply standard rules and regulations, courts to conduct their business of litigation and cross-examinations, compulsory education to operate as a national system, and soldiers to be drilled and commanded in an age of mass military conscription, the need arose to use a common standardized language accessible to, and understood by, all citizens. More importantly, the principle of the people's sovereignty which replaced that of the divine right of kings necessitated the establishment of representative local councils, and national parliamentary institutions, which made it all the more imperative to standardize the medium of communication and record-keeping.[52]

Hence the struggle to revive local languages or resist the imposition of an alien language on the inhabitants of a foreign-occupied country constitutes one of the longest chapters in the history of nationalism and nation-formation. To defend and preserve one's language, al-Husri concludes, amounted to safeguarding national identity and independence. Consequently, the loss of a particular language announces the death of the nation and its assimilation into another.[53]

As to history, it had a similar romantic beginning and a more mature end. Although language sometimes appeared to take priority ovr history in al-Husri's scale of things, it never relinquished its position as an equal partner in the making of nations. At first, it was an energized memory of glorious deeds and a spur to action, with its heroes and past achievements inspiring the new generation to a loftier ideal of nationhood, faith in the future and boundless sacrifices. Since the Arabs had had an impressive list of historical accomplishments, he argued, they did not need to falsify history or embellish misfortunate outcomes. All they had to do was to reconnect their past to their present by injecting a sense of pride and enthusiasm into its bygone episodes. Thus, in order to be inspired by history, one had to see it as a living entity teaming with outstanding statesmen, military leaders, poets and philosophers. This was, however, to be a necessary but preliminary step. Teaching history to the new generation and the youth of the nation ought to be akin to an act of tremendous national responsibility. As a moral and spiritual principle of nation-formation in its own right, it had to be dealt with in a spirit of utter commitment and devotion.[54]

Nevertheless, al-Husri made a sharp distinction between teaching and composing history. Hence, the mere requirements of teaching history within a confined space and the constraints of time, a tutor lecturing to the young generation of the nation had to exercise a certain discretion by selecting episodes and emphasizing events which are conducive to foster a sense of national awareness. It is this awareness, nurtured according to a rigorous programme of inculcation and judicious selection of material, that ensures the birth of a new movement; this movement, while drawing examples from the past, is nevertheless committed to the making of the future with modern ideas and advanced technological equipment. Moreover, highlighting or selecting certain events in order to instil national consciousness and make the young aware of their heritage or civic duties is not the same as falsification or distortion of facts. Western history textbooks, al-Husri asserts, confirm rather than refute such a contention. It would thus be only logical and natural to rescue Arab history from the doldrums of an inert list of names and dates and recreate a dynamic picture of movement and life.[55]

By contrast, writing history as a scholarly endeavour has to follow strict rules and adhere to a rigorous methodoly of objectivity and originality. Such a task requires the use of authentic primary sources and calls for studying all the details and facts relating to a particular event. In this respect, the historian should be fair as well as objective, having no purpose but 'to know, and make known, truth'.[56].

In a sense, al-Husri wrote and thought as a historian, but always with two different purposes and audiences in mind. When he approached history as a fundamental component of nationhood, he sought to impart a message of hope and recovery of dignity in a nation he knew to be divided, economically and socially underdeveloped, and politically not yet capable of building and institutionalizing a healthy and sustained national regeneration. On the other hand, his historical monographs and articles, addressed to an audience of specialists, and fully documented, reveal an earnest scholarly aptitude and a desire to offer his own view, while taking account of other plausible explanations. In other words, as a specialist in pedagogy and the psychology of education he was fully alert to the infinite possibilities of delivering a message in order to convey a certain connotation or take note of the human context as a receptacle of coded utterances.[57]

His nationalism was thoroughly modern with a pronounced secular dimension that saw religions, in particular Islam and Christianity, as moral and spiritual creeds which supersede national borders and identities. They were therefore to be dealt with as such so as to avoid the intrusion of one into the territory of the other.

Religion and nationalism were two separate entities each performing a function peculiar to its original purpose and outlook. They were, therefore, to be dealt with according to their own specific spheres of operation. Thus, Islam could generate a feeling of brotherhood and weave spiritual ties among believers across continents and different nationalities, but that is something other than the idea of using religion as a basis of political action and national identification. Although he recognized and stressed on various occasions the contribution of Islam to the historical achievements of the Arabs, and the crucial influence of the Qur'an in preserving Arabic as a language of high culture, he always differentiated between Arab history and the expansion of Islam as a global movement that embraced and converted a host of different nations and communities in Asia, Africa, Europe, and at a later stage, the Americas. The Arabs could not but be proud of their Islamic episode, but their pre-Islamic history had also to be included as part of the national heritage. Moreover, in the age of nationalities and nationalism it was no longer possible to reconstitute the Caliphate and reintroduce theocracy as a system of government. Those who argued otherwise were swimming against the current and wasting their much needed energies on a lost cause. It may well be, al-Husri once conceded, that Islamic unity could become a worthy cause, but before that could happen and become a plausible project,

Arab unity has to be achieved first. And this was by itself no easy task to accomplish.[58] Moreover, the Arab world includes a substantial minority of Christian Arabs who share with the Muslim Arabs their language, history and literature. In this context, al-Husri believed that Arab nationalism, as a cultural movement, 'achieved its first real victory', when the Arab orthodox community in Syria insisted on electing in 1899 a patriarch of their own nationality. This act of defiance put an end to the hegemony of the Greeks who had controlled local orthodox churches in Syria ever since the fall of Constantinople in 1453.[59]

In one of his historical works, *The Arab lands and the Ottoman Empire*,[60] al-Husri explains the rise of Arab nationalism in these terms:

> The Tanzimat (or reform movement) produced no tangible changes in the attitudes of the Christian and Muslim Arabs towards the Ottoman Empire: the Muslims continued to consider the empire as their own and manifest their allegiance to its rule, it being the state of the Islamic Caliphate, while the Christians persisted in considering it an alien power, in that it treated them as second-class subjects. Consequently, the last turned to European powers seeking protection and assistance and which they received on numerous occasions.
>
> The idea of Arab nationalism had simultaneously to overcome these two trends: it had to divert the attention of the Muslims away from the Ottoman state, and that of the Christians from European powers. It did so in order to draw both to rally under the banner of Arabism which derives its strength from language and history.[61]

It is not difficult to see that this was a pragmatic approach seeking to create a common ground for constituting a modern nation. Language with its emotional and practical networks provides a standard high culture, which in turn unfolds within an historical dimension fixing the present as the living link of the past and the political march towards the future.

He thus eliminated and subordinated other characteristics of nationhood to his dual structure of culture (language) and politics (history). Theories of racial purity were scoffed at and branded as fanciful concoctions, with no scientific basis or rational validity. Neither the French nor the Arabs were descendants of one single identifiable stock. All nations were formed out of an admixture of races, resembling a great flowing river which is being constantly fed by the waters of various tributaries and sources. To isolate a particular droplet or stream, and claim it to be a representative sample, is to fly in the face of common sense and scientific evidence.[62]

Added to the long list of eliminated factors were climate, geography and the common will. The first was deemed a mere hypothesis which did not stand rigorous investigation or direct observation. One only had to look to see that many nations had different and divergent climate zones, without in the least being affected in their common unity or cultural attributes. The same could be said of geography, although, as we have seen, he did not rule out altogether a complex relationship of interaction between man and his environment. However, man, in the generic sense, was always given the upper hand as the toolmaker, inventor and conqueror of geographic barriers.[63]

As to the factor of will, he discussed at length and on more than one occasion Ernest Renan's lecture 'Qu'est-ce-qu'une nation?', endeavouring to tie its theoretical premises to an incidental political contest between France and Germany over the fate of Alsace. To equate the nation, as Renan did, with an electoral process of daily plebiscites, was to degrade nationalism to a low form of politics and electioneering. Popular will, being thus liable to fluctuation and sharp swings of mood and taste, could not be taken as a solid foundation of nationhood. A nation had first to be formed in the course of a long history of events and constituted on the basis of its language and shared history in order for 'will' to make its effect. It is thus the outcome rather than the source of nationhood.[64]

Nor did he spare his Arab detractors who continued to harp on the peculiar characteristics of their own state or province to the exclusion of the common identity of the nation as a whole. He thus argued relentlessly against Egyptianism, Syrianism and the Phoenician brand of Lebanese nationalists. His chain of reasoning was often measured, accommodating and built on a long list of historical and factual illustrations. But he did not suffer fools gladly, a trait revealed in some of his refutations. He had an infinite faith in his method, logic, and the manner in which data are presented and made to conclude an argument. Thus, each engagement with the opposite camp is summed up by the phrase: this proves beyond the shadow of a doubt that my point is the only possible conclusion. In this way he conducted a long-running dialogue with a host of prominent members of the intelligentsia because of the influence he thought they wielded upon public opinion. In the course of these dialogues, argument and counter-argument, his articles and books can be seen as a huge dam meant to keep Arab nationalism from being swamped by what he saw as its most formidable and dangerous opponents: regionalism, communism and Islamism. The first two were often dealt with ruthlessly and in a manner designed to silence their proponents once and for all. As to Islamism, he had to tread more delicately, while at the same time not seeming to be compromising his secular position. This he did by pursuing a number of strategies, all designed to show how religion could benefit by recognizing its proper function as a moral force rather than a political instrument.[65]

In the early 1950s Arab nationalism scored one of its most spectacular victories. The president of the most powerful and most advanced, and the most populous Arab country, announced his conversion to Arab nationalism, adopting it as the guiding principle of his domestic and foreign policies. This was the Egyptian leader, Jamal 'Abd al-Nasir (Nasser). To al-Husri, this was seen as 'the happiest moment of his life'. And Nasser's newly-adopted pan-Arabism seemed to confirm his long-cherished dream of seeing Egypt, ever since his first visit to Cairo in 1919, leading the Arab nation to its unity.[66]

Al-Husri's primary concern was to formulate a secular concept of Arab nationalism capable of acting as a common denominator of a modern community. To that end, he defined the nation as a national organism formed out of a common language and a shared history. To him, language and history were the only twin pillars which had the moral potential and suitable structure to support a modern nation. All other factors, such as climate, geography, religion, economy and will, were deemed to be subordinate elements, oeprating within a prior set of rules. Hence, a nation may fall under foreign occupation, witness the utter devastation of its economic life, and inhabit divergent climate zones, yet it could continue to exist. It does so by ensuring the survival of its language and the living memory of its history. For if language embodies national culture and history represents its dynamic movement, the nation's political focus regenerates itself by linking both to the building of a new state.

In this sense, to him Arabism (al-'uruba) was not a theory or an ideology, but a national identity. And as long as it was recognized as such, it could accommodate a variety of ideologies and political programmes. Moreover, the recognition of this priority was no easy matter. This was all the more so since no single individual could see the vastness and varied regions of a nation all at once. A nation had, therefore, to become a mental image evoked by the power of the imagination and the knowledge of its historical evolution.[67]

5

In Search of Theory

On the eve of World War II there was a general feeling that Arab nationalism lacked a coherent theory grounded in a distinct philosophical substratum. It was felt that a mere descriptive list of outer characteristics would not be sufficient to launch a movement of national regeneration. Something more than a general definition was needed in order to effect a radical transformation of society and its socio-economic structures.

It is true that by that time the idea of embodying belief in Arab unity in a political organization had become a conventional tenet. Yet, even the emergence of a properly hierarchical organization, complete with its executive committee, consultative council, provincial structures and local cells, would still count as no more than another layer of visible and easily identifiable characteristics. It was thus believed that the time had come to penetrate more deeply, to discover 'the inner soul' of the nation, and express such a discovery in theoretical terms capable of creating a doctrine that would, in its turn, determine the direction of the struggle and define its ultimate purpose. A qualitative leap was needed in order to grasp the motivating force of events and animate a new generation with a nationalist mission.

At the global level, the 1930s were the decade of ideological movements par excellence. Ranging from fascism, radical social democracy to communism, an obsession with the necessity of possessing 'a world view' had taken hold of educated elites across the continents. Responding in large measure to the failure of liberalism and market forces precipitated by the Depression of 1929, in addition to the triumph of the Bolshevik Revolution in Russia and the rise of fascist regimes in both Italy and Germany, the professional elites of newly-emerging nations began to take for granted the necessity of adopting novel creeds and doctrines.

It seemed at the time that no nation could survive in the struggle for existence or independence without articulating to itself and others a clear set of theoretical guidelines. These guidelines were presumed to go beyond the mere enumeration of a number of commonsense demands spelt out in a programme of policies. It had now become imperative to develop a doctrine capable of explaining the trajectory of historical developments by illuminating present dilemmas and charting the course of the future. Furthermore, society was to be regulated, reshaped and rebuilt in a new venture of human engineering. Human beings could and should be remoulded within a system of coordinated institutions and political activities. At this juncture, re-educating the youth of the nation to render their personalities in tune with the ethos of the times asserted itself as one of the most urgent tasks.

The spirit of the age was thus thoroughly ideological, and the educated elite of a newly-emerging urban Arab middle class was part and parcel of this wave sweeping over entire societies. Since the mid-nineteenth century the educated Arab elites had articulated their hopes and aspirations in either cultural or political terms. Members and products of modern institutions thrown up by the Ottoman reform movement or its equivalents, they were largely content to put forward their demands in non-ideological programmes of action. In fact, some political societies made a virtue out of avoiding commitment to a particular doctrine. Culturally, this drive reiterated the ethnic and religious qualities of the Arabs as 'a race' that had once developed one of the most eloquent languages and propagated a noble world religion. Such qualities, revealed in great works of literature, architecture, science and empire-building, were deemed to qualify the Arabs to be treated on an equal footing with their Ottoman rulers, or to be masters of their own destiny once colonialism had loomed over the horizon. Hence the quest for gaining proper representation in the executive and legislative bodies as well as the insistence on the use of Arabic as their official language. In North Africa, French colonialism persisted to resist these demands down to the World War II and beyond. In Egypt, the agenda of the national movement after 1882 was centred on wresting independence or granting the Egyptians their constitutional rights, while the use of Arabic was no longer in question. It was only in the Ottoman provinces of Syria and Iraq that the question of Turkification loomed so large. In this way, the political agenda of various Arab societies and political parties varied from one region to another. The Ottoman state, for example, was held in high esteem and considered an ally against Western domination in the Maghreb and Egypt. In the Arab Asian region, where the Ottomans held sway, an ambivalent attitude prevailed manifesting itself in a multiplicity of practical endeavours. It could be safely assumed that the majority of the Arabs in 1915, one year after the outbreak of the war, were still hoping to preserve the Ottoman state, albeit in a revamped fashion based on their treatment as full and equal partners. However, the defeat of the Ottoman Empire, to which some Arabs contributed and worked for, redefined the political agenda of most Arab states. Political independence was claimed and fought for in Egypt, Syria, Iraq and parts of Arabia, while in North Africa and the Sudan it was still a matter of achieving some sort of autonomy. Egypt was granted semi-independence in 1922, an outcome which did not differ much in practice from the Mandatory systems introduced to govern Syria and Iraq in the inter-war period. Moreover, both Egypt's semi-independence and the Mandate systems underlined the fact that eventual recognition of Arab independence was no longer in doubt.[1] Meanwhile, Palestine was placed under a different category and Britain was selected by the League of Nations to be responsible for putting into effect the Balfour Declaration of 2 November 1917 'in favour of the establishment in Palestine of a National Home for the Jewish people . . .'. The Arabs of Palestine in the original Balfour Declaration and in its subsequent adoption by 'the Principal Allied Powers' and the Council of the League of Nations were simply referred to as those 'natives' whose 'civil and religious rights' were to be safeguarded and guaranteed. In other words, it was implicitly assumed that 'the natives', or the majority of the inhabitants of Palestine, had no 'national' rights in comparison with the Jewish community. This was confirmed by the so-called Churchill memorandum of 3 June 1922, which sought to allay the fears of the Palestinian Arabs regarding the establishment of a Jewish National Home in their country. Winston Churchill, who was then the Secretary of State for the Colonies, went out of his way in his Memorandum to explain at length the implications of the Balfour Declaration for the future of both the Arab and Jewish communities. The notion which certain Jewish leaders entertained to the effect that Palestine was to become 'as Jewish as England is English' was firmly refuted as being an 'impracticable' expectation. He went on to state: 'the terms of the Declaration referred to do not contemplate that Palestine as a whole should be converted into a Jewish National Home, but that such a Home should be founded in Palestine.'[2] What is of more relevance to our topic was the Memorandum's assumption that the Jewish community in Palestine 'numbering 80,000', with its 'distinctive intellectual life', 'considerable economic activity' and 'its political, religious and social organizations' possessed all the requisite '"national" characteristics'.[3] This only served to sharpen the Palestinians' own awareness of their 'national characteristics'.

By 1936 the Palestinian question had become a pan-Arab issue and was added to the list of accumulated political frustrations. It was thus thought that all the Arab world had become the target of European colonial penetration, and almost all foreign powers appeared to be either unreliable or lukewarm allies. The Arabs were thenceforth left to fend for themselves and work out a new strategy capable of checking the intensification of European domination. It was therefore perceived that earlier attempts, which aimed at achieving the independence of certain Arab countries, lacked both a comprehensive vision and a proper organisational framework that transcended local and regional boundaries.

One of the first Arab intellectuals to stress the need for a new philosophy of action was Qustantine Zurayq (1909–). Zurayq was born in Damascus and received his training as a professional historian at Columbia, Chicago and Princeton Universities. He taught history at the American University of Beirut, served as a Syrian diplomat, was President of Damascus University, and was one of the founders in 1934 of a clandestine Arab nationalist organization. He, furthermore, played an important role in his capacity as an advisor and spiritual guide to an entire generation of Arab youth. His association with the initial formation of the Arab Nationalists Movement under the leadership of George Habash is well known.[4]

In his book, *National Consciousness*,[5] published in 1939, Zurayq contends that Arab societies were in the grip of a 'nationalist resurgence' which promised and adumbrated a new renaissance. However, he argued that such a renaissance, in order to gather momentum and endure, had to be grounded in a clear theoretical vision. He went on to say;

> It would be useless to hope for a new Arab renaissance unless it was derived from a nationalist 'philosophy', capable of depicting its spirit, defining its direction, determining its goals and specifying ways and means. (pp. 6–7)

He was certain that political struggle had to be supported by an intellectual movement as the only instrument of delineating a clear strategy. In other words, action had to be performed according to 'a specific doctrine' and a comprehensive theory. He therefore put forward the idea of developing a three-pronged plan of praxis.

This consisted of, (1) building an intellectual foundation by pro-
viding a coherent, clear and comprehensive national philosophy;[6]
(2) distilling such a general philosophy into a nationalist doctrine;
and (3) organizing the nation and mobilizing its men and women
to embody its single will as the expression of one single doctrine
(pp. 7–9).

Such a call was confined to the preface, whereas the bulk of the
book dealt with more immediate issues such as Arab history, the
Arabic language and Arab culture. Nevertheless, Zurayq was clearly
trying to discover the true 'mission' of the Arab nation, and its ethos
as a motivating force. More importantly, he wanted the new generation of Arab nationalists to penetrate into 'the spirit' of their history,
as opposed to its letter. His call was the result of a conviction that the
world of the soul and its internal factors were more crucial in
determining points of strength or weakness.

To him, these internal factors, composed of historical experiences
and current conditions, do not exhaust the various ingredients which
have entered into the formation of the Arab nation. The other
elements are composed of western civilization in its domination of
modern society. The West is, in fact, the ultimate factor that domi-
nates the modern world and determines the pace of its development.
Understanding the West is thus an integral part of demarcating the
national identity of the Arabs.

Zurayq, therefore, undertakes to delineate his concept of the West
in order to demonstrate the importance of creating a coherent national
philosophy. The essence of the West consists of a number of interrelated institutions and ideas:

1. An interconnected economic system born out of the industrial
    revolution. Its aim is to exploit natural resources, human talent,
    and the capabilities of modern machines in order to increase and
    organise production. An organized and ever-increasing produc-
    tion is the secret behind a nation's power and its ability to
    dominate other nations. This meticulous system which unites all
    its parts in one single coherent order has infiltrated all aspects of
    life in the West, moulding personal traits in the cultural, social
    and political spheres.
2. Moreover, behind the economy of the West, there stands its
    science. Science is not knowing disparate facts by reading school
    books or pedestrian works. It is rather a method that consists of a
    continual search for truth, while at the same time maintaining a
    healthy doubt about aspects that do not accord with reason,
    correct induction and sound logic. Science is distinguished by a

spirit of modesty and a constant endeavour to arrive at new
solutions thrown up by new problems.
3. Behind the science of the West, there is its philosophy. In this
    philosophy all spiritual and intellectual currents meet and flow in
    one direction, and according to one consistent pattern. In order
    to understand the West in its true nature, one has to understand
    Plato, Aristotle, St Augustine, St Aquinas, Descartes, Kant, Hegel
    and Nietzsche, and other leading thinkers. By combining a true
    understanding of the modern economy, science and philosophy,
    with a true grasp of the personality of the nation, a well-formed
    theory would emerge which would chart the course of the future
    and the nation's mission (pp. 26–38).

This idea of a nation's mission was adopted by the Ba'th party after
its foundation in the 1940s.[7] To Zurayq such a mission superseded
the twin objectives of independence and unity as mere means towards
a lofty end. As to the exact nature of this Arab mission, Zurayq
proffers a tentative possibility consisting of assimilating the new
sciences of the West in addition to other elements which are thrown
up by local responses, turning both into a single unit (pp. 38–42).

As to the new bearers of this lofty mission, they are not to be
confined to statesmen and political leaders, but should include all
individuals – civil servants, workers, journalists, teachers and others.
Women have also to be included in this endeavour. Their contribution
as partners, wives and mothers is to participate in outlining the
objective and clarifying the message of a new nationalist ideology
(pp. 42–3).

As a historian, Zurayq was surprisingly insistent on directing
national efforts towards the future rather than the past. Without
belittling the importance of history, he nevertheless declares:

> I am concerned that this historical mentality has taken hold of us, and
> occupied in our thinking a higher place than it deserves. It is incumbent
> upon us to direct our attention – and more than we have previously
> done – to the impending future so that a vision of life could be formed
> expressing our hopes and needs. (p. 94)

Zurayq's pioneering call appeared in a book which was more of an
anthology of disparate articles, rather than a coherent study. However,
the theme of nationalism and its modern implications forms a connecting thread which touches upon religion, language, culture and
education. Apart from advocating the need for a new philosophy, the
text offers one of the first positive appreciations by a Christian Arab of

the Prophet Muhammad and the central role of Islam in the history
of the Arabs. This appreciation is, however, meant not to rehabilitate
Islam as a political system of government, but to underline its cultural
significance as a set of values and symbols. Zurayq delivered his
appreciation 'on the occasion of the anniversary of the birth of the
noble Arab Prophet', in order to clarify the relation between religion
and nationalism. He thus hoped by delimiting the respective spheres
of each entity to restate the function of each. In this scheme of things,
religion turns out to be a moral force which strengthens nationalism
when shorn of its fanaticism and confessionalism. In other words, the
religious spirit was to act as a source of inspiration. He next underlines
the pivotal role of the Prophet Muhammad as the messenger of Islam
and the builder of a solid state which for the first time united 'the
quarrelling tribes' of Arabia. Thus, Islam as an 'Arab heritage' is the
foundation of Arab culture both in the medieval and modern periods.
Nevertheless, what Muhammad established, and in conformity with
the spirit of the age, was a religious state. By contrast, nationalism is
the child of the modern age, and in spite of the appearance of a certain
'national sentiment' among the Arabs in the formative and mature
period of their empire. It was thus only in the modern era that
nationalism, as a cultural and political bond, became superior to all
other bonds, creating a community of equal citizens irrespective of
religion or sect (pp. 111–17).

Hence, the Prophet laid the foundations of Arab unity which later
developed into a nationalist movement. More importantly, the
example of the Prophet as a man of conviction and high principles
should serve as an inspiration to all the sons of the Arab nation
(pp. 117–18).

Zurayq's text, addressed in the main to the young generation, was
adopted by the Iraqi Ministry for Education as a textbook to be used
in all its schools. It was, moreover, widely reviewed and its contents
debated by prominent Arab intellectuals. Although most thought it
did not live up to its promise of offering a new theory on which Arab
nationalism could build its programme of action, it did stimulate a
lively debate which has not yet reached a final conclusion.[8]

Thus, after 1938, there was a clear shift towards formulating a
political doctrine whereby Arab nationalism would become an
expression of a coherent theory. This shift represented the advent of a
new political elite and the politicization of a wide section of urban
social groups. Adumbrated by Zurayq, the need for a new type of
nationalist movement was made into a central issue in a text published
in 1941 by a leading Sunni Muslim cleric from the Lebanon, Shaykh
'Abdallah al-'Alayili (1914–96).

In his text, *The National Constitution of the Arabs*,[9] the author depicts in an eloquent Arabic style[10] the urgent need for an Arab nationalist theory fit to bring about deliverance and liberation. While he acknowledges the existence of a glorious Arab nation in the past and a vigorous modern nationalist movement, he deplores the absence of 'a coherent theory' which the Arabs could claim as their own. This lack is characterized by a vague feeling which was generated by the advent of nationalism as a world movement, leading in the process to shallow political movements which failed to embrace the Arabs as a whole and link their disparate struggles to one single movement. Nevertheless, the mere birth of this feeling indicated, for him, the existence of an earnest desire which by itself constitutes the first stage of an intellectual and social renaissance (pp. 9–10).

So far the Arabs have lagged behind other nations, such as the Swiss, the Germans, the Italians and the English, in being not yet the recipients of such a doctrine either through education, the printed media or political parties.[11] In order for public opinion to be educated and won over and vague ideas turned into concrete action, the articulation of a political doctrine becomes one of the most urgent tasks, for it is an energy that infuses general principles with dynanism (pp. 10–11).

Even without a doctrine of their own, the Arabs would still have a relatively well-defined cause that is understood in one way or another by its adherents. The Arab cause was at first unified around a simple idea and a programme of action which found its clearest manifestation in the Arab Revolt of 1916. As the Allies reneged on their promises and imposed their Mandates on some Arab provinces in the wake of World War I, the Arab movement began to disintegrate. Hence, al-'Alayili singles out the Arab revolt as the turning point of modern Arab history. Despite its failure, it re-established for the Arabs a new history which inspires them to perform great deeds in the future. More importantly, it taught them to venture beyond their immediate demands and grievances by revealing the importance of basing their identity on a long chain of historical events linking them to the early Arab conquests.[12] It is this idea of resurrecting history and turning it into a living entity that furnishes the basis of a new doctrine (pp. 11–22).

Adopting social Darwinian terminology, al-'Alayili thought that the conflict of ideas would result in the survival of the fittest vision according to the laws of natural selection. The struggle for life in the realm of politics and ideas is an incessant activity that is both natural and more beneficial, whereas artificial selection is imposed by violence and external pressure. Thus, colonialism, autocracy, theocracy and other outmoded forms of rule and government are artificially induced and cannot withstand the force of natural selection. The value of a nationalist philosophy is then its suitability to, and direct connection with, a living social being within the parameters of a certain time and place (pp. 22–7).

In this sense, a philosophical doctrine has to be coherently articulated without robbing it of a certain malleability capable of adaptation and evolution. While scientific disciplines, such as physics, are based on straightforward laws formulated in the light of rationalist judgements, in human affairs rationality has to be preceded or accompanied by some inchoate means linked to the emotions and communal feelings. Moreover, the viability of this national doctrine, juxtaposing rationality and faith in an organic unity, is guaranteed when it becomes a new religion. This religion has to be flexible and profound at the same time (pp. 28–32).

Having outlined the need for a new philosophy, the author proceeds to offer his vision based on the assumption of creating the proper balance between the individual, on the one hand, and the community, or society, on the other. Such a balance has to derive from human choice whereby education in its broadest sense makes possible the achievement of homogeneity in its Gellnerian sense. Hence, he discusses the merits of political and economic systems of his day, rejecting modern socialism in its Bolshevik form as it stifled the individual and the right to private property and ownership. However, he supports the idea of 'co-operative socialism' or social democracy. What is more noteworthy in this respect is his articulation of a novel concept of immortality and which is of direct relevance to his nationalist creed. This is all the more interesting, as it is to be recalled that al-'Alayili is a Muslim cleric of sound and well-attested credentials. He thus thinks that the idea of immortality has so far gone through two stages. In the first stage, it grew out of a selfish inclination on the part of the individual to ensure his own salvation and life after death. The second stage finds immortality focused on the family as the locus of eternal life. It is only now in the age of nationalism that human beings have begun to seek their immortality in the survival and stability of their society. The last stage is still in its infancy and only by surpassing it could we think of a new stage in human development. This is all the more so since 'society does not become stable until thought itself has become social' (pp. 33–59).

The author alludes in the Introduction to contributions which preceded his own, singling out pamphlets put out by the League of Nationalist Action and Zurayq's book discussed above. He nevertheless makes it clear that these contributions, particularly that of Zurayq, did no more than reveal the importance of a new consciousness without succeeding in delineating its various aspects (p. 31). It is in this respect that *The National Constitution* breaks new ground by trying to offer a coherent vision based on philosophical premises, sociological categories and political analysis. The comprehensive nature of the text led some scholars to attach a 'totalitarian' label to its contents, which is largely unwarranted.[13] To al-'Alayili, there was no doubt that modern civilization was based on an industrial system in which the manufacture of innumerable goods and commodities would lead to a division of labour and the emergence of new social classes: capitalists, the working class and the middle class. Although he deplored the depletion of natural resources in an economy of industrialism, he identified productivity and constant growth as the engine of all national societies. Arab society had to become part of the same drive, albeit in a more gradual manner which would avoid the purely 'material and automated nature of the American system of production'. Production had to be on a small scale calculated to meet the needs of the national consumer rather than to enter into competition with other producing nations, and which was the cause of modern wars. Workers must be allowed to share in the profits of their industrial enterprises whereby rewards were given according to merit and effort (pp. 62–70).

As to modern education, American pragmatism has to be avoided as it preaches the gospel of material profit and immediate gain (p. 71). But how does nationalism figure in this scheme of things?

Nationalism is an integral part of the progress of social life, al-'Alayili asserts. It is the result of socio-economic and geographic factors whereby loyalty to the family and the tribe was superseded by loyalty to a particular territory. However, there are two types of nationalism. One is based on territorial affiliations, and another on 'imagined blood' kinship. The first grew out of feudalism in which social organisation revolved around a stretch of territory, whereas the second, which is properly speaking a species of sub-nationalism, grew out of tribal amalgamations and in which ethnicity took primacy over social factors. Hence, ethnic or racial nationalism is no longer viable as it harks back to primitive conditions of life represented by nomadism. Being purely racial, this nationalism is out of tune with the spirit of the age, leading to social fragmentation and segmentation. Nowadays, there ought to be only one nationalism built on the concept of social and territorial loyalty. Social nationalism is in accord with the laws of progress, and creates the right conditions for cooperation among peoples of various nationalisms. Ethnic nationalism is retrograde and reactionary, while nationalism, derived from the unity of language, territory, common interests and ideals is the only one that is destined to prevail (pp. 83–6).

Racism as a modern European phenomenon, particularly in its German variety, or belief in the supremacy of the Aryan race, is dismissed by al-'Alayili and judged to be a mere emotional reaction to the decline of religion, on the one hand, and a desire for power and domination, on the other. The German philosopher Fichte, the French author Arthur de Gobineau (1816–82),[14] Richard Wagner (1813–83) and Houston Stewart Chamberlain (1855–1927), who was Wagner's son-in-law, are shown to have preached a racist message that flies in the face of scientific and biological theories. Hence, racial purity is dismissed as a basis of modern nationalism. The Arabs themselves are shown to have clung to such myths during the early period of their imperial domination in the Maghreb and Andalusia, before embracing a sort of social nationalism towards the end of their domination (pp. 91–2). Other factors such as language, religion, economic ties and geographic location are shown to be of more direct relevance to the constitution of nationalism. However, except for language, no particular importance is given to either geography or religion.

As a matter of fact, religion is said to lack the proper requirements for creating nationalism and does not qualify as a primary factor, although it may play a secondary role, both positively and negatively (pp. 87–90).

Modern Arab nationalism found its first public expression in the proclamation of Sharif Husayn on 10 June 1916. Despite its failure, the Arab Revolt revealed the existence and maturity of a nationalist movement. It is true that the Arabs after 1916 failed to achieve the unification of their countries. However, they scored military victories in the battlefields and their revolt infused them with enthusiasm, manifesting itself in their separate confrontations with the new European masters. If Arab nationalism has become an irrefutable reality, how does one define it?

> Arab nationalism is the awareness of the Arabs of their complete social existence, an awareness which is subjective rather than objective, so that the imagined Arab community (*Khayal al-jama'a al-arabiyya*) as a spiritual and dynamic complex is everpresent to their conscience. Consequently, every Arab must experience with an instinctive compulsion the strong prevalent connections and ties, in such a way that the community is transferred for him from the surface of life to his innermost soul. (p. 101)

In other words, an imagined community, long before Benedict Anderson used the phrase, was being articulated as a concept corresponding to the existence of nationalism. What al-'Alayili meant was that nationalism should have 'the imaginative power of religion', becoming itself a new religious creed capable of stirring the individual in an instinctive manner and creating at the same time a homogeneous society whereby the entitlement to freedom and independence would become natural rights (pp. 101–2).

Having defined nationalism, al-'Alayili defines the nation as being a natural community of a group of people who are brought together by the unity of their territory, ethnic origins and linguistic ties. Their union in the future is confined to common interests and the will to live together whereby an idealistic spiritual unity and social awareness should prevail. Hence, the nation is a natural community, whereas the state is an artificial creation that may or may not coincide with the nation. More importantly, nationalism announces the arrival of the age of democracy and the end of former feudal, aristocratic and monarchical systems. It is thus the government of the community by the community, and contrary to what John Stuart Mill feared, there could be no tyranny by the majority which is composed not of one but a number of social classes (pp. 119–20).

In spite of his belief in a strong leader, al-'Alayili condemns personality cults and dictatorships. Writing during World War II he alludes to Germany, Italy and Japan as examples of states which because of their dictators, succumbed to warmongering, whereas Britain and France, being democratic, were more reluctant to be drawn into such activities. To be truly nationalist is to oppose both authoritarianism and imperialism:

> Nationalism is based on the general will which is the result of the drive to participate in a common social and economic life, and the nationalist state represents this will. Accordingly, the meaning of the state is transformed from being an oppressive ruling power to one in which the sovereignty and self-government of society are realized. In fact, the history of nationalism is the history of the emancipation of mankind from its shackles. Hence it [nationalism] made possible the separation of power, tipping the balance in favour of the legislative authority, which represents the will of the people, vis-à-vis the executive power which wields the means of violence. (p. 123)

It is true, al-'Alayili concedes, that nationalism is of 'modern European origin'. It was adopted after long and arduous struggles, and then became the established norm of modern systems in Europe. There are various political systems in the world today, but the

European ones are the most noteworthy. The Arabs have to swim with the European tide lest they drown. However, they should do so while keeping some links with 'our past, history and traditions. If nationalism is some kind of nourishment, one should not only chew it, but assimilate it and digest it as well' (pp. 123–4).

There is thus a clear modernist definition of nationalism based on three pillars: geographic location, common interests and language. Other elements enter into the equation as contributory factors, whereby ethnic ties become mere imagined ones, in the same way history, customs and belief-systems are part of nationalist myth-making (p. 116).

The rest of the text is devoted to the exposition of three interrelated topics: the precise role of religion in society, the practical steps of achieving Arab unity and the system of government that is commensurate with a nationalist vision.

As we have seen, al-'Alayili excluded religion as a primary factor in the creation of nationalism. Instead, he singled out three main constituents: geographic location, common interests and language, whereby the last two are rendered of decisive importance in a future polity. Ethnic ties, history and belief-systems were also said to enter into the equation as contributory factors, serving in the main to consolidate the imagined national community.[15]

Being a religious leader himself, al-'Alayili does not shy away from discussing the implications of religious faith in the modern world. His approach is significant as it allows us to observe how Islam was being reinterpreted by both Muslim and Christian Arabs to meet the requirements of the age of nationalism.

To al-'Alayili, the interaction between a certain society and its environment leads in the long run to the emergence and eventual consolidation of certain spiritual and mental traits. Religion, being a complex of particular spiritual and intellectual characteristics, is governed by the same environmental stimuli. Hence different environments produce different religions and which are in accord with their specific conditions. Islam, despite its universalist message, did not escape this geographic articulation which is most pronounced in its different legal schools (Malikite, Hanafite, Shafi'ite and Hanbalite).

Nationalism, being a practical endeavour, is often in need of idealist symbols capable of mobilizing support and generating enthusiasm. This symbolism is derived from either a moral principle, divine religion or natural religion.

The moral principle is the least qualified to act as an effective symbolism. This is the result of its liability to rapid change and the successive emrgence of different cognitive and biological theories.

Divine religion is represented in the Arab East by Judaism, Christianity, and Islam. Judaism by its very nature does not accept the other two religions, condemning both as heresies. Thus, it cannot be allowed to control them as it is highly likely to act as their oppressor. Christianity, while it accepts Judaism, deriving some of its theology and regulations from it, considers Islam 'an aberrant innovation and an atrocious heresy'. Hence, it may be suitable to oversee the affairs of Judaism but not Islam. Islam, on the other hand, does accept the first two, considering them as divine religions dedicated to the word of God and His worship. Both the Qur'an and early Muslims did not perceive Islam as a new religion, but as a synthesis aimed at unifying fractious religious sects. In this sense, Islam may be considered more qualified to take charge of the other two. However, while such a possibility is true in theory, in practice, the selection of Islam as the symbol of nationalism will inevitably lead to strong objections from non-Muslims. Moreover, Muslims themselves are not agreed as to the true interpretation of their original texts. Thus, the only other alternative, al-'Alayili asserts, is to have resort to natural religion (pp. 147–9).

Natural religion brings together, and acts as a common denominator of, concepts and beliefs shared by the three divine religions, such as the idea of God, the immortality of the soul, punishment and reward in the afterlife and the performance of good deeds. Moreover, natural religion springs from the depth of the human soul and all religions are in agreement as to its general precepts. It is in this sense that it could infuse nationalism with vitality, making its concrete idea more abstract and sublimely idealistic. Moreover, no one, al-'Alayili continues, should entertain the illusion that this is a new religion; it is merely the prelude to divine religion be it Islam or Christianity (pp. 149–50).

At this stage, al-'Alayili differentiates between religion as scripture and divine revelations, on the one hand, and religious leaders who misinterpret their texts to suit their own purpose, on the other. Religion in its original meaning is a philosophy related to heavenly ideals and metaphysical notions, while nationalism is a philosophy that prescribes earthly rules, having to do with organizing our lives in society and not in heaven. Thus, there are two separate spheres in which two different functions have to be specified: what is suitable for one sphere becomes harmful when transferred to the other. Modern Turkey and Iran (1924–41) did not succeed in achieving 'political freedom' until their religious leaders were sent back to their places of worship. Separation of religion and politics releases the former from the shackles of mundane pursuits, thereby restoring its true function as an ethical system of values focused on the idea of an eternal, wise and regulatory power that is inaccessible to the human mind. Religion forms an integral part of one's personality which is more durable and far superior to all rational systems of philosophy which attempt to confine the individual to material forces based on the sufficiency of the human mind. Only religion has the requisite qualities to render individuals ever willing to serve their community selflessly and continually (pp. 150–6).

Thus, religion is excluded at one level, only to be rehabilitated at another. Its restitution is, however, made on condition of its confinement to the realm of high culture, and which Gellner stipulated as the true hallmark of the age of nationalism, particularly in an Islamic environment.

Regionalism

In 1941, there were only a handful of Arab states which had achieved some kind of political independence. These were Saudi Arabia, North Yemen, Iraq and Jordan.[16] Yet only Saudi Arabia could claim to have unified under the leadership of Ibn Sa'ud a number of adjacent provinces in Arabia between 1912 and 1932 (Najd, Ha'il, Hejaz and 'Asir). Greater Syria, which before World War I and subsequently after the French Mandate was still striving to unite its disparate parts, had been divided into four separate provinces: Greater Lebanon, Jordan, Palestine and the Republic of French-mandated Syria. Iraq was perceived to have gained Mosul in the north after succeeding in fending off Turkish claims, only to lose Kuwait in the south. The rest of Arabia including Qatar, Bahrain, Oman, the Trucial Statelets known after 1971 as the United Arab Emirates, and South Yemen were under British occupation, protection or control; the Sudan had yet to gain its independence from Britain; Libya had been under Italian occupation since 1911; Tunisia, Algeria and Morocco were in the process of embarking on their drive for complete independence from French colonialism.

Arab nationalists in the 1930s and early 1940s began to articulate a new vision of Arab unity directly derived from their assumption that the Arab nation formed a single social entity which sought to be grouped into one political unit. This was plainly the political programme of the League of Nationalist Action, the views expressed by the Arab delegation to the Islamic conference in 1931, and various clandestine organizations.

Perhaps al-'Alayili was one of the first Arab nationalists to tackle the practical difficulties of achieving the complete and simultaneous unification of all Arab states.

He believed that 'the boundaries of the Arab fatherland' coincided with the historical and final expansion of the Arabic language. This was a natural development resulting from successive Arab conquests, migrations and settlement. The final triumph of Arabic followed the law of natural selection whereby other languages, spoken by various ethnic communities, were gradually wiped out and the Arabization process left behind a permanent imprint and a triumphant language. Regional or local nationalisms, calling for loyalty to a particular Arab country, to the exclusion of others and on the basis of more ancient or dead cultures, were thus artificial constructs destined to perish by the mere fact of their reactionary characteristics (pp. 130–2).

Nevertheless, social homogeneity was far from being complete in the Arab homeland. This was particularly the case in the undeniable divergence between the eastern and western parts of the Arab world, being divided as they were by the Libyan desert. Social homogeneity is said to signify a degree of mutual approximity in development and evolutionary progress. Hence, regionalism was an inevitable stage, provided all local movements considered their work to be of a transitory nature, and were at the same time imbued with the idea of Arabism. Provinces which were already socially homogeneous and were at similar stages of development, such as Iraq and Syria, are to unite and form one single Arab nationalist state. Such a state could form the nucleus of a wider Arab unity, closely controlled by gradual and measured steps and in accordance with the actual stage of social development. However, in order to hasten the desired outcome the best means would be the employment of nationalist propaganda, the foundation of nationalist clubs and the publication of books. The idea of forcible unification whereby military force is used by a powerful Arab state to compel others to join it is to be avoided, as it may lead to negative reactions in countries in which Arabism is still a weak force. The creation of a standardized Arabic language, the codification of a single law and the inculcation of a general culture, brought about by the consensus of various Arab governments, is the first right step.

Contrary to al-Husri's contention, who advocated as early as 1936 that Egypt should be the natural leader of a new Arab movement, al-'Alayili saw Iraq, with its vast natural resources (particularly oil) and abundant agricultural products as well as its direct links with Europe,[17] as the political leader of a new Arab union. It is to be remembered that in 1941, Iraq was witnessing a movement of resurgent nationalism centred on the Iraqi army and its opposition to British and French policies in Palestine and Syria.

An Arab Polity

It is perhaps appropriate at this juncture to underline the fact that Arab nationalism was associated in its political stage with a clear commitment to liberal democracy or to a system of parliamentary democracy in its various western models. Such a trend can be clearly seen since the early twentieth century, through the period of World War I, and the inter-war period. This remained the case until the mid-1950s when a gradual adoption of single party systems became a more attractive option. This preference for parliamentary democracy is apparent in al-'Alayili's text as well as in the constitution of the radical nationalist party, the Arab Ba'th Party, adopted by its founding Congress in 1947.

Although a form of social democracy in the economic field was being advocated, there was a marked antipathy towards communism and its advocacy of class struggle at the expense of national alliances. This antipathy became all the more pronounced when most local communist parties stood aloof from the idea of Arab unity, followed policies dictated by the Soviet authorities and did not object to the partition of Palestine or the foundation of a Jewish state. Hence, beginning in the early 1940s, Arab nationalists started to articulate their criticism of communism in general, and local communist parties in particular, on the basis of their defective appreciation of the idea of Arab unity and the centrality of nationalism as the ideology of liberation in under-developed countries.[18] This enmity towards communism remained a major characteristic of Arab nationalism until 1961. In the meantime, the Soviet Union had emerged by the early 1950s as a friendly power towards revolutionary Arab regimes and entered with fierce competition with the United States for strategic and political spheres of influence in the Middle East. This served to soften the Arab nationalists' assessments of Marxism as a major world ideology and led, as we shall see later, to a wide-ranging dialogue at the theoretical and practical levels.

It is no wonder then that a text written in 1941 takes for granted the general approach of the Enlightenment, the American and French revolutions, tinged with an emphasis on things purely Arab in the moral and spiritual history of Islam. Seen in this light, al-'Alayili opts for 'the middle class' as the carrier of his nationalist aspirations. It is this class which is credited with the ability and the right social and intellectual qualifications to represent the solid incarnation of the nation and its ambitions. In this respect, he cites the policies of Cardinal de Richelieu (1585–1642), those of Otto von Bismarck

(1815–98) and Giuseppe Garibaldi (1807–82) as examples of a clear tendency towards the creation of a strong middle class. The upper and lower classes are deemed unfit to bring about the regeneration of the nation, for social, cultural and economic reasons.

Nevertheless, al-'Alayili sees ownership of land and real estate by all Arab citizens as the key element in building a stable national identity. Land ownership and national loyalty reinforce each other. Moreover, by creating a vast majority of property-owners in the nation, extremist and subversive ideas are nipped in the bud, whereas the willingness to defend one's homeland becomes an ingrained trait. Hence, class cooperation rather than class struggle would distinguish social relations in the new polity. Racial, sectarian and ethnic divisions are as much inimical to the body politic as class conflict and should be dealt with by redistributing their elements. He singles out, among others, the Assyrians of Iraq and the Jews in Palestine, calling for a policy of population redistribution rather than expulsion (pp. 170–8).

Morality and civic consciousness are highlighted by al-'Alayili for their unquestionable benefit in a civil society that is both egalitarian and democratic. Herbert Spencer (1820–1903) is invoked in this context for his stress on moral consciousness as the foundation and framework of society (p. 185). The belief in a system of values transcends nationalism and it is a moral law that defines natural rights and duties. According to al-'Alayili, Arab culture itself is universalist and humanist in its adherence to high ideals of duty, virtue and generosity. Natural rights of the individual are nowadays enshrined in the constitutions and laws of the major states in the world. These include: personal freedom, the right of ownership, and the right to resist oppression. On the other hand, civil law prescribes certain duties incumbent upon the individual such as the payment of taxes and his acceptance of a higher authority as the ultimate power. The emergence of society, in contradistinction to the existence of an aggregation of human groups, was the result of the emergence of similarly-motivated individuals who could then coalesce because of their initial affinity and homogeneity (*tajanus*). Thus, preserving the independence of the individual means allowing each member of society to perform his/her function according to ability and competence. In this sense, political rights go hand in hand with economic rights. 'Political democracy' should be paralleled by 'economic democracy'.[19] Equality of means and opportunity entails the political right of the public to manage their own affairs. This introduces universal suffrage as an inherent right through the establishment of democratic rule. Side by side with political, civil and economic rights, the universalization of education is a general right whereby the exercise of one's duties and responsibilities is enhanced by knowledge. That is why all civilized nations have made primary education both compulsory and free. As to freedom of thought, al-'Alayili goes out of his way to underline his belief in an open society in which ideas interact, clash and are propagated, provided social order is not disrupted. He refers in particular to religious missionary work as being harmful when undertaken to convert the inherited religion of various groups (pp. 179–212).

Finally, equality before the law led inevitably to the political right of the public to control their own system of government, rather than being governed by the will of the select few. This right is enshrined in the democratic form of politics and the acceptance of universal suffrage. In this sense, in order for the majority to exercise its rights and be truly representative, it has to enjoy the freedom of participation in public affairs. Nation and state, although having two different origins (one natural and another artificial), do not merge into each other until the community governs itself by itself, becoming the source of authority. Democracy is the best method of government without exception, particularly when it is properly applied. In fact, democracy exists only in name if the wealthy classes and notables are allowed to run for parliament. By the mere fact of their wealth and deceptive promises, they end up in charge of legislation which they invariably distort to favour their interests. Thus, 'capitalists' should be prevented from entering parliament as representatives of the people. Their only role is to be members of consultative parliamentary committees, whose function is to propose rather than vote (pp. 216–20).

A constitutional monarchy or a republican system are two preferred options, provided the monarch is himself elected from among the members of the royal house by the people and is considered a functionary of the state, or the president of the republic is not a member of the wealthy classes (pp. 220–1).

Al-Arsuzi: Language and Industry

Between 1943 and 1958, Zaki al-Arsuzi (1899–1968) published a number of booklets and tracts with the aim of offering a new Arab philosophy of nationalism. Born in the Syrian coastal town of Latakia, al-Arsuzi grew up during the last and final phase of the Ottoman empire. The advent of the French Mandate in both Syria and Lebanon in the early 1920s sharpened his political awareness and turned him into a militant activist. After completing his elementary and secondary education in Syria, he spent three years (1927–30) in Paris, studying philosophy at the Sorbonne. Upon his return, he was appointed a secondary-school teacher of history and philosophy in Antioch, Aleppo and Dayr al-Zur. Attempts by the Turkish government to annex the Syrian province of Alexandretta,[20] in collaboration with France, transformed al-Arsuzi into a defender of Arab rights and Arabism. Thus, between 1934 and 1938 al-Arsuzi became a symbol of national resistance and a champion of a new generation of Arab nationalists. Having joined the League of Nationalist Action, an Arab nationalist party founded in 1933, he represented the emergence of new social forces: the western-educated young men of provincial towns. However, Alexandretta was annexed by Turkey in 1939 and renamed Hatay, despite the fact that it had a clear Arab majority.

After 1938, al-Arsuzi settled in Damascus and began to articulate his idea of Arabism in a new direction. Disillusioned with existing political parties, he gathered around him small groups of secondary-school pupils, who were to form a new vanguard. According to the poet Sulayman al-'Isa, who was a member of these groups, al-Arsuzi discussed with them the origins of the French Revolution, the Italian and German unification movements and the Japanese industrial miracle. More importantly, the ideas of Nietzsche, Fichte, Hegel, Marx, Spengler and Bergson were explored and explained. Moreover, Fichte's *Addresses to the German Nation* was widely discussed and circulated in a provisional Arabic translation.[21] In 1940, al-Arsuzi adopted the name of *al-Ba'th al-'Arabi*, the Arab Renaissance or Resurrection, for his group of pupils and students.[22] It seems that during the same period, two other school teachers, Michel 'Aflaq (1910–89) and Salah al-Din al-Baytar (1912–80), and both were, like al-Arsuzi, French-educated, the first specializing in history and the second in physics and mathematics, initiated a similar course of intellectual and political action, centred on secondary-school pupils. Whereas al-Arsuzi published pamphlets under the title of *al-Ba'th al-'Arabi*, al-Baytar publicized the idea of the other group in pamphlets carrying the title *al-Ihya' al-'Arabi* which could mean Arab resurrection or revivification. While 'Aflaq and al-Baytar resigned their teaching posts in 1942 and dedicated their efforts to full-time political activity, al-Arsuzi continued to teach philosophy at various Syrian schools until his retirement in 1959. In the meantime, the Arab Ba'th party was officially founded in 1947 by 'Aflaq and al-Baytar, and al-Arsuzi's group joined as individuals in the conspicuous absence of their master.

In 1943, al-Arsuzi published what he considered to be an entirely original study of the genesis of the Arabic language and consequently the uniqueness of Arabism as a philosophy of life. The title of his study was *The Arab genius in its language* (or tongue).[23]

Before discussing al-Arsuzi's linguistic theory, it is worth stressing at this stage that his analysis of nationalism in its Western origins bears striking similarities to what Kedourie would allude to as Kant's concept of the autonomous individual as well as the Cartesian emphasis on the rationality of human beings. However, this particular strand merges in al-Arsuzi's depiction into another and more encompassing strand which bears unmistakable Gellnerian overtones. The third strand is peculiarly unclassifiable, focussing as it does on the unique function of Arabic as a system of grammatical originality. Needless to say, al-Arsuzi expounded his views long before those of either Kedourie or Gellner. In fact, one is tempted to assume that Kedourie, a keen Arabist, was already familiar with al-Arsuzi's texts, particularly those published in the 1950s. In his edited book *Nationalism in Asia and Africa* (1971) Kedourie lists in addition to Kant, already discussed in his *Nationalism* (1960), the French philosopher Descartes as being responsible for endowing the individual with the ability to achieve independence in the intellectual, moral and economic realms. He goes on to say:

> And it is of course a fact that this aspiration is peculiarly European . . . Kant and Descartes may be considered to offer a reasoned philosophical justification of this European ideal, Descartes who doubted everything except the scope and power of man's reason, who proclaimed man nature's lord and possessor, and Kant who taught that no action was moral unless it was a freely accepted commitment.[24]

As for al-Arsuzi, he attributed the rise of nationalism in Europe to a series of intellectual, social and economic revolutions. First, the medieval idea of a hierarchical system of beings gave way to a modern concept of causality and relative relationships. Second, the Copernican revolution which deprived Earth of its centrality in the solar system and Galileo's laws sealed the fate of the medieval conception of nature and man. It was now believed that 'man was qualified to know the truth, since what is constructed by reason can be verified by experiment'.[25] This particular aspect of modern civilization, al-Arsuzi continues, was summed up by Descartes in his memorable phrase: 'Common sense or reason is naturally equal in all men.'[26]

Thus, if the human mind is endowed with the ability to grasp the true nature of things, and the human soul is endowed with a conscience which enables it to determine its moral commitment, 'it becomes the right of every individual to organize his way of life according to his will and to participate, as a citizen, with his compatriots in the management of the affairs of the state. Consequently, communities got together to demand independence and freedom, and peoples defied colonial rule and oppression, affirming their will to life.'[27]

According to al-Arsuzi, modern life is underpinned by the twin factors of science and industry. Science eliminated chance and superstitious beliefs, and created standard criteria which lent matter a common identity by reducing it to spatial extension. In other words, instead of a hierarchy of beings, the dominant notion of the medieval culture, a homogeneous world was now conceived in conformity with the laws of causality. Observation and objective experiments replaced a priori notions of mind and matter. As for industry, it made possible the achievement of common goals by bringing about uniformity and organisation in society. It was thus possible as a result of science and industry to turn equality and liberty, or democracy, into a permanent feature, being the end-product of a long process which established the rule of law and the accountability of political leaders. Both the English and French Revolutions confirmed the right of the individual to conduct his own affairs according to his will, leading in due course to the demand of nations to enjoy the right of independence and sovereignty.[28]

Hence, nationalism, despite its rootedness in human nature, has only become dominant in the current historical period. Moreover, it is only now that one can see how all aspects of public life, such as language, law, arts and philosophy, seem to be mere manifestations of a nation's true identity.[29]

This diagnosis of nationalism as a recent phenomenon created an unbridgeable gap between two cultures: the medieval and the modern.

The medieval world, al-Arsuzi explains, believed in a system of hierarchical beings, in society, nature and the cosmos. This chain of being dictated that authority emanated from God who communicated its essence to a messenger or a prophet. The messenger would, in turn, impart the message to the Pope in Christendom and the Caliph in Islamdom. The messenger is, moreover, accountable for his actions to God and not the community. The transmitted message constitutes revealed laws in the form of injunctions and commands. God alone has the right to amend or abrogate these laws: the messenger merely explains them, whereas lesser human beings, such as religious scholars, may use the technique of analogy or personal interpretation to elucidate certain points. This was compounded in western Europe by the idea of Original Sin, which led to the expulsion of Adam from Paradise. It was accompanied by another idea, namely the inadequacy of reason, and the need of revelation in order to achieve salvation, and the existence of a qualified body of men or an institution, such as the church, to offer guidance. Thus, social and cultural inequality was an integral part of this hierarchical chain of being.³⁰

This medieval scheme of things was swept away under the impact of the new scientific theories of Copernicus, Galileo and Newton as well as the discovery of the New World. Henceforth, the law of causality, based on standard general principles of necessity, made natural events equal and uniform. This equality spilled over into the human realm, giving rise to the notion of the equal right of all human beings in the management of the body politic under one general law. The community became the ultimate source of authority whose right it was to elect the head of state who is, in turn, accountable for his actions to the representatives of the nation. Moreover, laws ceased to be immutable: expressing the general will, they had to evolve with the evolution of the community and in conformity with the nature of social life. Revealed laws had become redundant. Equality of opportunity and freedom of movement and thought announce the emergence of nationalism as the creed of a new humanity intent on achieving limitless progress and under the emblem of equal citizenship for all members of the national community.³¹

This secular interpretation of the national idea and its centrality in the modern world sits uneasily with al-Arsuzi's third strand: his attempt to explain the uniqueness of the Arab nation by means of singling out the characteristic structure of its language.

He thus argued that the derivation of an Arabic word consisted of the vocalism of its syllables and in its expression of a direct representation of natural objects. Unlike languages of Latin origin, which are purely conventional and use arbitrary signs to denote the meaning of a certain object or referent, Arabic is essentially in conformity with nature itself. It is an intuitive language whereby what it signifies is not mediated by the concept which gives meaning to both signifier and signified. Rather, the word and its meaning are both united in their signification of a referent that is itself fully absorbed in this direct operation.³²

The authentic identity of the Arab nation, al-Arsuzi explains, is embodied in its language. In the same way a cell grows and multiplies in a living organism, the Arab person derives his personality from his nation, which is itself a living organism in nature and society. Arabic, as a natural and intuitive language, discloses what the national spirit implies and in so far as it aspires to accomplish acts of idealism, prophecy and heroism. Moreover, whereas the constituent component of society is the family, that of Arabic is its roots of basic syllables. These basic syllables, together with their sound, determine the meaning of a derived word. There is thus a natural sympathy between the vocalism of Arabic words and their meaning, leading to an organic unity of cognition and activity. It is in this sense one could say that the Arab vision of the world is spontaneous, whereas the modern European approach is based on the principle of causality.[33]

Needless to say, Plato's dialogue, *Cratylus*, discussed the same topic with the aim of ascertaining whether words or names were merely conventional arrived at by some agreement or custom, or whether they were natural whereby the label given to each object is embodied in letters and syllables. *Cratylus* reveals Plato's ambivalent attitude towards one view or the other, although he lets Socrates indulge in discussing the merits of both theories. At one point, Socrates seems to argue that words were mere 'imitations of their objects', then shifts the argument by showing his agreement with the consideration that assigned names were simply the result of an arbitrary convention.[34]

Furthermore, *Cratylus* was translated into Arabic in the 'Abbasid era, and its contents were well known to Arab grammarians.[35] However, al-Arsuzi's comparative study of Latin and Semitic languages and his theory of Arabic etymology, as a natural reflection of objects and the expression of a unique national character, remains part of a novel contribution.

Shahbandar: Leadership and Revolution

In a sense, the 1930s announced the emergence of Arab nationalism in its full political dimensions. It was also the decade of rapid transition from a familiar world of upper-class politics to a new scheme of educated middle-class elites grappling with social change and economic crises.

One Arab leader who represented the transition from an old style of politics to a new one was the Syrian statesman and renowned orator 'Abd al-Rahman Shahbandar (1879–1940). He combined an active political career with an intellectual curiosity which led him to espouse, in the early 1930s, the concept of Arab nationalism embracing the entire Arab nation, rather than his own Syrian homeland.

A medical doctor by profession, his political career epitomises the gradual maturation of a new approach wedded to a plan of action and a theoretical framework. Upon his graduation from the Syrian Protestant College (later renamed the American University in Beirut) in 1906, he joined in Damascus a 'literary circle', brought together by Tahir al-Jaza'iri (1852–1920). Its ostensible aim was to revive Arab culture within the Ottoman Empire, and instil in the young generation a sense of national pride and a good knowledge of 'the modern sciences'. This literary circle, dating back to the late nineteenth century, gave rise in due course to 'a secret political circle' which was formally established in Damascus in 1903. Its main purpose was to ameliorate the position of the Arabs within the Ottoman empire by demanding a decentralized system of government and the use of Arabic as an official language in its Arab regions.[36]

However, the 1908 Young Turk Revolution prompted him to join its leading organization, the Committee of Union and Progress. His enthusiasm for the revolution turned gradually into disappointment and disillusionment as he observed, along with others of his generation, the creeping 'Turkification' of the state. As Ottoman rule in Syria became increasingly repressive, especially after the outbreak of the war, he avoided detention by fleeing to Iraq and India before moving to Cairo, as his final destination. It seems that during the war he initially supported the Arab Revolt of Sharif Husayn. Moreover, he and several Syrian leaders formed a committee in June 1918 to conduct direct negotiations with the representatives of the British Government regarding the future of Arab Asia. In reply to a memorandum they submitted to the Foreign Office, through the Arab Bureau in Cairo, His Majesty's Government reaffirmed its intention to uphold the right of the Arabs to self-determination and independence.[37]

This British Declaration, known as 'The Declaration to the Seven', since it was addressed to seven Syrian leaders, was not implemented in either its spirit or letter.

The seven Syrian leaders,[38] had approached the British Foreign Office as the representatives of a newly-formed political organization, the Syrian Union Party (SUP). It was set up in the wake of the publication of the Sykes–Picot Agreement by the Bolshevik government (see chapter 2), and the publication of the Balfour Declaration. By seeking renewed assurances from the British government as to the future and independence of 'liberated Arab lands', their demands were more defined than those of Sharif Husayn and revealed a clear Syrian dimension.

Reliable Arab sources attribute the formation of a Syrian Party, at a time when the Arab Revolt was still proclaiming as its ultimate aim the independence and unification of all Arab Asia, to a growing rift between Sharif Husayn, on the one hand, and the leaders of the Arab movement in both Syria and Iraq, on the other. Antonius alludes to the concern of Shahbandar and his colleagues 'as to the form and character of the Arab governments to be set up in Syria, Palestine, and Iraq after the war'.[39] Amin Sa'id, who quotes a version related to him by one of the seven leaders, Kamil al-Qassab, indicates that the Syrian leaders resident in Egypt formed in early 1918 a national committee after it had become apparent that France intended to add Syria to its colonial possessions. At first, Sharif Husayn was made aware of the committee's programme and its intention to pursue Arab demands for complete independence under his leadership. However, as the Arab Revolt, under Faysal's command, swept northwards towards Damascus, the rift between Iraqi and Syrian officers in the regular Arab Northern Army began to widen. This rift, centred on Syrian objections to serve under the command of an Iraqi officer, Ja'far al-'Askari, while Damascus was about to be liberated, was compounded by the objection of Syrian civilian leaders, formerly associated with the Decentralization Society, to the rigorous application of Islamic law as envisaged and practised by Sharif Husayn. Consequently, the seven Syrians set up their political party under the leadership of Michel Lutfallah, a wealthy Christian Syrian landowner, resident in Egypt.

Be that as it may, the SUP turned out to be an ephemeral affair, especially after the return of Shabandar to Syria in 1919 and his subsequent appointment in 1920 as Minister of Foreign Affairs in Faysal's government. His appointment was cut short by the dismemberment of Faysal's Kingdom and the dispersal of his associates and team members.

However, the application of the Mandate system by the League of Nations in the former Ottoman Arab territories was the decisive factor in forcing various Arab leaders and organizations to readjust the focus of their national demands on the basis of the new territorial divisions. Furthermore, the failure to achieve the unity of Greater Syria was to lead in the 1930s to the emergence of political parties and ideologies calling for a wider unity embracing the entire Arab world. Shahbandar was one of those Syrian leaders who tried at first to implement an exclusive national programme centred on the twin demands of independence and unification of Greater Syria. To that end he established in 1924 the People's Party. In his inaugural speech he chose to concentrate on the importance of coordinating all national efforts to achieve self-determination. Moreover, he underlined the debilitating economic policies of the French Mandatory power, linking its practices to a colonial system of exploitation. 'Almost all revolutions in history', he explained, 'were the result of the economic factor.' 'The French as well as the Russian Revolutions had as their root causes the exploitation of the working class by the aristocracy.'[40] Although, the doctrine of communism, he went on, was not in accordance with the cultural heritage of the east, 'prudent socialism' could not be antithetical to the beliefs of eastern nations.[41]

The eruption of the Syrian revolt against French occupation under the leadership of the Druze chief, Sultan al-Atrash, transformed Shahbandar from a statesman into a national hero. As the revolt spread from southern Syria and started to engulf Damascus in violent clashes with French troops, Shahbandar joined the ranks of the rebels, turning in the process a local dispute originally centred on Druze grievances, into an armed insurrection for Syrian self-determination. The repressive and harsh measures taken by the French to quell the revolt reverberated across the Arab world. Egyptian reactions at both the official and popular levels were all the more remarkable for the future implications and the gradual emergence of Egypt as a leading centre of Arabism.[42]

By the end of 1926 the Syrian revolt had been crushed and Shahbandar left Syria once again and settled in Egypt. From his exile in Cairo, he began to publish a series of articles in the local press, designed to articulate a new approach to the political problems in the Arab world.[43] This approach was significantly sociological in its premises and concepts. It dealt with culture, civilization, the role of woman and man in society and the family, before tackling the function of the state, citizenship, political ideologies, nationalism, leadership and revolution. Last, but not least, religion is discussed as an important moral factor in the social development of humanity. This system of prioritization and arrangement of topics after the collection and publication of his articles in book form was meant to signal a clear shift towards a secular attitude having society as its main focus. In this respect, political activity was shown to be the result of a complex network of culture, social structure and economic conditions. Moreover, the latest western sociological theories were used to back up an argument or illustrate a point.

Having experienced 'democracy' in its Ottoman application during the first decade of the Young Turk Revolution, and another 'liberal' phase of politics under Faysal's brief sojourn in Syria, Shahbandar contended that an Arab society in the process of its emergence from a long period of subjugation and disorder could not afford the slow and cumbersome machinery of multi-party politics and electoral competition. It was thus permissible to insist on free elections and open democratic practices as long as colonial France continued to rule Syria. Once independence was achieved, Shahbandar argued, a newly-liberated country should be governed by 'an enlightened dictator' for a limited and provisional period. The enlightened and just dictator would use his talents and political wisdom to fashion a coherent society out of disparate regions and social groups. All Arabs should, first of all, rebuild their national personality and restore a sense of cultural homogeneity before turning their attention to the elaborate and delicate business of democratic government and constitutional processes.[44] Shahbandar was at pains to concede the benefits and undoubted suitability of democracy in a fully developed society. Nevertheless, given the intermittent and fairly brief Arab experience of constitutional rule, he believed that the inculcation of pan-Arabism on the basis of a comprehensive social programme should precede, and was a precondition of, democratic governance and accountability.

However, Shahbandar believed that violent revolutions were unlikely to erupt in countries with a long tradition of parliamentary democracy. Radical change in a well-established democracy, such as Britain, was simply achieved through 'the ballot box and without resorting to violence and widespread upheaval'. By contrast, Latin American countries, where parliamentary principles were still in a nascent state of development, governments used the constitution to perpetuate their oppressive rule in the absence of organised public opinion and the lack of a common will.[45]

Turning to the 1916 Arab revolt as the expression of a nationalist movement, he reveals his negative appreciation of its 'primitive' practices, the prevalence of 'medieval notions' in the ranks of its leaders as well as the public at large, and the low degree of its political organization. More importantly, the Arab revolt failed to gain popular support in a number of Arab countries which clung to the Ottoman Caliphate 'until its last dying moments'.[46] Nevertheless, he went on to justify the necessity of revolution in an Arab world dotted with colonies, protectorates, mandates and foreign military bases. In other words, gradual and peaceful change had become virtually impossible. It is in this context he, as a medical doctor, conducts a comparative analysis between the animal kingdom and human societies, seeing in both a number of similarities. At first, he explains, when Darwin put forward his theory of evolution, most biologists were converted to the idea of slow development, in the sense that change was a long drawn-out process which an organism undergoes in its response to a new environment. Hence, 'mutation' was ruled out. However, Shahbandar asserts, recent scientific discoveries proved that in both the animal and plant kingdoms 'mutation' did occur, making the birth of a new organism capable of passing on its newly-acquired characteristics as one of the most startling phenomena. In human societies, mutation is none other than revolution itself, not as mere probability but the necessary mechanism of political life. In this respect Islam itself was such a mutation which created totally new conditions 'within one generation'.[47]

Shahbandar was certain that with the new means of printing presses, education systems, and communication networks, the ability to effect radical and enduring social change had become much more feasible. He cites in this context how Atatürk had succeeded within a short period of time in introducing the secular Swiss personal status code, turning thereby monogomy into a normal state of affairs rather than an innovation.[48]

In discussing religion, Shahbandar reveals his belief in a universal moral code of conduct and which all religions are said to embody in their core values. The school of Sufism in Islam is, moreover, singled out for its tolerance, open-mindedness and exemplary belief in 'the unity of all religions'. Ibn al-'Arabi (d. 1240), the most renowned but highly controversial representative of this trend of thought and practice was, thus, commended for holding the view that all religious experiences were legitimate ways of worshipping one single God.[49]

Shahbandar returned to Syria from his exile in Egypt in 1937. By that time, he had established himself as the most prominent leader of the Syrian opposition to French occupation. The 1936 Treaty between France and Syria, which was negotiated by the leaders of the traditional National Bloc Party and the French Socialist government of Leon Blum, gave Shahbandar the opportunity to appear as the champion of complete Syrian independence. Although it was modelled on the Anglo-Iraqi Treaty of 1930, Shahbandar thought that France had been offered too many concessions[50] despite its recognition of Syrian independence.

However, the Treaty was never ratified by the French parliament and was subsequently abrogated in 1938. French colonial officials, following the downfall of the Popular Front government, became more concerned with the repercussions of recognizing the independence of two Arab countries (Syria and Lebanon) upon their colonial presence in the Maghreb. Furthermore, the French government perceived the treaty as an implicit recognition of the rising tide of Arab nationalism and which it thought was gaining the support of British officials and Mussolini's Italy.

Upon his return to Syria, Shahbandar was received with popular acclamation and seemed destined to lead a new movement of national renewal. However, as the Syrian socialist leader Akram Hawrani was later to observe: 'We admired Shahbandar because he was an eloquent orator and a leader far ahead of his generation in culture, mentality and approach. However, Shahbandar's energy and popularity began to wane as a result of the opportunistic nature of those who formed his entourage. Moreover, he did not reorganise his former People's Party, nor did he come up with a plan of action or a clear vision.'[51]

On 6 July 1940, Shahbandar was assassinated in his surgery by a gang of hired killers. Hawrani, and others who heard the news, wept bitterly at the death of the national leader. Hawrani later learned that a religious society under the influence of Shukri al-Quwwatly, the leader of the National Bloc, was behind the assassination.[52]

The assassination of Shahbandar, who had, so to speak, a foot in both camps, bridging the gap between the old and the new generation, left the door open for the consolidation of radical trends which had already appeared on the scene.

Michel 'Aflaq: The Vanguard

One of those who took upon themselves the task of introducing a new style of politics and leadership was the Damascene writer, school-teacher and co-founder of the Ba'th Party Michel 'Aflaq. In the early 1940s 'Aflaq established himself as the ideologue of a new political movement, the Arab Ba'th Party (see above). His contribution to the theory of Arab nationalism consisted of a series of articles which were later collected and published in book form for the first time in 1959. As a matter of fact, all his published works were originally either newspaper editorials, political statements on a particular topic, or speeches addressed to the party faithful. Moreover, he insisted on more than one occasion that what he had to say was a viewpoint (*nadhra*) rather than a full-blown theory (*nadhariyya*).

Nevertheless, his terminology and pronouncements did become part of the political discourse of an entire Arab generation. His lively and concise style seemed to convey a message of urgent action and a call for total change in Arab societies. It spoke the language of revolution as a moral task to which the individual was expected to dedicate all his efforts. There is thus a celebration of energy and self-sacrifice embodied in a relentless drive for eventual triumph and conquest. This inexhaustible energy was said to animate both the individual and the nation albeit in a potential state of readiness. The party, in its ideology and discipline, was simply a rational instrument and a highly-motivated agent capable of tapping the inner potentialities of the nation.

Consequently, 'Aflaq's contribution to the new style of politics resided in suffusing his audience, be it a group of students or party followers, with a spirit of limitless confidence in the future and an air of revolutionary optimism. He did so by sidestepping all available political parties and ideologies and by staking his claim to a novel vision of a bright future. Using Hegelian metaphors, he differentiated between reality and mere appearances, existing conditions and their prescribed course to be transformed into a higher order of things. In most of his articles, he repeatedly refers to the necessity of resurrecting and rebuilding 'the Arab soul' in accordance with the requirements of the modern age. Instead of tabulating the characteristics of the Arab nation with mathematical precision, or exerting one's efforts in an academic exercise designed to prove its existence, he stipulated 'faith' in one's cause as the highest moral criterion in political struggle.

In this sense, 'Aflaq's eyes were fixed on the future rather than the past. It was a future to be immediately realized, since time itself was no longer 'to be calculated in months and years', but evaluated as a 'spiritual dimension' that could be actuated in the present, ensuring thereby 'the attainment of eternity'.[53] In other words, the future was to be embodied in a new recruit of the party so that what the nation would be like could be glimpsed in his person.

After his return from Paris in 1933, having studied history at the Sorbonne, he worked as a school teacher until 1942 when he decided to dedicate his energies, together with his colleague Salah al-Din al-Baytar, to the foundation of a new political party. As we have seen, the 1930s ushered in a new era in the development of Arabism. Apart from the foundation of a number of pan-Arab organizations, and the intensification of the struggle for independence throughout the Arab world, economic and social issued began to colour all political discourse. By 1936, the League of Nationalist Action, one of the first pan-Arab parties to be established, seemed to be losing its appeal and political direction. The death of its charismatic leader in 1935, coupled with a wavering attitude towards traditional political parties such as the National Bloc (al-Kutla al-Watniyya), made it look less and less attractive to the new generation of the Arab educated elite. More importantly, Arab communist parties had already been part of the political scene for more than a decade, and were openly engaged in trade union activities, and espousing class struggle as a concomitant of national liberation. In the spring of 1934, a Syro-Lebanese group of Arab nationalist and Marxist-oriented writers, journalists and school teachers held a meeting in the Lebanese town of Zahle to discuss common issues of interest. Those who attended from Syria included Michel 'Aflaq, his colleague Salah al-Din al-Baytar, Ibrahim Kaylani, Jamil Saliba, and Kamil 'Ayyad. From Lebanon, there were, among others, a number of communist activists[54] who had become disaffected with the official line of their party and its subservience to the Soviet Union. At the end of the meeting, the delegates issues a statement entitled: 'In the Path of Arab Unity'. It defined the Arab cause as a nationalist endeavour aimed at uniting the Arab nation on the basis of language, culture, history, customs, and common interests. 'The Arab Fatherland' was said to extend from the Taurus mountains and the

Mediterranean in the north, the Arab [Indian] ocean, the Ethiopian mountains, southern Sudan and the Great Sahara in the South, the Atlantic Ocean in the West, and the Zagros Mountains and the Gulf of Basra in the East.[55] When the Ba'th Party was officially founded in 1947, it stuck to the same geographic boundaries as the national territory of the Arabs. Furthermore, the delegates called for the establishment of one unified Arab party 'as powerful as the force of a volcano upon its eruption', and the publication of a journal to act as a platform for 'all unionists and progressive nationalists'. The single party had to wait for more than a decade or so to come into existence. As for the journal, it began its short-lived journey in mid-August 1935 until it was banned, along with other publications, by the French authorities on the eve of World War II in 1939. It was significantly called al-Tali'a (the Vanguard).

Thus, from that early date 'progressive nationalists', considering themselves 'the vanguard' of the nation, were differentiating themselves as the voice of a new generation which had the lofty mission of educating and defending 'the popular masses'. Although the members of 'the vanguard' drifted apart after 1939, this largely intellectual encounter between Arab nationalists and Marxists served to impart a socialist dimension into the core of a hitherto purely nationalist message.

'Aflaq's early articles had no particular nationalist flavour, their main theme being socialism, idealism and the pivotal role of youth. He set out to underline the intellectual and political rupture between his generation of young, educated and progressive men, and the older generation of selfish politicians and short-sighted leaders. To stand outside one's own immediate environment, to be in opposition to the current and take the necessity of revolution for granted, these were the watchwords of an awakened Arab spirit. Revolution was more than political or social change: it places 'the future' in opposition to 'the present', revealing thereby the existing backwardness and defects of the nation as being temporary, alien and fabricated. Although an Arab nationalist could not divest himself of his past, it should be rescued from its relapsed existence and placed at the head of a progressive march as a guiding light towards a better future. In as much as the past of the Arabs was a revolution in its own time, the need for a new revolution under different conditions was all the more compelling. In this sense, 'Aflaq believed the 'eternal Arab mission' was to turn the dismembered Arab nation into 'a wholesome natural entity', whereby human dignity would be restored and justice reestablished. In other words, by becoming part of a revolutionary process, with all its responsibilities and travails, the Arabs would rejoin humanity, and as worthy members of its belief in the popular will and social progress.

Socialism

As early as 1936 'Aflaq singled out 'the educated youth' for his endeavours to articulate a vision of 'a new revolutionary society'. His purpose was to explain his adoption of 'socialism' as an ideal that surpassed mere material gain. Its aim, he insisted, was not to increase the production of factories but to release the inherent gifts of each individual and restore faith in human life. It was thus a positive doctrine motivated by a free-giving spirit rather than an attitude of vengeance and feeling of envy. It was thus not 'a religion of pity' and philanthropy, but an instrument of 'satisfying the hungry and clothing the naked' so as to enable them to perform their proper human function. Furthermore, 'the deprived masses' were entitled to the dignity of a full life not as a charitable act but by rights. He concluded:

> If I was asked to define socialism, I would not seek its definition in the texts of Marx or Lenin. I would rather say: it is the religion of life, and the triumph of life over death. By opening the door of employment for everyone, and allowing the gifts and virtues of all human beings to blossom, flower and be fruitful, it preserves what rightfully belongs to life, leaving to death nothing but dried meat and rotten bones. (pp. 24–6)

This definition of socialism was to remain undisturbed in its relatively broad and indeterminate consequences until the early 1960s.[56] In 1960, for example, and in an address to a gathering on the occasion of Labour Day, 1 May, Arab unity rather than socialism formed the main theme. It was, he said, 'for all the people: an independent socialism which does not follow a particular doctrine; . . . it benefits from all theories and experiments . . . and is determined to be in conformity with the spirit of the nation' (p. 110).

In other words, this was *Arab* socialism as opposed to Marxist socialism and found its raison d'être in its subordination to nationalism. By subordinating socialism to Arabism 'Aflaq intended to reduce communism to an alien western creed. Writing in 1944, he thought that the communist theory would continue to pose a serious threat to Arab nationalism unless the last managed to formulate 'a comprehensive', coherent and scientific theory, capable of being achieved through 'organised action' (p. 195).

Communism was thus the product of peculiar European conditions. No Arab, on the basis of his history, past or present traditions, could conceivably accept its philosophical or economic premises. It, moreover, repudiates 'the eternal Arab mission' which is an expression of the unique qualities of a great nation. In order for the Arabs to rejoin the world in its modern civilization, the assertion of their independent nationalist personality, rather than communism, would be the only choice open to them. Socialism in this context became 'a mere economic system', and not an internationalist movement which forms a totalitarian system subsuming in its purview politics and economics, as well as morality and religion (pp. 198–9).

As to Arab socialism, it is the product of the objective conditions of a divided Arab nation. It could, therefore, be said that 'Arab nationalism is synonymous with socialism in our present time' (p. 204). This is so because 'the nationalist struggle necessitates a socialist vision', which is equivalent to saying that 'the Arabs cannot achieve progress unless they feel and believe that their nationalism would guarantee justice, equality and a decent standard of living for all citizens' (p. 204).

In the past, 'Aflaq continues, the driving force of Arab solidarity was the religion of Islam. Nowadays, it is nationalism. In the case of Islam, economic reform was the result of a deep faith in the power of religion. In the same way, the achievement of social justice and freedom for the Arabs in the modern world has to spring from nothing else but 'nationalist faith'. Furthermore, if socio-economic issues seem to dominate the politics of western countries, the reason is not far to seek. These countries have already achieved their independence and unification so that the history and future of the nation have ceased to be a source of contention. The Arabs have still to achieve cultural rejuvenation and national sovereignty, whereas western nations are mainly occupied with 'the distribution of wealth' (p. 205).

More importantly, unlike communism, Arab socialism does not seek to obliterate 'the personal incentive of individuals'. On the contrary, it affirms the right of private ownership, albeit in a restricted and regulated manner. It also recognizes 'the right of inheritance' within certain limits designed to protect both the individual and the wealth of the nation. Furthermore, Arab socialism cannot possibly be fully achieved except in a future 'single unified Arab state'. Thus, echoing debates in the Marxist camp, socialism in one particular Arab country, such as Syria, was an impossible task. On the other hand, 'national socialism', as applied in the inter-war period in Germany and

Italy, had as its philosophical premise, the idea of racial superiority and the right of one superior race to world domination. Nazism and fascism, 'Aflaq points out, were geared towards a policy of discrimination between the citizens of their nations, and ended up by installing the dictatorship of one individual or one class (pp. 211–13).

This perspective led 'Aflaq to acknowledge class struggle as a factor of social conditions under capitalism. However, he redefined social polarization in its Arab context to include capitalists, feudalists, politicians opposed to Arab unification, and obscurantist religious leaders, on the one hand, and the rest of the people, on the other. Nationalism is then said to be a positive sentiment of sheer love rather than class hatred. But this love is imbued with a spirit of 'brutality' which does not flinch from facing down the enemies of the people (pp. 223–4).

Nationalism

Hence, socialism in its Arab dimensions was firmly established as the child of Arab nationalism and its legitimate offspring. By 1941, 'Aflaq had coined his trinitarian slogan of the Arab revolution: unity, freedom and socialism. It almost instantly became synonymous with the ideology of Arab nationalism in almost all its schools and trends. The slogan, however, was said to be 'a spontaneous expression of faith', rather than 'a scientific theory' or 'a mathematical equation' (p. 30). It sprang from 'the living virtues' of youth, in contrast to the cold calculations of elderly gentlemen or the manoeuvres of corrupt politicians (pp. 36–8). Hence, nationalism had ceased to be a mere theory, or a fashionable topic that was liable to be replaced by a more exciting craze. It is not to be compared to communism or a religious call. Springing from the depths of the Arab soul, and slowly growing like a well-planted seed, it defies definition and dry commentaries in the manner of theological treatises. To discuss nationalism by referring to books and journals imported from Europe is tantamount to distorting the Arab national personality and neglecting the real conditions of the nation. Abstract reasoning, 'Aflaq asserts, was never able to initiate a true renaissance or grasp the complex nature of the real world. Comparing and contrasting nationalism with religion, art or social customs amounts to an arbitrary act which fails to see nationalism as an all-encompassing entity and the soil which nourishes 'all the talents' of the nation. Hence, the presumed conflict between religion or Islam, on the one hand, and nationalism or Arabism, on the other, is a false assumption. Islam in its origins grew out of Arabism and as 'the most eloquent expression of its genius'. Thus:

Arab nationalism is not a theory but the source of all theories. Nor is it the offspring of pure thought but its foster mother. Instead of enslaving art it constitutes its fountainhead and soul. (pp. 41–3)

The act of interpreting Arab nationalism correctly, 'Aflaq continues, is akin 'to the sprouting of a plant out of the soil or a spike out of a wheat kernel'. To ignore context, time and place and concoct a theory that could be equally applied to eighteenth-century France or Plato's Greece, would be 'a false and artificial' operation. Hence nationalism is not an idea, nor is it a matter of 'love, faith and will', although these are necessary conditions of nationalism. Nationalism 'is not knowledge, but an act of active remembrance' (p. 44).[57]

By a process of elimination, 'Aflaq put aside all previous and current endeavours to define nationalism. His negative exercise, which yielded one positive statement, opted for a definition which encompassed the virtues of love and the certitude of faith. And nationalism became 'love above all else' and faith in its sanctity and eventual triumph. Nationalism was, furthermore, said to be inscribed in human societies like 'a desirable destiny'. In the same way, a person acquires a name or the features of his face, so does a people, without choice and irretrievably. Thus, there was no point in lamenting one's fate or regretting what might have been. In other words, nationalism is not a choice but an inevitable destiny that has to be embraced in the battle of patriotic survival (pp. 46–9).

To serve one's nation and make the ultimate sacrifice was the duty of the new generation. Such a generation in order to come into being, had to become convinced of its 'new' mission. This mission consists of creating an ideal society as an idea and a criterion with which 'the old society' is judged and rejected: this act of imagining one's ideal society does not consist of 'the present marching towards the future, but of relaying the future to the present' (pp. 69–73).

Moreover, the new generation has to enact 'a complete rupture with the old one', not in the conventional sense of age and time, but in a psychological and spiritual sense. This rupture of transcending one's immediate surroundings allows the act of segregation to pave the way for a more sound union based on the idea of the nation as a living ideal (pp. 69–74). In this sense, the nation is not simply the sum total of its members. Rather, it is an idea that could be represented by a few individuals, irrespective of their total number. As long as the idea of the nation exists in a potential state, it could be embodied by a single individual. This is the more so, when a particular 'leader' is faced with a situation of weak national consciousness. Under such circumstances, his task is to translate quantity into quality by representing 'the idea of the nation' in his own person, and in the face of fierce opposition. As long as 'the new generation' believes in itself as the carrier of 'an eternal mission', sooner or later, the nation is bound to respond to its true vocation by discovering its authentic nature (pp. 74–5).

According to 'Aflaq, Arab nationalism, represented by the youth of the nation, cannot be but a revolutionary force. The greatness of the Arab nation in the past is matched by its weakness in the present. Furthermore, compared with other advanced nations in the contemporary world, its miserable underdevelopment is immediately apparent. To remedy such a state of affairs, revolution is the only available option. In this context, the analogy of advanced and backward nations[58] is used by 'Aflaq to account for the absence of revolutions in the former and its inevitability in the latter. Hence, gradual evolution, the hallmark of sound systems of governments in developed countries, is ruled out in a nation still struggling for independence and unity (pp. 76–82).

The advent of a new generation, imbued with confidence in the future of its nation and motivated by the idea of revolutionary change, constituted the decisive rupture between the past and the present. Seen in this light, all regional, cultural and social variations within a divided Arab nation became of secondary importance. Differences in the level of political and economic development between Saudi Arabia and Syria, for example, were not to be used as an excuse against total Arab unity (pp. 244–5).

According to 'Aflaq, Arab nationalism was not to be defined by reference to racial and blood ties. It was an idea articulated on the basis of common history and culture, and has as its aim 'the defence of one single fatherland' as well as 'the building of one future'. Divisions based on racial assumptions, such as the one between Berbers and Arabs in the Maghreb, were manufactured by western imperialism. The unity of the Arab nation is forged in creating a state of relentless struggle againswt backwardness and stagnation (pp. 244–50).

In fact, 'Aflaq concedes, the Arab nation was still 'an abstract notion', tied up with the dreams and struggles of the new generation. In other words, this 'imagined community' had yet to be achieved in concrete terms; its existence depended on the belief of its faithful youth to be reborn as a vigorous nation. Those who struggled faced death, arms in hand; they embodied the Arab nation and possessed all the qualifications to hasten the birth of their imagined community (p. 250).

Furthermore, Arab nationalism could not be reduced to its immediate aims. The struggle for 'unity, freedom and socialism' imposed itself because of their absence at this stage of the nation's history. Their achievement would not signal the end of Arab nationalism, but the beginning of a different set of goals (p. 338).

Religion

In April 1943, marking the anniversary of the Prophet's birthday, 'Aflaq delivered at the Syrian university one of his most quoted and memorable addresses. Reprinted in numerous editions as a separate booklet, and considered the Ba'th's definitive statement on the relationship between Islam and Arabism, it continues to form a source of inspiration and controversy.

As we have seen, both Miqdadi and Zurayq singled out the Prophet Muhammad for his special and heroic role in the history of the Arabs. However, 'Aflaq's address remains the most articulate statement made by an Arab nationalist leader on the subject. We also know from internal evidence offered by innumerable disciples that 'Aflaq's theoretical formula had an emotional charge that continued to inspire and attract new adherents. A former Ba'thist, for example, informs us that he used to feel a shiver go down his spine, every time he read the following sentence: 'Muhammad was the epitome of all the Arabs. So let all the Arabs today be Muhammad.'[59]

'Aflaq saw Islam as a universal message, and an expression of Arab humanism at the same time. Moreover, 'the glorious past' of Islam was in sharp contrast to 'the shameful present' of the Arabs. Thus, there was no historical continuity between past and present, but complete 'rupture'. In order for the Arabs to relive their moment of glory, they had to renew themselves and perform a creative leap in their entire social and political conditions. To commemorate the Prophet's birthday, conventional utterances by politicians and religious leaders were mere hollow words with no real connection with present-day life. Only those who approached Islam afresh, enthralled by a new discovery and a reborn faith, could convey to others the utter beauty of the message and its endless possibilities. Hence, Islam is not mere rituals or a historical phase bounded by its causes and outcomes. Rather, it is 'an eternal and perfect symbol' of the Arab spirit, its authenticity and rich potentialities. For this reason, Islam could always be reinvigorated as a spirit of experience and a symbol of moral values (pp. 50–2).

Reliving the Prophet's experience in an act of empathy represents the task of a nation embarking on its new renaissance. In the same way, 'Aflaq contends, Islam represented in the past the renewal of Arab life, Arab nationalism should become the ideal of a different age. Nevertheless, Islam and Arab nationalism could not be separated in a mistaken analogy with modern European culture. For in Europe, religion was imported from the outside and thus remained 'alien to its nature and history', whereas for the Arabs Islam formed part of their innermost personality (pp. 53–8).[60]

As for Christian Arabs, like himself, 'Aflaq urged them to love, understand and cherish Islam as the most precious ingredient of their Arabism. Once they were awakened to their true identity, Islam would become for them 'a national culture' and an expression of their living heritage. The new Arab generation was thus entrusted with a mission far superior to politics and enthused with a faith that recognized 'God, nature, and history as being on our side' (p. 60).

Does that mean that the Ba'th was intended to be a mere religious movement preaching a nationalist message to the modern Arabs?

In 1950, the Syrian Constituent Assembly was convened to approve a new constitution of the independent republic. The first article of the draft constitution stipulated Islam to be 'the religion of the state'. Several members representing various shades of opinion and political parties objected to such an article of a democratic constitution meant to express the interests and rights of a modern society. Following heated and lengthy sessions, a compromise was adopted whereby Article One was amended to read: the religion of the President of the Republic is Islam. Amongst those who approved the new article was the Ba'thist representative of the district of Dayr al-Zur, Jalal al-Sayyid. As for 'Aflaq, in his capacity as the General-Secretary of the Ba'th Party, he expounded his views in an article entitled: 'The Arabs betwixt their past and future'.[61] In it 'Aflaq sought to pinpoint the exact nature of Islam as well as the spiritual and legal foundations of his envisaged Arab nationalism. He also sought to show how an Arab country, like Syria, with a multiplicity of sects and religions, should consider Islam as a religion and a culture.[62] To his mind, the Arabs were divided into two camps: conservative and progressive. The conservative camp simply wanted to maintain the status quo with all its accumulated traditions, while the progressive one represented a nationalist trend bent on effecting radical change. Moreover, the first were in the minority, whereas the second stood for an overwhelming majority and its wishes for a better future. Religiosity as practised and preached by the first camp was a mere mask, hiding all the outworn trappings of a dying tradition and all the vices of 'hypocrisy, opportunism and selfishness'. The progressive camp, by contrast, looks forward to a new dawn armed with a sound knowledge of the unadulterated spirit of religion as a sublime value of renewal. In this sense, the Ba'th movement operates 'a decisive rupture' between the defects of the status quo and the struggle to relive the purity of the religious mission before its corruption. By doing so, this political creed becomes 'a positive spiritual endeavour', which simultaneously embraces religion and combats stagnation (pp. 84–9).

Consequently, Arab nationalism addresses itself to all Arabs, irrespective of religion or sect, and is equally respectful of all religious traditions. However, it singles out Islam for its spectacular role in the history of the Arabs, considering this particular aspect of special significance in their spiritual heritage. In other words, Islam as a religion is equal to other religions in an Arab nationalist state. It only becomes more significant as the spiritual, cultural heritage of the nation and its source of inspiration. To be inspired by Islam, 'Aflaq reiterates, is totally different from being committed to a religious state. By opposing both a religious and an atheistic system of government, the future Arab state introduces 'secularism' which emancipates religion from the shackles of politics, and allows it to perform its proper function in society (pp. 89–91).

However, this secularism is peculiarly political, stopping short of including the civil space or the legal implications of personal status laws. It is secularism with a difference: equality of all citizens in the political arena, and no radical interference in the application of the law in the civil sphere of marriage, inheritance and custody.

New Politics

The texts of Zurayq, al-'Alayili, al-Arsuzi and 'Aflaq allow us to explore the arrival of a number of new developments in the Arab world and to glimpse at the same time the configuration of new social forces. It is in this context that one may speak of the second generation of Arab Nationalists, born in the first or second decade of the twentieth century. If Sati' al-Husri (b. 1879) represents the culmination of the first generation in its quest for a modern Arab nation, Zurayq (b. 1909), al-'Alayili (b. 1914), and al-Arsuzi (b. 1899) articulated concepts and prescribed solutions which would dominate Arab discourse and activities throughout th 1950s and '60s. Indeed, the very terminology used in their texts was appropriated by political parties and leaders, particularly the Ba'th Party and the Movement of Arab Nationalists.

It would thus be appropriate at this stage to underline the novelty and freshness of a nationalist approach that began to assert itself in the 1930s and 1940s. One of its salient features was the selection of a new audience, summarized by the term *shabab* or youth. Another facet consisted of an intellectual and practical attitude that was vehemently contemptuous of traditional politics and politicians. Hence democracy was to be redefined and made conditional on achieving certain reforms, which in turn delayed its application and turned it into a mere slogan. More importantly, in this scheme of things the new discourse was to a large extent inspired by an organic view, a biological paradigm that saw society as a living organism governed by the laws of adaptation, growth and even mutation.

6

Socialism and Pan-Arabism

Between 1945 and 1962 most Arabs gained their independence and were grouped under the umbrella of the League of Arab States. More of a coordinating agency than a federation or confederation, the League was deemed by most Arab nationalists to be a weak and inefficient organisation incapable of meeting the political, social and economic challenges of the post-war era. This diagnosis received further confirmation in the disastrous outcome of the decision of its seven founder members to confront the nascent Israeli state. However, this official pan-Arabism is still the dominant pattern of inter-Arab relations both in its political mode of operation and its entrenchment as an affirmation of the sovereignty and territorial integrity of member states.

Although there were, between 1950 and 1978, numerous official and non-official projects and attempts to unite two or more Arab states with each other, no concrete or lasting results have ever been achieved. The only exception that proved the rule came a decade later when South and North Yemen did succeed in achieving unification in 1989. Hence, this was to a large extent a confirmation of limited territorial patriotism which has so far resisted pan-Arab pressures to extend its vision beyond internationally sanctioned and recognised borders. Yemeni unification was in this sense a success story which has stood the test of time, particularly in 1994 when southern dissidents tried to secede and were crushed by the national Yemeni army.

The World of Social Arab Nationalism.

The most spectacular achievement of Arab nationalism was the brief union between Syria and Egypt (1958–61) under the leadership of Jamal 'Abd al-Nasir (Nasser). In 1963, there occurred another attempt to unify Syria, Egypt and Iraq. Political differences and the legacy of the previous Syro-Egyptian merger turned it into a stillborn endeavour. After the death of Nasser in 1970, and perhaps as a result of the leadership vacuum he left behind, Syria, Egypt, the Sudan and Libya announced in 1970 and 1971 their intention to form a federation. Although the Sudan, under its military leader Ja'far Numairy, who came to power in 1969, withdrew, a constitution of the Federation was approved by referenda in the other three countries in September 1971. Moreover, the federation was officially proclaimed on 1 January 1972 and much was made of it by its architects, but no practical results followed and no concrete institutional instruments were ever set up. A similar experiment was attempted by Syria and Iraq in October 1978, when Egypt under its new president, Anwar Sadat, embarked on a bilateral policy of reaching a separate peace deal with Israel which culminated in the Camp David Agreement in September of the same year. Perhaps in response to the Israeli-Egyptian peace deal, a 'national charter for joint action' was hammered out envisaging political and economic union between Syria and Iraq. However, by July 1979 Iraq withdrew when it announced the discovery of 'a conspiracy' designed to jeopardize the political character of the Union.

However, the fact that after 1945 several Arab countries began to engage in projects for Arab unity, albeit in varying degrees of genuine commitment, indicates the existence of an underlying popular current that was becoming hard to ignore, as well as an official recognition of the numerous ties that cut across the boundaries of Arab countries from Morocco to Iraq. Furthermore, the drive for Arab unity, or at least the mere appearance of being engaged in an attempt to bring about the unification of a number of adjacent states, seemed to confer political legitimacy on regimes which lacked secure foundations or were in the grip of social and economic crises. Thus, in response to the formal proclamation, on 1 February 1958, of the merger of Egypt and Syria into the United Arab Republic, the monarchical regimes of Jordan and Iraq came up with their own scheme of Arab unification. On 14 February 1958, barely two weeks after the founding of the United Arab Republic, the two Kingdoms of Jordan and Iraq were hastily brought together to form the Arab Federation. Furthermore,

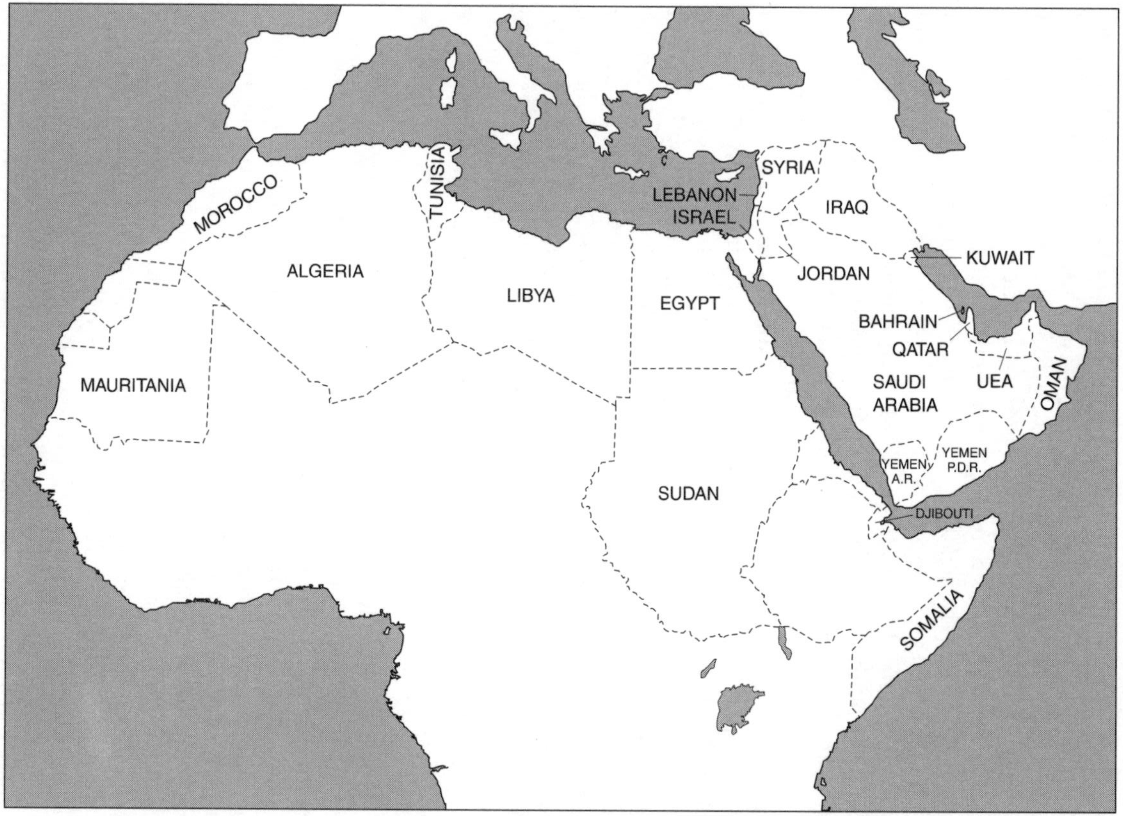

Map 6.1 The Arab World in 1985

earnest negotiations were conducted with Saudi Arabia to join the Union, but failed to reach a positive conclusion. This federation turned out to be an abortive affair and was formally dissolved when army officers in Iraq took over power on 14 July 1958, and abolished the monarchy.

Another gesture towards Arab unity, and which was largely perceived as a political response to the drive for Arab unity, took place in the Moroccan city of Tangier towards the end of April 1958. There representatives of the ruling parties of the newly-independent Tunisia and Morocco, the Neo-Destour and the Istiqlal respectively, in addition to a delegation from the Algerian National Front (FLN), which four months later formed the Provisional Government of the Algerian Republic,[1] called for a federated state to include the whole of Arab North Africa. Although the Tangier Conference was convened in the midst of an intensifying struggle against the French in North Africa, it situated this struggle within a wider political framework which was said to 'emanate from the unanimous will of the peoples of the Arab Maghrib to unite their destinies'. Its resolution thus proposed to set up 'common institutions' in the form of a federal structure, with particular emphasis on the need to establish an 'Arab Maghrib Consultative Assembly'.[2] However, no practical consequences, apart from assisting Algeria to gain its independence, were achieved. More importantly, on 17 February 1978, North African Heads of State (Libya, Tunisia, Algeria, Morocco and Mauritania) signed an agreement in Marrakesh to form 'the Union of the Arab Maghreb'. King Hasan of Morocco was appointed its first President. The new Union was mainly concerned with facilitating economic cooperation and establishing joint ventures. However, divisions between Algeria and Morocco over the Western Sahara, which was divided between Morocco and Mauritania after the withdrawal of Spanish troops in 1976, but opposed by Algeria,[3] in addition to other regional tensions, have so far prevented the Union from carrying out the terms of the agreement.

That said, the mere fact that such projects for unifying five Arab states were still being discussed signified the continuing relevance of pan-Arabism as a force to be reckoned with. The preamble of the Agreement defined 'the solid bonds' of the people of the Maghreb as being based on their common 'history, religion and language'. It went on to relate the foundation of their union to the wider effort of 'establishing complete Arab unity'. One of its provisions stressed the need to preserve 'the spiritual and moral values which are derived from the tolerant teachings of Islam' and to safeguard 'the Arab national identity' of its constituent members.[4]

These repeated reaffirmations and continual endeavours since 1945 do indicate the persistence of pan-Arabism and its adoption as something more than a rhetorical device. This is all the more so, when we examine the texts of the various constitutions of the Arab states. Both monarchical and republican states, such as Bahrain, Jordan, the United Arab Emirates, Kuwait and Qatar in addition to Algeria, Yemen, Libya, Egypt, Syria and Iraq, declare their respective countries to be 'an integral part of the Arab nation' or 'the Arab homeland'.[5]

If one turns to political parties in the Arab world, and leaves out those which adopt radical Arab nationalism as an essential doctrine, one finds traditional parties of a decidedly conservative nature, adopting goals ranging from 'Arab solidarity' to 'complete Arab unity'.[6]

One may well ask, given the above evidence which tends to show that the movement of pan-Arabism is so widespread and so publicly and fervently proclaimed at both the official and unofficial levels, why is the Arab world still divided into more than twenty states and no Arab unity is anywhere in sight? As a matter of fact, one could provide examples to prove the gradual fragmentation of certain Arab countries and a general regression in earnest attempts to stem the tide of creeping divisions in the ranks of all Arab states.

As we have seen, Arab unity culminated at the official level in the foundation of the League of Arab States and which, in effect, strengthened the separate independence of its members. Such an outcome was dictated by a number of factors and considerations. The foremost of which was the recent orientation of Egyptian official policy towards a wider pan-Arabist sphere which it perceived to be of direct benefit to its own national interests. When earnest inter-Arab consultations were finally entered into in 1943 to form what was first proposed as a federation of independent or semi-independent Arab states, there emerged four conflicting proposals representing the views of Iraq, Syria, Saudi Arabia, and Egypt. The Iraqis, under the leadership of Nuri al-Sa'id, were first and foremost working for their Fertile Crescent project, which was submitted to the British government for consideration in 1943. Their decision to widen the scope of pan-Arab consultations by including Egypt was meant to win political support for this particular scheme, thereby making it more difficult for the British to turn it down. However, once Egypt was approached in the shape of its prime minister, Mustafa al-Nahhas, the Iraqi proposal was transformed and its priorities rearranged. Egypt, not satisfied to be a mere mediator, and sensing a timely opportunity to reinforce its emerging role as the natural centre of pan-Arabism, put forward a much wider proposal envisaging cooperation across the entire Arab world. By so doing, it brought in for the first time the possibility of including North African states into the deliberations, despite the fact that they were still under French Colonial rule. Moreover, Egypt's idea of Arab unity did not contemplate complete mergers of separate states, but simply an alliance of existing regimes under its leadership. Although no North African representatives were allowed to attend, owing to French objections backed by British support, which also entailed barring Libya still under Allied occupation, the Egyptian signal towards North Africa shifted the future of pan-Arabism away from its Greater Syria and the Fertile Crescent orbits. Syria, in keeping with its radical Arabism, and led by its recently-installed veteran pan-Arabist president Shukri al-Quwwatly, was opposed to both the Greater Syria and the Fertile Crescent projects, proposed by Transjordan and Iraq respectively, and resurrected the idea of the unity of Arab Asia, but added to it Egypt, which was becoming hard to ignore.

Saudi Arabia was instinctively inclined to oppose all schemes emanating from the Hashemite courts in Amman and Baghdad. Ibn Sa'ud's destruction of Hashemite power in western Arabia in 1926 made him look with suspicion upon all Hashemite schemes for Arab unity. He interpreted such proposals, whether hatched by 'Abdallah or Nuri al-Sa'id, as mere preliminary steps towards regaining and reclaiming dynastic rights in Arabia itself. His policy was, therefore, to insist on the complete independence of each Arab state, while at the same time favouring cooperation as the need might arise – a view which found resonance with the Lebanese delegation and its desire to assert their country's independence in its relation with Syria which still thought of reducing Lebanon to its former Ottoman size. Moreover, Ibn Sa'ud, more than any Arab leader, was always anxious to cultivate the goodwill of both Great Britain and the United States, and refrained from any action that could be interpreted as a hostile move towards his western allies. To that end, he did not harbour dynastic ambitions outside his Kingdom and was prepared, to counter Hashemite claims, to accept and work with republican regimes such as Syria and Lebanon.

The so-called Alexandria protocol, which was finally drafted in October 1944, envisaged the League of Arab States as a political structure capable of steering Arab countries towards unified action in foreign affairs, cultural coordination, and economic development. However, its formal formation in March 1945, following the dismissal of Mustafa al-Nahhas as Prime Minister by King Faruq immediately after the Alexandria protocol, was drafted by a preparatory committee of Arab delegates; it told a different story. The official Pact of the League, as it was finally approved, expressed the lowest common denominator as represented by the Saudi monarch. At this stage both

Egypt and Saudi Arabia emerged as partners who saw to it, for their different reasons, to check Hashemite ambitions in the Fertile Crescent, be they Iraqi or Jordanian. Moreover, King Faruq still entertained the idea of resurrecting the Islamic Caliphate under his auspices or in his person, and failing that, the emerging Arab order was obviously ripe for Egyptian leadership. Since the Saudi monarch at that juncture did not have either the means or the inclination to pursue a pan-Arab policy, but was fiercely opposed to Hashemite schemes nonetheless, this made his friendship an ideal field to cultivate. It thus came as no surprise that the first Secretary General to be appointed to head the League was the Egyptian 'Abd al-Rahman 'Azzam (b. 1893) who enjoyed the goodwill of both Faruq and Ibn Sa'ud. As a veteran pan-Arabist,[7] he also won the support of Syria, which in turn softened Iraqi objections to his appointment.

Thus, at this early stage there were two rival Arab states, Egypt and Iraq, each vying with the other for influence in the Arab world and putting forward conflicting ideas of how best to harness the drive for Arab unity. By and large, Saudi Arabia and Syria tended to side with Egypt, and this remained the case until 1957 when Saudi and Egyptian policies began to diverge, and Syria was on the brink of merging with Egypt. By that time the Egyptian monarchy was no more and Nasser, the President of the Republic, had left behind the pan-Arabism of an entire class of notables, royal families and absentee landlords. In 1958 the Iraqi monarchy was swept away by a group of army officers who once again, albeit under a different configuration of national and international factors, chose to chart an independent course of action. Furthermore, the new Iraqi leader of the revolution, 'Abd al-Karim Qasim, took Iraq out of the Arab sphere altogether, with the exception of his interest in annexing Kuwait to his country.

In 1948, the repercussions of the defeat of seven Arab armies by the burgeoning Israeli state signalled a turning point in the fortunes of the Arab ruling elites. These elites who came together under the umbrella of the Arab League, and in spite of their regional rivalries, shared a number of common traits which coloured their attitudes and served to group them into privileged members of one political club.

All these countries, with the exception of Saudi Arabia and Yemen, had adopted parliamentary democracy as the form of their government. This entailed multi-party politics, and free regular elections, as well as freedom of the press and association. The political parties in question, such as the *Wafd* in Egypt, the People's Party in Syria and the National Democratic party in Iraq, were established and controlled by a handful of politicians who were either absentee landowners, lawyers with extensive commercial interests or notables who had inherited status, power and wealth by learning the art of manipulating urban crowds clustered around particular leaders of city quarters. The fact that Saudi Arabia and Yemen shunned parliamentary democracy and opted for a more traditional and less fragile scheme of things, did not alter the basic ingredients of political practice in a significant way. Their traditional Arabian and Islamic culture was itself based on a vast network of direct access which made members of the royal families political bosses in their own right. Beginning at the local tribal or village level, passing through the different regions of the country and leading up to the very top of the political hierarchy, the system reproduced and reinforced its brand of legitimacy by means of its informal institutions known as *majlis*. *Majlis* in this context meant either a session room or a social gathering whereby the ruler or his direct representatives were supposed to make themselves available to receive their subjects and hear whatever grievances they wished to raise.[8]

In this sense, a common patronage system, with its urban notables, large merchants and absentee landlords, dominated the political life of Arab communities. By manipulating loyalties and perpetrating a particular type of governance, it deflected horizontal stratifications, forcing the emerging middle classes to readjust their modernist allegiances in their daily affairs. Hence family ties, regional identifications, as well as ethnic, tribal and sectarian grievances, were either reconstructed or reactivated. In the search for electoral support, or pledges of renewed loyalties, the family, the neighbourhood and the tribe were expected to solidify their structures rather than suppress them. Jobs, loans, access to education, legal rights, and even marriages, were supposed to become available or be withdrawn according to the rules of patronage. To escape such a world, Arab nationalist parties, few in number but vociferous in proclaiming their message, sought to bypass the patronage system, often by condemning liberal politics as a clear example of corruption or collaboration with western powers.

This type of politics, operating within an economic system that lacked a solid industrial base and dominated by agrarian products, had, in its turn, to respond to international pressure brought to bear on its operators in different forms of diplomatic manoeuvres, military threats and the fluctuating market prices of the advanced western world.

Apart from food processing plants and textile industries, most of the Arab urban economy became increasingly dependent on government policies and state employment, which were seldom forthcoming or sufficiently imaginative. The slow pace of economic development was further aggravated by the influx of rural migrants into urban centres looking for work or seeking better living conditions. By the early 1930s, the population of most Arab cities began to grow at rapid rates, which resulted from a combination of natural growth and rural migrations. Cairo, for example, which had a population of 374,000 in 1882, by 1937 had become home to 1,312,000. It thus replaced Istanbul, the old capital of the Ottoman Empire, as 'the largest city in the Middle East and the focus of the Arab world'.[9] Most migrants lived on the edge of poverty and recreated, to a large extent, village life by settling in quarters which already housed former relatives or neighbours.

In the social field, the old quarters of cities built around a grand mosque, a bazaar and narrow streets, began to give way to a new type of city, moving away from the centre and expanding in new directions. The new districts were modern, based on European models, and had regular streets and more open spaces. They offered better amenities, schools and hospitals. There the new members of the professional middle classes took up residence. University teachers, pharmacists, medical doctors, lawyers and engineers mingled with Europeans and other wealthy residents, and began to plan for a new age of politics. Added to the new districts were the mushrooming shanty towns and districts teeming with occasional, landless and seasonal labourers. As modernization continued its march, it became urban-centred, creating sharp social bifurcations between big cities and small towns and villages.

Occupational divisions, based on access to university and specialization abroad or accumulated wealth, were also rapidly growing into a feature of city life. The role of women became more visible, as girls were increasingly being educated in new schools and made more widespread by the relatively tolerant attitude of the professional middle classes. Women's Associations began to appear and voice demands ranging from social to political issues. Although still deprived of the right to vote, their voices were being increasingly heard as they occupied public positions as teachers, journalists, nurses, and in a few cases, civil servants.

Middling farmers and peasants also entered the social scene as a political force to be reckoned with. Issues of land distribution and better rural conditions claimed the attention of a number of political parties in the 1930s and 1940s, and 'socialism' was being frequently debated as an alternative system to capitalism. Societies representing purely rural interests were, for example, set up in both Syria and Egypt. In Syria, the Youth Party (Hizb al-Shabab), led by the lawyer Akram Hawrani since 1939, devoted most of its activities to the problems of the peasants in the Syrian district of Hama and elsewhere. It advocated a radical programme of land distribution, prevention from eviction and a more representative electoral system. Its members often clashed with landlords and their retainers and resorted to a militant policy of agitation. In 1952, having changed its name to the Arab Socialist Party in 1950, the Youth Party joined forces with the newly-established Arab Ba'th Party. In Egypt, a less militant and effective society, the Social Peasant Party, promoted rural interests and the peasants' social welfare between 1938 and 1945. In 1945, it adopted socialism and began to call for land distribution as part of regenerating national life and ensuring the dignity of the majority of the population. In 1952, the Free Officers, led by Colonel Nasser, implemented the first agrarian reform in the Arab world.

Political independence brought with it the question of national defence and the need for a sizeable army in possession of modern weaponry and trained along western lines. The required manpower, particularly in the lower ranks, was often met by recruiting rural elements or recent arrivals in the city from the countryside. In due course, and after 1948, the political implication of the social background of Arab armies would make themselves apparent in the 1950s and 1960s. Furthermore, the modernization and professionalization of military forces made them an attractive recruiting ground for nationalist and radical parties. Thus, the army came to be perceived as an appealing force: disciplined, operating within a coherent structure, and economically attractive. By 1949, Egypt had a standing army of 70,000, the Iraqi army numbered 45,000 and the Syrian army, the most recent of the three, was rapidly approaching 30,000. Once the army became broadly-based, drawing recruits from all segments of society, it lost its attractiveness to upper-class families, who began to concentrate their efforts on more lucrative and prestigious pursuits such as commercial transactions with foreign companies or investment in the construction sector, property and industrial projects. So it was that by the early 1940s, the army officer, the teacher and the lawyer, representing in their own way the universal principles of order, education and law, allied themselves to the cause of the peasant, claiming to be his true voice and representatives.

In this new era, in countries which did not possess their own armies as a result of direct colonial rule or settlement, political parties were formed to act as instruments of national liberation. This was the case in Algeria whose urban-based civilian political parties had failed to budge French intransigence, leading to the establishment in 1954 of the National Liberation Front and its armed wing, the National Liberation Army. In addition to socialism, the Algerian FLN integrated Arab nationalism into its programme and turned Algeria, after its independence in 1962 into a regional power in its own right.[10]

The war in Palestine ended with the creation of Israel. It was followed in 1949 by armistice agreements between the Jewish state and four Arab countries – Jordan, Lebanon, Syria and Egypt. Moreover, the Palestinians were left with no state of their own, and what was left of Palestine was either annexed by the Kingdom of Jordan (old Jerusalem and the West Bank), or came under the control of Egypt. The defeat of the Arab armies, numbering 21,000, came as no surprise as they confronted a better-equipped and highly motivated Israeli force of 30,000.

The war in Palestine ended with the creation of Israel and the forceful eviction or displacement of over 700,000 Palestinians. Most of these, totalling three-quarters of the population of Arab Palestine, became refugees in neighbouring Arab countries, living in makeshift tents and dreaming of returning to their original homes, towns, cities and fields. By 1952 the number of Palestinian refugees had climbed to 850,000, with the following distribution per country or district: 460,000 in Jordan (including the West Bank), 200,000 in the Gaza Strip, 104,000 in Lebanon, 80,000 in Syria and 4,000 in Iraq and 19,000 inside Israel. Although the Jordanian, Syrian, Lebanese and Egyptian governments had signed armistice agreements with the Jewish state between February and July 1949, a state of war still existed, turning the Arab-Israeli conflict into a major issue of Arab nationalism. Repercussions of the defeat of seven Arab armies and the plight of the Palestinian refugees sent shock waves through the Arab and Islamic world and made intellectual and political debates on the future of the Arab nation more tangible and infused with a message of urgency and the need to initiate immediate action and long-term plans.

After 1950, oil revenues were beginning to exert a growing impact, leading in the next two decades to the emergence of Saudi Arabia and other Gulf states as centres of financial wealth with political muscles to flex in their immediate region and beyond. By 1952 the dependence of Saudi Arabia on British and American subsidies had become a thing of the past, as its oil revenues had risen to $172 million and kept on climbing, reaching $22,573 million in 1974. Moreover, the Arabian oil-producing region began to open its doors to immigrant workers and their families, with the result that in some states, such as Kuwait and Qatar, the native population was reduced to a minority in the overall population.

Moreover, the Arab world was home to a number of minorities who had their own national or ethnic grievances. As more Arab countries gained their independence and embarked on programmes of economic, cultural and political development, these minorities, in particular the Kurds in northern Iraq, southerners in the Sudan, and Berbers in Algeria, began to articulate their own demands, ranging from autonomous rule to the right of using their own local languages. Moreover, Jewish communities had been living in the Arab world for centuries and some of their members had occupied ministerial posts or managed to become successful businessmen, bankers and retailers.[11] The rise of Zionism and the foundation of the state of Israel led to mass migrations or evacuations of entire Jewish communities. In 1950, for example, 40,000 Yemenite Jews were airlifted from the British Protectorate of Aden to Israel. However, upon Algeria's independence in 1962, the majority of its Jewish community, who had been admitted to French citizenship in the nineteenth century, opted to go to France.

The old colonial powers had emerged from World War II weakened and largely dependent on the goodwill of the United States to rebuild their shattered industries. The election of a British Labour government in 1945, with grand ideas of economic development and a new relationship with the Arab world, did not amount to more than theoretical discussions. For better or for worse, both Britain and France were being eased out of the Middle East by the new superpowers: the United States and the Soviet Union.

American interests in the Arab world, apart from missionary schools and colleges in Lebanon and Egypt, were mainly to be seen in the activities of oil companies in Saudi Arabia known as Aramco, or the Arabian-American Oil Co. Moreover, the Israeli-Arab conflict and the decision of Britain in 1947 to withdraw from Palestine and refer its Mandate to the United Nations in New York, left the United States largely in charge of working out a solution to the conflict. This coincided with the decision of the Zionist movement to make the United States its main centre of diplomatic and fund-raising activities as early as 1942. The end of the war and the revelations of Nazi atrocities in eastern and central Europe generated a wave of sympathy for the victims of the Holocaust. In 1947 and 1948 the American administration under President Harry Truman was actively involved in the deliberations of the United Nations on the Palestine question. On 29 November 1947, the United Nations General Assembly voted in favour of partition, paving the way for the creation of the Jewish state. The fact that the partition plan and the subsequent recognition of Israel in May 1948 was supported in the United Nations by both the United States and the Soviet Union did not signal the onset of an era of cooperation between the two superpowers. The cold war, the term attached to US–Soviet rivalry throughout the world in the following decades, entered the Arab arena with full force in the early 1950s. Arab nationalists, initially reluctant to join either camp, and professing a policy of non-alignment, discovered at a later stage a more positive Soviet attitude towards their radical policies of social change. Thus US–Soviet rivalry in the 1950s and 1960s unfolded in the Arab world as a set of political approaches closely associated with programmes of economic development, the balance of military power between Israel and the Arabs, and the issue of self-determination for the Palestinians. Polarization at the global level found its local articulation in the division of the Arab world into progressive and conservative states, Arab nationalist or pro-western regimes. Although these divisions were sometimes surmounted and certain Arab alignments or coalitions were dictated by other factors, such as the confrontation with Israel, this polarization remained an internal feature of Arab politics until the end of the Cold War and the collapse of the Soviet Union.

In this sense, the intensification of the struggle for Palestine, the socio-economic aftermath of World War II, and the onset of the cold war, define the main characteristics of this phase in the fortunes of Arab nationalism.

In this third phase, Arab nationalism acquired wide popular support and managed, with varying degrees of success, in implementing its own radical programme in the economic, social and cultural fields. Although Arab unity, embodied in political and institutional structures, remained an elusive goal, its legitimacy as an imperative drive became more difficult to question or dislodge. As it crossed the threshold of its third phase, the programme of Arab nationalism took on a decidedly socialist dimension, combined with an emphasis on centralizing political authority under one-party rule. In other words, discussions on the validity or viability of multi-party politics and pluralistic systems of government resurfaced throughout the 1950s in one form or another, only to be totally eclipsed by the early 1960s. Thus, democracy in its liberal varieties was either suppressed or considered a legacy of colonial domination and the exclusive monopoly of a class of semi-feudal lords and comprador capitalists.

The 'golden age' of Arab nationalism is generally associated with this social phase. Some scholars see it as a climax that had reached its ultimate intensity and was bound to find expression in a milder mood,[12] while others interpret its consequent phase as the end of Arabism in all its implications.[13] As with all such appellations conferred on movements and personalities after their disappearance, myths and realities intermingle, rendering a specific historical context an abstract notion of questionable validity. Nevertheless, by the early 1970s new political and social forces in the Arab world were heralding the end of one period and the beginning of a novel constellation of ideological doctrines and economic trends. As long as these forces continue to surge forward, their final destination appears to be somewhat reluctant to reveal the contours of its exact location. It would thus be immature at this stage to give a definite answer as to what the future might bring.

Be that as it may, pan-Arabism in its 'golden age' asserted itself as a triumphant movement, eclipsing all other ideologies, such as Communism and Islamism, throughout the Arab world. This was particularly the case between 1956 and 1970, when Nasser, the Egyptian President, dominated the Arab world in his policies, initiatives, activities and speeches. In addition to Nasserism, pan-Arabism was in this phase represented by two main organizations: the Arab Socialist Ba'th Party and the Movement of Arab Nationalists. All three had their origins in the 1940s as a new generation of Arab activists considered both the army or a tightly-knit ideological party the ideal instruments of revolutionary change.

Nasserism

Although the political label of Nasserism was not initially attached to the movement of the Egyptian Free Officers who came to power in 1952, the fact that Nasser initiated, organized and led what became known as the revolution made the designation inevitable. Moreover, it was, as its founder repeatedly stressed, a pragmatic ideology responding to political and economic developments as they unfolded; the ideology adjusted itself accordingly. Consequently, its early emergence as a cluster of army officers organized in separate cells, and each linked to an executive committee, headed by Nasser, was primarily an Egyptian affair with no particular pan-Arabist dimension. Egypt in the second half of the 1940s was still ruled by King Faruq who in contrast to his early popularity was now seen as incompetent and surrounded by a corrupt entourage. His humiliation in February 1942 by the British Ambassador, Miles Lampson, was still fresh in the memory of many Egyptians. The British, having reoccupied Iraq in May 1941 to crush what they considered a pro-Axis nationalist government in Baghdad, wished to forestall a similar development in Egypt. Suspecting the Egyptian king of such sympathies at a time when the German General, Erwin Rommel, was threatening to advance towards Alexandria from the Western desert, the British ambassador decided to act. At that time, Cairo was the Allies' headquarters of the Middle East

Supply Centre and the capital of the most advanced Arab country. Lampson surrounded Faruq's palace with tanks and troops and presented the king with a clear ultimatum which gave him the choice of abdication or the formation of a government sympathetic to the Allies' cause. As Faruq chose the second option, he was forced to appoint the leader of the popular Wafd Party as his new Prime Minister. The King's capitulation, the circumstances surrounding the appointment of al-Nahhas to the premiership, and the direct intervention of a British ambassador in the internal affairs of an independent country, tarnished the image of the entire Egyptian political system. Moreover, ever since its semi-independence in 1922, and despite the 1936 Treaty which granted it formal independence, Egypt's political life was dictated by the struggle between the king, the Wafd and the British.

Nasser at the time had already graduated from the Military Academy and had been promoted to lieutenant after his service with other Egyptian officers in the Sudan. It was in this period that the future leaders of Egypt and close friends and associates in the Officer Corps began to plot their rise to power. With the exception of a few officers, they all had a lower-middle-class background or a foothold in the countryside. In his student days, Nasser had toyed with the idea of joining a number of radical political organizations, such as Young Egypt, the Muslim Brotherhood, or the Wafdist Youth Organization, but never did. Nevertheless, his schooldays in Alexandria and later in Cairo were punctuated by active involvement in student demonstrations and the occasional brief jail internment. By 1935, most Egyptian political parties had formed paramilitary youth organzations, which had their parallels in Syria and Iraq but were too weak to effect radical change. His acceptance into the Military Academy was facilitated by the decision of the Wafdist government to recruit young officers from outside the restricted circle of landowning families. It was in the Military Academy, shortly before the outbreak of World War II, that he established close ties with a number of young officers who were to abolish the monarchy and turn Egypt into a republic.

However, apart from a desire to free Egypt from British influence and remove the King, the Young Officers had not yet developed a clear political programme. Their involvement in the Palestine war was to make them more aware of the need of political change as a set of interrelated reforms. It also widened their outlook in relating the security and defence of Egypt to its strategic links with other regions of the Arab world. This view was widely shared by most Egyptian pan-Arabists who hitched their political preference to a practical calculation rather than an ideological commitment. As we have seen, this brand of Arabism began to develop in Egypt in the mid-1920s and 1930s, and had by 1945 entrenched itself in official circles as an additional, but not dominant, strand. In this sense, unlike Syria or Iraq which gave birth to political parties advocating a clear ideology of pan-Arabism.[14] Egyptian nationalist allegiances developed at a different pace and under strong provincial interests. Hence, the Egyptian educated elite seldom discussed Arabism in theoretically precise terms, in the manner of al-Husri or 'Aflaq, for example. Their political espousal was often couched in utilitarian and pragmatic arguments, based on strategic considerations, economic benefits and the desirability of union in a world dominated by supranational blocs.

Thus, when the Free Officers finally seized power on 23 July 1952, their decisions and measures were largely dictated by the requirements of their immediate situation. The Executive Committee which prosecuted the coup renamed itself the Revolutionary Command Council, and placed at its head a non-free officer, General Muhammad Najib. Born in 1901, Najib was a senior army officer who had been selected in January 1952 as a figure head whose seniority and amiability were an asset for an unknown group of junior officers. But as he did not belong to the Free Officers' inner circle, his ultimate alienation and resignation on 14 November 1954, were to be expected. In the interval, Nasser held the reins of power while acting as deputy Prime Minister and then Prime Minister. The Monarchy was not abolished until 18 June 1953 and Nasser in his intricate manoeuvres to edge Najib out of the way did not officially assume the Presidency of the new Republic until June 1956, shortly before the nationalization of the Suez Canal. In the meantime all political parties, including the Muslim Brotherhood which had initially endorsed the revolution, then turned against it for its radical social programme, had been dissolved and their assets confiscated. At the end of what was termed 'the transition period', which ended in June 1956, martial law was terminated and the Revolutionary Command Council was replaced by a civilian government.

The 1956 Constitution declared 'the Egyptian people' to be part of 'the Arab nation' and Egypt 'an Arab state'. The 1971 Constitution, approved by referendum almost one year after Nasser's death, reaffirmed the same principle.

All these steps were preceded by one of the most momentous measures of the revolution. Within two months of coming to power the government, on 9 September 1952, promulgated its agrarian reform law. It limited landownership to 300 acres per family leaving the door open for expropriating and redistrirbuting all excess holdings. 120,000 sharecroppers and landless families received their allotted share out of approximately 500,000 acres reclaimed by the government for distribution. The measure only affected a fraction (0.5 per cent of all proprietors), but who owned 34.2 per cent of cultivable land. Nor did it solve the problem of landlessness which kept increasing despite further reductions in the maximum entitlement to ownership in 1961 and 1965. More importantly, the land reform swept away the political power of an entire class of landlords who had dominated the countryside and the electoral process long before independence. It would perhaps be useful to add that land reform was not part of a socialist programme or an expression of ideological commitment to socialism. Following the defeat of Japan in World War II and its occupation by American forces, it was General MacArthur[15] who implemented a large-scale redistribution of land owned by absentee landlords.

It was only in January 1953 that the Revolutionary Command Council came up with a set of 'six Principles' which were said to form the broad guidelines of its political programme. These were: (1) the liquidation of imperialism; (2) the abolition of feudalism; (3) an end of monopolies and of the domination of capital over government; (4) the building of a strong army; (5) the achievement of social justice; and (6) the establishment of a healthy democratic life.

Thus, within a few months of announcing the land reform law, promulgated in the early days of the revolution to abolish 'feudalism', and break the political hold of the absentee landlords over the countryside, Nasser turned his attention to settle Egypt's relations with Britain. This involved the settlement of the status of the Sudan and the British military base in the Suez Canal zone.

Unlike the politicians of the old regime, who insisted on linking the two issues of the Sudan and the Suez base, Nasser preferred to tackle them separately. For in the past, the monarchy and the various political parties advocated the unity of the Nile Valley as a single Kingdom under the Egyptian crown. In January 1953, the RCC and the leaders of the Sudanese political parties agreed on the principle of granting the Sudan the right of self-determination. Then, both Egypt and Britain agreed to implement the same principle in deciding the future of the Sudan. This meant that the Sudanese people after the withdrawal of Britain from their country could either opt for complete independence or decide to join Egypt to form the Nile Valley Union. In the event, the Sudanese chose independence which was formally inaugurated on 1 January 1956. The evacuation of 80,000 British troops from the Canal Zone turned out to be less easy to achieve, owing to Britain's insistence on maintaining its defence links with Egypt. Consequently, negotiations with Britain were punctuated by guerrilla raids against British installations and soldiers. While Nasser was willing to consider the prospect of Anglo-Egyptian cooperation in the years to come, he stuck to his demand of complete evacuation. At the time Britain's Prime Minister was its wartime hero, Winston Churchill, who still harboured ambitions of imperial dimensions. To that end, he sought to enlist the support of the American President, Dwight Eisenhower. However, the American administration did not show much enthusiasm for a British military presence in Egypt, which had become untenable. Negotiations dragged on until July 1954, when an agreement was finally reached. British forces stationed in the Canal Zone were to complete their withdrawal over the next twenty months, while Egypt took control of their installations. British civilian technicians would be recruited to ensure their maintenance. The agreement was to remain in force for seven years during which Egypt committed itself to allowing Britain 'to reactivate' the base in defence of Egypt or Turkey against an attack by an aggressor. Israeli aggression, however, was considered to fall outside the reactivation clause of the agreement. The 1888 Constantinople Convention which guaranteed freedom of navigation through the Suez Canal was upheld and reaffirmed by Egypt. Although the Agreement generated much criticism from some political quarters, with the Muslim Brotherhood taking the lead, Nasser stuck to his guns and moved on to the next stage of his political programme. This turned out to be one of his most intractable problems, leading in the end to far-reaching consequences in Egypt's regional and international alignments.

Nasser's effort to 'build a strong army' coincided with the intensification of the cold war and western attempts aimed at containing Communism. The Iraqi Prime Minister, Nuri al-Sa'id, was particularly responsive to such western overtures and arranged a meeting with Nasser on 15 September 1954 to convince him of their feasibility and benefit to the protection of the Arab world. Nasser responded to the Iraqi proposal by putting forward an alternative policy based on the Treaty of Joint Defence and Economic Co-operation signed by the member states of the Arab League on 13 April 1950. In other words, Egypt wished to join other Arab countries in a collective security pact capable of strengthening the pursuit of an independent foreign policy. Nevertheless, Iraq went ahead with its plans and linked itself to a new defence treaty known as the Baghdad Pact. Signed in 1955, it eventually brought together Iran, Pakistan, Turkey and Iraq, under the leadership of Britain and with the tacit support of the United States.

Nasser's refusal to join the Baghdad Pact and his diplomatic and propaganda campaign against its implications in the Arab world at large, was deeply resented by both Britain and the United States.[16]

Moreover, sporadic fighting flared up along the Israeli–Egyptian border further north, as Egypt was now in control of the Palestinian Gaza Strip. One incident occurred in February 1955, during which an Israeli force attacked an Egyptian army camp in the Strip, killing thirty-eight soldiers and civilians. Nasser's determination to rebuild the Egyptian armed forces and equip them with modern weapons became as a result all the more urgent. At that time, France was the main supplier of arms to Israel, including tanks, fighter aircraft, radar systems and guns. His approaches to the British and the Americans to purchase arms having repeatedly been rebuffed, he therefore turned elsewhere. During his attendance of the Bandung conference in April 1955,[17] he met the Chinese Prime Minister, Chou En-lai, who lent a sympathetic ear to Nasser's grievances against the western powers and promised to convince Moscow of Egypt's need for modern weaponry. Thus was born the 'Czech Arms Deal' which was signed between the Soviet Union and Egypt in September, 1955.

The Arms Deal, negotiated with Moscow but delivered through Prague, hence its name, drove another wedge between the Free Officers and the West. Its implications, the onset of the Algerian armed struggle for independence in 1954, and Nasser's open support of its just cause, strengthened France's cordial relations with Israel and resulted in a widening rift between Cairo and Paris. A similar rift was soon to develop between Egypt, on the one hand, and Britain and the US on the other.

Since 1953 the Free Officers had been trying to arrange a loan with the World Bank to help towards the cost of building a huge dam in Upper Egypt to harness the Nile waters and bring more land under cultivation. What became known as the High Dam was initially welcomed as a sound economic project by both Britain and the United States, which offered, towards the end of 1955, to support Egypt's request for a $200 million loan from the World Bank. The building of the dam was supposed to take ten years and cost no less than $1,300 million. In the meantime, the Soviet Union had made known its willingness to offer Egypt financial and technical aid for the High Dam. Thus, western delivery of the grants and loans were made conditional on Egypt's refusal to accept Soviet aid for the same project. Moreover, the World Bank, in conformity with its own rules and standard procedure, wished to see stringent fiscal policies designed to curb inflation and reduce public expenditure. As negotiations proceeded, Jordan was being persuaded by the British to become the second Arab member to join the Baghdad Pact. Such a step contravened earlier assurances given by the British to abstain from applying pressure on Arab countries in that direction. Nasser counteracted by unleashing a propaganda campaign designed to intimidate Jordan's King Husayn and undermine the validity of the Pact. Strikes and demonstrations erupted in the Jordanian capital, leading to the downfall of the government, and in March 1956 King Husayn dismissed General Glubb, the British commander of the Arab Legion (Jordanian army). Anthony Eden, who had then become Britain's Prime Minister, blamed Nasser for the Jordanian decision, so much so that all British interests in the Middle East were considered under threat and had to be protected from the rising menace of Arab nationalism. To make things worse, Nasser extended diplomatic recognition to Communist China two months after Glubb's dismissal, a move which served to alienate the American administration, considering its refusal to recognize other than Formoza (later Taiwan) under Chian Kai-Shek. On 17 July 1956, the United States announced the withdrawal of its own offer to build the High Dam, pleading Egypt's inability to cope with building such a huge project. Britain followed suit with a similar declaration.

On 26 July, the fifth anniversary of the revolution, Nasser announced towards the end of a long speech, the nationalization of the Suez Canal Company. The Company, largely under Anglo-French dual control, had a concession which was due to expire in 1968. Since its construction and formal opening in 1869, the Canal had acquired an important strategic and economic importance for the maritime nations of Europe. In 1875, the Egyptian Khedive, Isma'il, decided to ease the burden of his accumulating debts by selling his shares in the company (176,602 out of a total of 400,000 shares). The British Prime Minister, Disraeli, bought them for £4 million with a loan from the House of Rothschild. In 1910 the Company, under its British and French directors, proposed the extension of the concession beyond the original 99 years. Egyptian political leaders and public opinion defeated the proposal. Nasser had already decided in the early years of the revolution not to extend the concession after its expiry, thereby regaining Egyptian control of the Company. Although he was interested in increasing Egypt's share of its gross profits, he ruled out the idea of nationalization and preferred to press ahead with getting a bigger slice of its revenues. The Anglo-American abrupt decision to withdraw their High Dam offer forced him to reconsider his position.

In his above-mentioned speech Nasser dwelt at length on Arab grievances against Israel and the West. He justified his prompt action by linking the use of the Canal's annual revenue to the construction of the High Dam.[18] He went on to argue the case for economic independence as a prerequisite of political independence. More significantly, in the course of his speech he welcomed the recent decision by the Syrian parliament to unify Egypt and Syria in one single state.[19]

Britain and France did not question the legality or validity of the Egyptian decision to nationalize the Suez Canal Company. Nor could they accuse Nasser of confiscating an international asset.[20] Instead, their argument concentrated on the inability of the Egyptian government to operate the Canal on its own, or sufficiently trustworthy to ensure the efficient functioning of such a vital and international waterway. Amid the flurry of diplomatic meetings and conferences held to force Egypt to rescind its decision and accept an 'International Authority' to operate the Canal, Britain, France and Israel began a series of secret meetings to prepare a military operation against Egypt. The United States, on the other hand, while not willing to aid Egypt economically, was genuinely opposed to a military solution.

In order to dispel suspicions of collusion between the Anglo-French alliance and Israel, an elaborate but deeply flawed scheme of military operations was agreed on 25 October 1956. Israel was to take the initiative by launching an attack on 29 October across the Sinai Peninsula, with the ultimate aim of reaching the Suez Canal. Following the Israeli attack, Britain and France were to deliver an ultimatum to both Egypt and Israel to agree to a ceasefire and withdraw their forces to a distance of ten miles either side of the Canal. By thus assuming the role of peacekeepers, British and French troops were to begin to occupy the Suez Canal zone in order to enforce the ceasefire. When Israel had signalled its willingness to accept these terms, and Egypt, as was expected, had defied them, the Anglo-French invasion would be put into effect. The invasion was to be preceded by an intensive air campaign by British bombers in order to destroy or disrupt Egypt's air force, vital communications and military installations. Having assured themselves of air supremacy, a combined Anglo-French force would be in a position to land at the Canal zone. According to the account of a British minister, who later resigned in protest, another attack was planned to occupy Cairo in the hope of ensuring the downfall of Nasser.[21]

The first stage of the agreed military operation went ahead as planned and an Anglo-French ultimatum was duly delivered. Most of the Egyptian air force was destroyed and Nasser reacted by preparing for a long-drawn guerrilla war and ordering the closure of the Canal by the sinking of blockships. Protests, riots and demonstrations erupted all over the Arab world. Arab countries broke off diplomatic relations with either France or Britain. More importantly, both the leaders of the United States and the Soviet Union were infuriated and ordered a complete cessation of hostilities and the withdrawal of

Israeli troops. Nevertheless, Port Said, in the vicinity of the Canal, was occupied by an Anglo-French force on 6 November. The Soviet Union threatened 'the aggressors' with a nuclear rocket attack and offered to send volunteers to repulse the invasion of old colonial powers. Thus, immediately after the fall of Port Said, the British government decided to abide by the UN ceasefire resolution. By the end of December, the Anglo-British troops had departed, while the Israeli withdrawal from Sinai and the Gaza Strip was not completed until 6 March 1957. The Suez Canal was reopened on March 29 under the full control and management of the Egyptian government. The temporary coincidence of US–Soviet attitudes towards 'the tripartite aggression', as it was dubbed in the Arab world, was soon replaced by the rhetoric and political imperatives of the cold war. French colonialism reached its lowest ebb and was soon to sink further, while the British retreat from empire was accelerated.

Nasser, on the other hand, had emerged as the undisputed leader of the Arab world. His status within Egypt soared above all his colleagues, particularly as some of them had shown signs of panic and disarray during the invasion. Henceforth, Nasser's leadership of the movement of Arab nationalism was to turn his Egyptian base into 'the nucleus state' that was expected to bring about unity, social progress and represent the hopes of 'the nation' as a whole. Consequently, Nasser, the leader of 'the Arab revolution', was detached from his immediate political system so much so that his personal prestige and stature entered the Arab arena with such popular acclaim that dwarfed other local or provincial allegiances. In this sense, conservative Arab regimes interpreted the impact of his charismatic leadership as a direct challenge to their legitimacy and survival. By bypassing normal channels of communication and diplomacy, this direct and ever growing bond, with what became known as 'the Arab masses', evolved into a highly personal admiration charged with emotional overtones. It was also fraught with all the dangers built into such an equation of popular appeal.

As Nasser turned his attention once again to rebuilding the Egyptian economy, he introduced a number of measures designed to 'Egyptianize' banks and insurance companies, on the one hand, and promote industrial production, on the other. Various decrees were issued to raise the standard of living and create a number of agencies charged with implementing a plan of economic development. These measures and steps, covering the period between 1957 and 1960, conformed to Nasser's principle of operating a 'controlled capitalistic economy' or what was later considered to be 'guided capitalism'.[22] New land reform cooperatives were established in the rural areas with a view to coordinating and improving methods of cultivation among farmers. It was hoped that by extending cheap credit facilities, educational and health amenities, productivity would be raised, and the tide of migration into urban centres curbed.

Political Orientations

The Egyptian political elite which consolidated its grip on power in the course of the revolution constituted to a large extent a bureaucratic layer with no particular ideological cohesion. On the contrary, various shades of political views and orientations were allowed to emerge and compete with each other. However, the various networks of political activity, operating under the towering figure of Nasser, were enmeshed in a world of their own. Hence, there slowly developed a perception, both in Egypt and the Arab world, that the leader and the political system over which he presided, were two separate entities: one charismatic and self-sacrificing, and the other cumbersome and liable to corruption. This dichotomy which was to manifest itself at moments of national crises, such as the 1967 military defeat at the hands of the Israeli armed forces, continued to shelter Nasser against adversities and setbacks.

The three mass organizations established by Nasser between 1954 and 1962 (the Liberation Rally 1954–57, the National Union 1957–61 and the Arab Socialist Union 1962–77),[23] were not meant to act as political parties in the ordinary sense of the term. They were rather broad coalitions intended to mobilize society at large and channel social, economic and political demands. Moreover, each organization represented a particular moment in the development of Nasserism as it moved from its early phase of Egyptian national liberation to Arab unity and finally Arab socialism. Thus, in the aftermath of the Suez crisis and the introduction of his Egyptianization economic policy the Liberation Rally was dissolved, to be replaced by the National Union. The new organization was to be composed of 'all the citizens' in order to work for 'the economic, political and social construction of the country'.[24] After 1956, Nasser repeatedly stressed the linkage between the 'political' and 'social' revolutions, and the building of 'a co-operative, democratic and socialist society'.[25] With the exception of 'a small minority', all classes were supposed to work together for the common good. In conjunction with the foundation of the National Union, an elected National Assembly[26] came into being as stipulated by the 1956 Constitution. It consisted of 350 representatives who included, for the first time in Egypt's modern history, two women. Moreover, the Assembly was a mirror image of the new political elite, predominantly middle-class professional men upholding a wide spectrum of political views. It was the same National Union which became the sole political organization in the United Arab Republic of Syria and Egypt between February 1958 and September 1961. The Arab Socialist Union, formed after the secession of Syria, was conceived as a 'mass organization' with a hierarchical structure. It was meant to be based on elected committees representing local districts as well as places of work. Moreover, it specified more clearly its social character by defining itself as the alliance of 'The People's Working Forces'. This coalition consisted of peasants, workers, the intelligentsia and national capitalists. Thus, former 'feudal lords', reactionaries and 'exploiting capitalists' were to be excluded from its ranks. Furthermore, it was also to reflect in its elected organs a definite shift towards the majority of the citizens by ensuring that peasants and workers enjoyed a 50 per cent representation at all levels. Within a few years of its establishment, the ASU membership rose to over five million members. The new National Assembly, elected in 1964, operated on the same principle of allocating half of its 350 seats to peasants and farmers. Following the national elections, a provisional constitution was approved which defined the Egyptian state, which had retained its former name under the union with Syria,[27] as a 'democratic socialist state'. The revolution was now endowed with a definite socialist identity and all organs and agencies of the state were to operate accordingly. Moreover, a political organization of revolutionary cadres was to be set up within the ASU to coordinate its activities and ensure its adherence to the new socialist principles of the revolution.[28] By 1963, the foundation of such an organization, to be known as the Socialists' Vanguard, was being considered on the basis of recruiting and creating 'active political cadres' who were supposed to operate as a secret group charged with an ideological mission. Its executive committee included a number of Marxists who were afforded the opportunity to engage their intellectual talents in the new task of transforming Egypt into a socialist society. However, the Secretary-General of the Vanguard was a government cabinet minister, Sha'rawi Jum'a, and who later occupied the same post in the wider ASU.

By the mid-1960s, a number of political trends had crystallized around prominent personalities in the government or the ASU. Broadly speaking, Zakariyya Muhyyi al-Din (b. 1918), one of the original Free Officers, represented a right-wing faction which often leaned towards 'conservative' policies and was actively engaged in improving relations with the United States of America. Consequently, whenever Nasser promoted or appointed Muhyyi al-Din to a crucial post in the government, this was taken to signify an attempt to patch up differences with the West. This was, for example, the case in 1965 when Muhyyi al-Din was elevated to the position of prime minister. However, his premiership lasted less than a year,[29] and he is better remembered as Minister of Interior (1953–62), and the person Nasser named to take over the presidency in the wake of the Six-Day War in 1967. In 1968, this trend was temporarily eclipsed with the resignation of its foremost representative. However, it seems that by that time, Anwar al-Sadat, another Free Officer and Nasser's successor, was silently preparing himself to become the new mentor of the conservative trend.

The 'leftist' trend was largely identified with the second-level Free Officer, 'Ali Sabri (b. 1920), particularly during his chairmanship of the ASU between 1965 and 1969. He was entrusted by Nasser with various missions to the Soviet Union and China, acting as a reliable representative of the new socialist policies. He was known for his emphatic support of the public sector and the benefits of nationalization. Sabri was essentially a talented technocrat who was adept at manipulating the administrative machinery to push through his strong belief in state-controlled planning and economic development. However, by 1969 his star had been eclipsed owing to unspecified allegations of corruption, but he remained Nasser's principal link with the Soviet Union and their trusted liaison officer. Moreover, this official leftist trend was mistrusted by Marxist and ex-communist intellectuals and civil servants who advocated a more radical programme of socialist transformation.

The fortunes of the above-mentioned trends were largely dependent on the goodwill of Nasser and his political alignments or domestic policies. In this sense, the third trend represented a more formidable 'centre of power', as these political factions were labelled. Curiously, what may be called the 'centrist' trend was represented by Nasser's most trusted and intimate colleague, Field-Marshal 'Abd al-Hakim 'Amir (1919–67). 'Amir concentrated his efforts on building a network of followers and supporters within the armed forces. This became his only base, which he cultivated with his constant attention to the social and family needs of the officer corps. He thus jealously guarded its inner world and was resentful of those who tried to intrude into its mode of operation. No less so than when Nasser himself sought to reorganize the armed forces in the new socialist stage. This he intended to do by replacing 'Amir as Commander-in-Chief with a professional soldier with no political office. 'Amir dug his heels in and refused to budge. Although he was finally persuaded to be appointed

Vice-President with special responsibility for military affairs, and a deputy Supreme Commander, he continued to act as the effective Commander-in-Chief. In 1967, Egypt suffered its worst military defeat and claimed 'Amir as its first victim. In 1968, he committed suicide. It was his sudden disappearance which made it easier for Nasser to rebuild his armed forces on a more professional basis. This was clearly demonstrated in 1973 when the Egyptians crossed the Suez Canal and destroyed the Israeli defence line on the east bank.

Theory and Practice

The term 1961 marked the advent of a new revolution in Egypt and the Arab nationalist movement at large. It denoted the arrival of social revolution and expressed a wider shift which began to gather momentum by the late 1950s. Socialism, in various guises and modes of application had become by that time an alternative system of economic development and political organization in the newly-emerging non-aligned Third World countries. In the Arab world, both the Soviet Union and the United States had entered the political arena with their own ideological recipes and aid programmes.

In 1957, Dwight Eisenhower, the American President, came up with the idea of an updated version of the Baghdad Pact. Formally approved by the US Congress, the Eisenhower Doctrine, as it became known, was based on the premise of the Soviet Union's 'desire to dominate the Middle East'. This desire, as he explained in his address to a joint session of the Senate and the House of Representatives, on 5 January 1957, was not the result of economic need or lack of oil resources, but part of a drive to communize the world. However, the Suez Canal and Middle Eastern oil were of vital importance to the 'prosperous economies' of the nations of Europe and Asia. In order to deter the aggression of 'international communism' and ensure 'the continued independence' of the free nations of the Middle East, the United States would offer economic and military assistance and employ its armed forces to deal with the possibility of direct or indirect aggression. On 8 February 1957, the US and Saudi Arabian governments, following King Sa'ud's visit to Washington, issued a joint communique indicating their agreement to widen cooperation in the military and economic fields.[30] Although Nasser's popular influence and political pressure served to limit positive Arab responses to the new American plan, the Eisenhower Doctrine increased the pressure on the Arab states to define their positions in the language of American–Soviet rivalry. Within three years, the Arab world became sharply divided into a progressive camp, led by Egypt, and a conservative camp, with Saudi Arabia as its most effectie financial powerhouse. The fact that Eisenhower projected the existence of a 'vacuum' in the Middle East, waiting to be filled by either communism or American plans of development, made Arab nationalists all the more conscious of their neutrality and the need to formulate their own solutions, irrespective of cold war rhetoric. Furthermore, most Arab states, including Saudi Arabia, were more concerned with the growing military might of the Israeli state and its 'secret' nuclear programme. It was under these domestic and international conditions of increasing tensions that the Syro-Egyptian Union was proclaimed on 1 February 1958.

The difficulty of navigating a neutral course was demonstrated by the repercussions of the Iraqi revolution on 14 July 1958. Within a few months of coming to power, its leader Brigadier 'Abd al-Karim Qasim was at loggerheads with Nasser. Although the Iraqi Free Officers, who took over power and abolished the monarchy, were of a similar social background to that of their Egyptian counterparts and were inspired by Nasser's revolutionary ideals, they shunned an open commitment to Arab unity. Unlike Nasser, the Iraqi leader was unable to carry with him all the members of his Revolutionary Command Council. This was particularly the case of his deputy, Colonel 'Abd al-Salam 'Arif, who considered himself to be the real spirit of the revolution. The fact that Iraq had at the time a well-organized communist party was to add further complications, in view of its opposition to Arab unity and nationalist slogans. The communist's focus on a purely Iraqi agenda made them natural allies of the Kurds in northern Iraq who were clamouring for an autonomous province of their own. Furthermore, Iraqi political parties, the National Democrats, the Ba'th and the Independence, in addition to the communists were, directly or indirectly, represented in the new government.

Years of repression and corruption under the old regime had sharpened social divisions in Iraq and served to harden the determination of underground ideological parties. Qasim's initial courtship with the communists in order to counterbalance his deputy's Nasserite sympathies and reliance on Arab nationalist support split the country into two rival camps. Both resorted to demonstrations and acts of violent reprisals. On 30 September 'Arif was relieved of his post and a month later was sent abroad. When he attempted to return to Iraq, Qasim had him arrested, put on trial and sent to prison. He was not to be released until the break-up of the United Arab Republic in 1961. 'Arif's fall from power prompted six ministers of various Arab nationalist persuasions to tender their resignations in February 1959. This was followed by an abortive coup led by the veteran pan-Arabist, Rashid 'Ali al-Kaylani. What became known as the Mosul uprising (8 March 1959), represented the culmination of a power struggle pitting Qasim and his communist supporters against an urban-based constituency led by army officers and pan-Arabists. The leader of the uprising was Colonel 'Abd al-Wahhab al-Shawwaf. What was meant to be a military operation leading to Qasim's downfall degenerated into violent clashes between communists and pan-Arabists. Shawwaf was assassinated and a combination of governmental, Kurdish and communist forces took over the city of Mosul, and unleashed against their opponents a reign of terror which lasted for four days.

It was in this context that Nasser, throughout 1959, repeatedly attacked communists in his speeches and entered into heated debates with the Soviet leader, Khrushchev. Several communist officials were arrested and sent to prison. However, one year later Qasim consolidated his grip on power as 'the sole leader' and began to distance himself from his erstwhile friends. Nasser's anti-communist rhetoric was correspondingly toned down, and the Soviet Union committed itself to shouldering the burden of constructing the High Dam.

In 1961, shortly before the secession of Syria, Nasser inaugurated his socialist revolution by nationalizing all Egyptian banks, heavy industrial plants and public utilities. New measures were implemented to increase workers' participation and their share in the profits of their employers. A lower ceiling on landownership was introduced. However, land was still privately held and so was the urban real estate sector which became a refuge of former landowners to invest their capital in and escape confiscation. Real national income increased by 40 per cent between 1960 and 1965. However, the 1967 war put an end to ambitious plans of economic growth. Shortly before Nasser's death, the construction of the High Dam was completed in July 1970. In this respect, socialism was meant to operate a centrally-controlled system of economic activities. It, moreover, denoted the emergence of a set of political ideas which turned Arab nationalism into an ideology based on a radical programme. In other words, socialism was perceived as the ideological core of nationalism and its true identity. To be an Arab nationalist was immediately linked to a socialist plan of reconstruction and regeneration. This vision, which would cut across political parties, took a grip not only of Nasserism, but of the other pan-Arab organizations, the Ba'th and the Movement of Arab Nationalists (MAN). This ideological vision of a socialist future received theoretical articulation in the National Charter, published in May 1962.

The official approval of the Charter was preceded by wide-ranging discussions in the media and by means of holding a national congress in which Nasser participated.[31]

The Universal and the Specific

In the same way, al-Husri worked out a theory[32] whereby nationalism was depicted as a universal phenomenon, originating in nineteenth-century Europe, then spreading throughout the world, so did *The Charter* in the case of socialism. Thus, whereas nationalism in al-Husri's analysis was an inevitable outcome of substituting people's sovereignty for the divine right of kings, Nasserism identified socialism as the inevitable result of a new revolutionary age of social change.

Hence, *The Charter* alludes to the unity of the Arab nation as a foregone conclusion. It simply rehearses al-Husri's definition of the nation as a unity of 'language, history and hope'. Moreover, it makes the political achievement of this unity the responsibility of 'popular progressive forces' throughout the Arab world. The fact that the Arab world was split into two camps, one 'progressive' and the other 'reactionary', indicated the onset of 'social struggle', and the expression of a new revolutionary stage. It was now the masses (*al-jamahir*), and not Arab governments, who were in the process of bringing about unification under the banner of one single objective. This 'unity of objective' transcends the former phase of 'political revolution' and ushers in that of 'social revolution'. The twin adversaries of the Arab masses, namely 'imperialism and local reactionaries', have to be tackled as one enemy who still delays the advent of social revolution in certain parts of the Arab world (pp. 195–9).[33]

In this sense, the achievement of total Arab unity became conditional on a prior revolutionary process linking political independence and radical social change in each Arab country. Nasserite Egypt was then offered as a living example of both. In order for nationalism to survive as a viable movement in the 'modern scientific age' it had to reinvent itself and become part of a global march of events. Thus, *The Charter* offers a general survey of Egyptian history and the various stages of its struggle against Ottoman oppression, British occupation and despotic rule so as to arrive at definite answers to the problems that still lay ahead. The answers it provides are couched in a determinant set of rules which are said to derive from the lessons of history and the prevalent new circumstances in the world at large. These include:

1. The rise and spectacular strength of national liberation movements in the Third World. Spanning the three continents of Asia,
   Africa and Latin America, 'they have now become an internationally effective force'.
2. The new material and moral presence of the communist countries.
3. Technological and scientific achievements which made it possible
   to create efficient 'methods of production' and sustain unlimited
   economic growth. Moreover, physical and intellectual barriers
   between countries have, as a result, collapsed.
4. International relations are no longer governed by traditional
   methods derived from a bygone age. The foundation of the
   United Nations, together with the emergence of non-aligned
   nations and the gathering strength of public opinion in the world
   at large, have added weight to the impact of 'moral forces'.
   (pp. 32–3)

However, traditional colonialism has been replaced by imperialism
which resorts to different methods of indirect control in order to
undermine the independence of the new nations (p. 33).

Under these circumstances, it was no longer feasible to build a
socialist system by borrowing models developed in the nineteenth
century. Socialism has to adapt its general concepts to the specific
conditions of the second half of the twentieth century. The same was
true of achieving the unification of a nation divided into several states.
Consequently, the methods of Italian and German unification movements have become obsolete. A new approach to unification imposed
itself based on 'the need for a peaceful appeal' as well as the desire to
secure 'the unanimous approval of the whole people' (p. 27).

The objectives of the Arab nation would still be 'freedom, socialism
and unity', with Egypt acting as the 'nucleus' state, but priorities and
methods of struggle have to be clearly indicated in this new endeavour.
Thus, each Arab country has to achieve political independence and at
the same time embark on bringing about a radical transformation of
its social system. All methods of struggle are permissible in order to
create the proper conditions for the next stage. Arab unity, being the
ultimate goal, becomes in this respect restricted to 'a peaceful endeavour' with the aim of generating its unanimous acceptance as 'a
crowning achievement' (pp. 30–1).

In this sense, 'revolution' becomes a necessity that obeys certain
laws of progress and conditions of 'material and social underdevelopment'. This revolution is then both democratic and socialist: it asserts
'the sovereignty of the people' and creates an egalitarian society, based
on equal opportunity, sufficiency and production. Moreover, social

freedom has to precede political freedom: one is a pre-condition of
the other and ultimately linked to the elimination of 'class distinctions'
by peaceful means. In order for 'class struggle' to be resolved,
'reactionary' social groups have to be deprived of their weapons in the
form of wealth monopolies (pp. 77–9).

Moreoever, *The Charter* explains, the history of capitalist development, based on looting the wealth of other people and the exploitation
of their labour, is no longer a viable model to be copied. Furthermore,
the advent of imperialism, as a form of indirect domination, serves no
other purpose but to perpetuate the underdevelopment of newly
independent states. Hence:

> The socialist solution was a historical inevitability imposed by reality,
> the broad aspirations of the masses and the changing nature of the
> world in the second part of the 20th century. (p. 109)

These broad principles formed the basis of a new trend which
turned Arab nationalism into a socialist movement. This socialism was
considered to be scientific, modern and inevitable. However, its
Nasserite version was taken a step further by the Ba'th party in its re-
emergence as an independent political force in the early 1960s. The
Movement of Arab Nationalists, on the other hand, remained for
most of its history within a Nasserite orbit, both in theory and practice
until the Six Day War. It then began its rapid disintegration and
reorganization into separate Marxist groups oeprating within their
own national states or territories.

Nasserism was essentially a populist movement linked to a charismatic leader and a set of policies, political pronouncements and
domestic or international activities. Its most articulate ideological
outlook was embodied in the National Charter of 1962. The theoretical thrust of the Charter highlighted the central function of socio-
economic factors in determining the development of nations and the
necessity of the socialist solution. Moreover, Nasserism reversed the
order according to which Ba'thism desired to achieve its goals, thereby
turning socialism into a prerequisite of freedom and unity. By giving
primacy to socialism, Nasserism after 1962 demarcated its own ideological territory within the Arab nationalist movement. Thus, with
hindsight and the failure of union between Syria and Egypt, Nasserism
underlined the importance of effecting internal transformations within
each Arab country as a necessary prelude to achieving unity of purpose
and aims. Democracy was, moreover, defined as 'political freedom',
and socialism as 'social freedom'. Both were deemed to form one
organic unity. Arab unity was thus thought of as the culmination of a

long process of economic, social, political and cultural change, brought about by a new generation of Arab leaders, operating in the context of their own independent countries, and relying on organizations similar to the Arab Socialist Union of Egypt.

Furthermore, the goal of Arab unity, as far as Egyptian policy was concerned, had to be accomplished by peaceful means, based on a strategy of persuasion, mobilization and propaganda, leading in due course to voluntary approval by the vast majority of Arab citizens. The civil war in North Yemen which lasted from 1962 to 1970 pitting republicans against royalists, represented the only direct military intervention by Egyptian forces. However, it was perhaps this intervention which paved the way for Yemeni unification two decades later.

Ba'thism

Ba'thism represents the ideology of the Arab Ba'th Party. This party was formally founded by two Damascene school teachers, Michel 'Aflaq and Salah al-Din al-Baytar, in 1947. It was renamed the Arab Socialist Ba'th Party in 1952 after its merger with the Arab Socialist Party of Akram al-Hawrani. The last championed the cause of the peasants against their landlords in the city of Hama and its environs. The Ba'th recruited among students, workers, peasants and minorities, and was gradually built into a well-organized party endowed with hierarchical structures: cells, sections, divisions, branches and regions. From its base in Syria, it spread to Iraq, Lebanon, Jordan, Palestine, Tunisia and the Arabian Peninsula. It did not establish a foothold in other Arab countries until the 1970s. Even then it had only a small organization in the Sudan, and Yemen, while Egypt, Algeria, Libya and, to some extent Morocco, remained outside its ambit. However, its ideology, based on Arab unity, freedom and socialism, was adopted, in one form or another, by a number of Arab parties, particularly the Arab Socialist Union (ASU), set up by Nasser in 1962 in the wake of Syria's secession from the United Arab Republic.

Up to 1960, the Ba'th was satisfied with playing the role of the king-maker, rather than being the king. The 1958 union with Egypt was largely due to the rise of the Ba'th party as an effective political force able to exert pressure on the old regime through its civilian constituency and the adherence of a number of army officers to its ideology. The merger between the Ba'th and the Arab Socialist Party in 1952 to form the Arab Socialist Ba'th Party signalled the end of its elitist phase and afforded it a wider rural constituency which Hawrani had nurtured since 1938. Another new ingredient which the merger provided, consisted of a network of army officers who owed their loyalty to Hawrani as a leader of the peasants' movement in Syria, as well as a parliamentarian since 1943 and Minister of Defence in 1950. The three coups d'état which Syria witnessed in rapid succession between 1949 and 1950 were launched by non-ideological colonels who accused the two principal political parties of the day, the People's Party and the National Party, of corruption, nepotism and inefficiency. The first coup was engineered by Husni al-Za'im on 30 March 1949; it was rapidly followed by the second on 14 August 1949. The leader of the second coup, Sami al-Hannawi, was in his turn deposed by Adib al-Shishakli on 19 December 1949. The third military dictatorship was destined to last until 25 February 1954. Initially, al-Shishakli, like his predecessor, chose to reconvene parliament and appointed a succession of civilian governments. But on 2 December 1951, he asserted his full authority and took control as a military dictator. He then dissolved all political parties on 6 April 1952. The Ba'th and the Arab Socialist Party offered their initial support then fell out with the three military leaders. When they were finally banned in 1952, their leaders, 'Aflaq, al-Baytar and Hawrani, fled across the border to Lebanon and then went to Rome. Before their departure they had decided to amalgamate the two parties in order to organize a more effective opposition against al-Shishakli. Although they eventually succeeded in their aim, and al-Shishakli was deposed by a combination of civilian resistance based on an extended political campaign and the effective intervention of Ba'thist army officers, Hawrani and 'Aflaq refrained from installing a military regime. Instead Syria was once again a parliamentary democracy.[34]

The old traditional system was fully restored and political life seemed to be returning to a familiar pattern which had established itself in the 1940s in the wake of Syria's independence. The two major parties, led by large landowners and wealthy merchants, resumed their activities oblivious to the growing influence of the other ideological parties and their insistence on land reform, non-alignment and the necessity of building a strong army. Moreover, Syria at the time had become a bone of contention between Iraq on the one hand, and Egypt as well as Saudi Arabia, on the other. While the People's Party, with its strong base in the northern district of Aleppo, leaned towards Iraq, the National Party, controlled by Damascene politicians, favoured stronger ties with the Saudi–Egyptian axis. The fact that Egypt had in the meantime abolished the monarchy and introduced a programme of land reforms did not lead to drastic changes in inter-Arab coalitions.

In the Syrian national elections held in 1954, the ideological parties won a substantial minority of parliamentary seats. Moreover, whereas the Communists managed to gain one seat, and the Syrian Social Nationalist party two seats, the Ba'th emerged with 16 parliamentary deputies headed by Akram Hawrani. However, out of a total of 142, the People's Party and the National Party won 32 and 25 seats respectively, with the largest contingent being secured by 'Independents' (55 seats).

As the People's Party drifted towards closer ties with Iraq and its pro-western policies, the Ba'th and the National Party sought to strengthen their position by upgrading their relations with Egypt under its new regime. The 1956 Suez crisis, during which a pro-Iraqi plot to topple the Syrian president Shukri al-Quwwatli was uncovered, shifted the balance of power in favour of the pro-Egyptian camp. High-ranking members of the People's Party were accused of instigating the plot, put on trial and convicted of treason. The exclusion of the People's Party from parliament opened the way for the Ba'th to dictate the formation of Syrian governments, especially after the election of Hawrani as Speaker of parliament in 1957 and the appointment of another Ba'thist leader, Salah al-Din al-Baytar as Foreign Minister a year earlier. Thus both the Syrian parliament and pan-Arabist army officers declared their intention to achieve an immediate union with Egypt. On 1 February 1958, the Syro-Egyptian unity was proclaimed as the culmination of a long-drawn struggle to launch Arab nationalism on the road to full victory.

One of the preconditions which Nasser stipulated for joining the union and becoming its president was his insistence on the dissolution of all political parties in Syria. The National Union Organisation, set up by Nasser in 1957, was to act as the only political party in both countries. 'Aflaq, in the apparent hope of transforming the National Union into an ideological instrument similar to the Ba'th, signalled his agreement to Nasser's stipulation. Hence, the Ba'th dissolved its Syrian branch, but continued its activities in other Arab countries, particularly in Iraq, Jordan and Lebanon. In the first cabinet after the formation of the Union the Ba'th was allocated four ministries, and Akram Hawrani became one of the four vice-presidents. However, Nasser's attempt to govern Syria on a largely non-partisan basis and rely on non-Ba'thist personalities, such as 'Abd al-Hamid Sarraj, Chief of Intelligence, began to sow doubts in the ranks of the Ba'th as to their role as an ideological party in a union which did not seem anxious to use their talents.

Moreover, Nasser's efforts to neutralize the Syrian army by reducing its infiltration by ideological parties created another difficulty, and was widely perceived as a deliberate attempt to cut the Ba'th down to size. As scores of Syrian army officers were transferred to Cairo, the rift began to widen and grievances of discrimination multiplied. As the National Union remained firmly in the grip of its Egyptian leaders, who were themselves a motley of bureaucrats, Ba'thist members lost hope of effecting radical change in its structure or amorphous ideology. On the other hand, some leading Ba'thists, such as 'Abdallah al-Rimawi, head of the Jordanian Regional Command, became openly pro-Nasserite and began to challenge 'Aflaq's leadership. In August 1959, al-Rimawi was expelled from the party and declared a renegade. A year later another leading Ba'thist, Fu'ad al-Rikabi, who had virtually established the party single-handed in Iraq and turned it into an effective organisation, was expelled for similar reasons. By the end of 1959, the Ba'th leaders, Akram Hawrani and Salah al-Din al-Baytar, had resigned their posts in the government with the full agreement of 'Aflaq. In the same year, a number of Syrian officers who had been transferred to Cairo began to organize themselves into what became known as the Military Committee. Organized by Lieutenant Colonel Muhammad 'Umran, it included in its ranks two future leaders of Syria, Salah Jadid and Hafiz al-Asad. Salah Jadid dominated Syrian politics between 1966 and 1970 when he was ousted by al-Asad in 1970.

It was the Military Committee that transformed the Ba'th into a more radical party and ousted its veteran leaders, 'Aflaq and Baytar.[35] According to Batatu, the social origins of its members, 'the middling or lesser rural or village notability', were to lead in the 1960s and 1970s to the 'ruralization' of the armed forces, the party machinery and substantial sectors of the political and administrative structures of the Syrian state.[36]

The Military Committee of Ba'thist officers played no part in the secessionist coup d'état on 28 September 1961. The coup was led by a coalition of moderate Damascene officers, led by Lieutenant Colonel 'Abd al-Karim al-Nahlawi and supported by the old political parties. However, both Hawrani and al-Baytar gave their blessings to the secessionists. As Syrian politics reverted to a pattern harking back to the 1950s, the scene was set for another coup, which took place on 8 March 1963. Although Akram Hawrani was expelled from the Ba'th on 21 June 1962, the remaining two veteran leaders of the Ba'th, 'Aflaq and al-Baytar, were no longer in a position to exercise effective control over their party. The balance of power had shifted to the Military Committee, which over the next two years whittled down their authority and then removed them altogether in 1966.

The Iraqi branch of the Ba'th underwent a similar process of radicalization and ruralization in the 1960s. However, the radical civilian leadership of the Iraqi branch, unlike its Syrian counterpart, failed to establish a strong foothold in the armed forces.

Nevertheless, 'Aflaq, as the Secretary-General of the Ba'th Party did play a significant role in turning his organisation into an instrument of government. As we have seen, up to 1959 the Ba'th had been satisfied with wielding its influence by political and military pressure, while abstaining from entertaining the possibility of clutching the reigns of powers on its own. As its relations with Nasser began to deteriorate in the wake of the Syro-Egyptian Union, it began to reorganize itself by tightening its internal regulations and stressing its ideological credentials as the only credible pan-Arabist organization. To that end, it convened its third National Congress in Beirut between 27 August and 1 September 1959.[37] One of its resolutions reaffirmed the existence of the Ba'th Party as a pan-Arab organization, and 'the only party which is able to tackle the various problems of our nation in all its regions'. Furthermore, it called for the need of 'a political plan' in order to align daily tactics with a long-term strategy.[38] In its fourth National Congress in August 1960, the delegates condemned the decision to dissolve its branches in Syria and Egypt after February 1958 and called for rebuilding the Party on 'a revolutionary basis'. While the Congress rejected the reliance on military coups as a method of struggle in principle, it recommended the possibility of a working relationship with the leaders of such a coup provided they adhered to national principles and accepted domocratic rule. It, moreover, stepped up its criticism of Nasser accusing his system of confiscating political freedom. More importantly, it singled out Iraq as being objectively ripe for a new system to be set up by the Ba'th.[39]

Thus for the first time the Ba'th party declared itself to be ready to take over state institutions. Those who considered the party 'a school of mysticism and asceticism and self-abrogation' were branded as defeatist and unworthy to carry on the mission of Arab nationalism.[40] Thus, by the time the Ba'th held its fifth Congress in mid-April 1962, Syrian secession was well-established, whereas the determination of its Secretary-General to seize power in the name of his party for the first time in its history had become a foregone conclusion. Although it continued to call for restoring the Syro-Egyptian union on a basis of equality between the two countries, whereby 'federalism' rather than complete integration was the preferred method, it was now embarking on a more cautious approach.

As we have seen, in 1958 the monarchical regime in Iraq was abolished under the impact of a radical revolutionary tide, spearheaded by the army. In the ensuing struggle for power various political parties and groups, espousing ideologies ranging from communism to nationalism, were pitted against each other. At first the leader of the revolution, 'Abd al-Karim Qasim, attempted to play a balancing act, trying to reconcile demands for Arab unity with a growing movement for Kurdish autonomy, coupled with the incessant pressure of a vigorous communist party to act as his mentor. He finally decided to restrict his programme to an inclusive Iraqi agenda centred on the army and the implementation of his land and social reforms. Of all his opponents, it was the Ba'th party which managed in 1963 to put an end to his brand of Iraqi socialism. However, the Ba'th itself, owing to internal strife in its ranks, did not manage to hold power for more than a few months. By early 1964 Iraq came to be ruled by a coalition of army officers, nationalist activists and civil servants who looked to Nasser for legitimacy and moral support. This state of affairs, alternating between radical socialism and right-wing nationalism, finally came to an end in 1968. It was then that a reorganized Ba'th Party returned to power and proceeded to establish its grip on the institutions of state and society by purging the army, building a national network of Party activists and creating a vast array of civilian organizations.

The regional command of the Ba'th Party which took over power in Iraq on 8 February 1963 was led by a second-generation activist, 'Ali Salih al-Sa'di. The Party which he took over in 1960 had been driven underground as a result of an assassination attempt it organized in 1959 against Qasim, the Iraqi dictator. The fact that those who were caught and put on trial defended their action as a revolutionary step based on ideological principles won them the admiration of Iraqis who were seeking to replace Qasim.[41] Consequently, al-Sa'di was able to form a National Front composed of pan-Arabist groups and personalities, in addition to student associations. The Iraqi regional command was entirely composed of civilian members with a pronounced provincial background. However, they did not form a coherent group either politically or ideologically. While some were loyal to the traditional leadership of 'Aflaq, others, including al-Sa'di, looked forward to a different leadership armed with a quasi-Marxist ideology. The army officers who spearheaded the revolt against Qasim were either full members of the Party or sympathetic to its cause, but were not very enthusiastic about al-Sa'di's scheme of things. The fact that he concentrated his efforts on organizing the National Guard as his own militia and contrary to the wishes of the army officers created a sharp division between him and the military at large. Hence his reliance on the National Guard, a civil militia originally set up to defend the revolution, increased his isolation from other members of the leadership. Moreover, the National Guard became embroiled in a

SOCIALISM AND PAN-ARABISM

terrorist campaign against the pro-Soviet communist party and Qasim's erstwhile ally.[42]

Matters were further complicated by the fact that the President of the new regime was none other than 'Abd al-Salam 'Arif, Qasim's one-time deputy. Thus, Ba'thist army officers, opposed to al-Sa'di, entered into alliance with 'Arif and the National Command of the Party represented by 'Aflaq.

The fall of the Iraqi Ba'th regime in November 1963 was preceded by a momentous event in the internal history of the Party. Between 5 and 25 October 1963, the Sixth National Congress of the party was held in Damascus, following the failure of the Tripartite Unity talks held in Cairo between 14 March and 17 April of the same year. These talks between Nasser and two delegations representing Syria and Iraq under their new Ba'thist regimes concluded with an accord to establish a federal state of the three countries, with Cairo as its capital. However, having tasted power and unwilling to relinquish it and place it again in the hands of Nasser, Ba'thist leaders in both Syria and Iraq found themselves in confrontation with all non-Ba'thist groups, including Syrian and Iraqi Nasserites. Nasser's withdrawal from the proposed federation on 22 July 1963 left the road open for a bilateral union between Syria and Iraq. The Sixth National Congress was convened to seal the final agreement between the two branches of the party. And the Congress did pass a resolution supporting a federal union of the two countries to be known as 'the Popular, Democratic Arab Republic'.[43]

The Sixth Congress was attended by representatives of all the factions in the party. Members of the Syrian Military Committee (see above) and the Iraqi civilian leadership were both seeking to undermine the authority of the founders of the Ba'th, 'Aflaq and al-Baytar, despite the fact that al-Sa'di was opposed to the ascendancy of the military in Iraq.[44] The left-wing, better organized and thoroughly prepared to impose its own agenda on the Congress, succeeded in getting its 120 delegates to approve their new ideological proposals for rebuilding the Party. A new National Command was elected and dominated by a second-generation of young Ba'thists, while both the Syrian and Iraqi Regional Commands fell under the domination of leftist elements.[45]

According to Hani al-Fukayki, a member of the Iraqi Regional Command and a delegate to the Sixth Congress, what became known as the 'theoretical resolutions' were drafted by the ex-communist Syrian intellectual, Yasin al-Hafiz (1930–1978).[46] Their underlying assumption was to stress the fact that nationalism was 'a stage in the transition to socialism'. Consequently, the aim was to 'Arabize' Marxism by blending its class analysis with the idea of Arab unity. As for the idea of liberty or freedom, the resolutions condemned the party's earlier support of parliamentary democracy and pluralistic politics. This criticism was premissed on the notion of equating 'liberal democracy' with bourgeois concepts 'imported by western imperialism'. 'Popular democracy' was put forward as a revolutionary alternative based on the principle of one-party rule.[47]

More importantly, Arab socialism was said to be 'an empty slogan deprived of any scientific meaning'. There was thus only one socialism but with different modes of application. Furthermore, 'private property' was no longer to be sacrosanct as the 1947 constitution of the party stipulated. It was now to be 'the common ownership of the means of production and distribution' as the solution to economic underdevelopment and social conflict.[48]

'Aflaq's fortunes as secretary-general became increasingly linked to the Iraqi branch of the party, following al-Sa'di's ousting. After 1968, when the party returned to power in Iraq under a new leadership, 'Aflaq decided to settle in Baghdad. Thus after 1966, the Ba'th was split into two wings, one Iraqi and one Syrian, and each with its own National and Regional commands.

Apart from Ba'thism and Nasserism, pan-Arabism was adopted by the Movement of Arab Nationalists (MAN). This organization was founded by a group of Palestinian students at the American University of Beirut in 1952. The mentor of this movement was a professor of history and an Arab nationalist, the Damascene Qustantin Zurayq. Although Zurayq had called as early as 1939 for a new philosophy of pan-Arabism, the MAN was more distinguished by its stress on immediate action rather than subtle theoretical issues. Its leading figure was the medical doctor, George Habash, who advocated a policy of revenge and armed confrontation against the state of Israel, after its foundation in 1948. Thus, its policies are reminiscent of those pursued by pan-Arabists in the 1930s.

Politically the MAN became a close ally of Nasserism, while its ideology depended on the theoretical analysis of 'Ali Nasir al-Din (1892–1974). Organizationally, it had branches in Jordan, Iraq, Kuwait, Oman, Qatar, Bahrain, South Yemen, Syria and Lebanon. By 1963, and following Nasser's shift to radical social policies, it began to adopt socialist notions of class struggle and armed insurrection. It also split into regional organizations centred on particular Arab territories: Kuwait, South Yemen, Lebanon and Palestine. After the defeat of the Syrian, Egyptian and Jordanian armies by Israel in 1967, most of its cadres adopted Marxism and renounced their former nationalist attachment. This was particularly the case of the Popular Front for the

Liberation of Palestine (1967) headed by Habash, and the Popular Democratic Front for the Liberation of Palestine (1969) led by the Jordanian Nayif Hawatimah (1969). Its branch in South Yemen, the National Liberation Front, seized power in 1967. By January 1969, it had ceased to exist as a pan-Arab movement.

Initially, the Movement of Arab Nationalists conceived of itself as 'a select elite' of dedicated Arab youth. Its task consisted of confronting three interrelated threats: political fragmentation, imperialism and Israel. It was thus reluctant to adopt socialism until the early 1960s.

However, for most of its history, MAN became a close ally of Nasserism, while it reserved for itself the right to use violence. Its violent methods were designed to incite 'the masses' into political action and raise their material awareness. Its slogan – unity, liberation, revenge – summed up its ideology.

By unity it meant the unification of the Arab countries into one single or federal state. Liberation denoted its resistance to imperialism and the necessity of combatting western imperialist presence. Its most effective and peculiar concept of 'revenge' was a powerful statement directed against the usurpation of Palestine by Zionism. This slogan did not initially differentiate between Zionists and Jews, lumping the two together and considering both fair game. Thus, 'revenge' was intended to be directed as a method of armed struggle or terrorist attacks against the State of Israel and its Jewish inhabitants.

Its association with Nasser, which began in 1955, finally came to an end in 1967 and the Movement ceased to exist one year later.[49] The fact that the main centres of its activities were in countries still struggling for independence – Palestine, Kuwait and South Yemen – explained to a large extent its failure to compete ideologically with Syrian or Egyptian pan-Arabism.

Following the death of Nasser in 1970, Nasserism split into a number of factions and political parties, both in and outside Egypt.

The Ba'th Party, on the other hand, underwent a process of radicalization, characterized by the influx into its ranks of provincial or lower-middle-class members. However, this radical trend was reversed in Syria after 1970 and the advent to power of President Hafiz al-Asad (d. 2000).

In Iraq, the Ba'th passed through its radical phase between 1958 and 1966. By 1968, and following several attempts, it had become the dominant force in Iraqi politics. After the triumph of Khumayni against the Shah in 1979, the Iran–Iraq War (1980–8), and the brief occupation of Kuwait in 1990–1, the Iraqi President, Saddam Husayn, began to adopt a new political discourse in which pan-Arabist and Islamist notions intermingled.

After 1973 and the ascendancy of Saudi Arabia as a regional power, pan-Arabism went into a state of relative decline. It was the oil-producing Gulf states, with their stress on Islamic values and concepts of governance, as well as their financial clout, that dominated political and economic affairs.

With the rise of Islamic Fundamentalism in the 1970s and 1980s, Arab nationalism or pan-Arabism split into three trends:

1. An official trend represented by states which advocate ideas of pan-Arabism, while being extremely reluctant to enter into hasty or uncertain unions. Colonel Mu'ammar Gaddafi of Libya represents in this particular case an exception to the rule. However, it seems that his advocacy of Arab unity has been toned down in response to economic sanctions by the United Nations and repeated failures to merge his country with neighbouring states.

2. An Arab nationalist ideology tinged with Marxist notions of class struggle, socialist construction and Leninist-type activities. However, this trend has been largely discredited after the collapse of the Soviet Union and the pursuit of capitalist policies in the Republic of China.

3. A neo-Arab nationalism that seeks gradual unity according to the diversity of the Arab world in its geographic, ethnic, economic and cultural aspects. It also places democracy in the forefront of its objectives, stressing the need of freedom of speech, multi-party parliamentary systems and collective leadership. This trend is represented by neo-Nasserite groups in Egypt, Syria and Lebanon. It has also established itself as an intellectual current throughout the Maghreb.

7

Epilogue: Civil Society and Democracy

The Syro-Egyptian unity, formed in 1958, did not last for more than three years. In 1967 the armed forces of both Egypt and Syria, two radical Arab nationalist states, suffered their worst defeat in living memory. As a result of its victory, Israel emerged as the dominant military power in the Middle East, and in direct occupation of the West Bank, Gaza Strip, the Gloan Heights and Sinai. This humiliating defeat, inflicted in the first hours of the outbreak of the war[1] on 5 June, led the foremost and most revered leader of the Arab national-ism, President Nasser of Egypt, to accept full responsibility for the 'setback' and to announce his resignation from public office. Nasser's decision on 9 June, relayed by radio and television, stunned the Arab world at large. Millions of Egyptians responded by pouring into the streets in spontaneous demonstrations calling on their president to stay in office. It was as if military defeat had given the ordinary civilian population the opportunity to assert its own national defiance. The symbol of Arab nationalism was thus reclaimed in the name of a determined nation. Nasser withdrew his resignation and went on to rebuild his armed forces with the aid of the Soviet Union. Two years later, Egypt began its 'war of attrition' against Israeli positions on the east bank of the Suez Canal. In the meantime, the Palestine resistance movement emerged as a new Arab force calling for a long strategy of armed struggle against Israel as the alternative way to Arab unity.

However, Nasser's sudden death on 28 September 1970 seemed to bring to an end a long chapter in the history of Arab nationalism. Shortly before his death, Nasser had been tirelessly exerting his efforts to avert a final showdown between the Palestinian Resistance Move-ment, under the leadership of Yasser Arafat, and the Jordanian army. The civil war which nevertheless engulfed Jordan in September 1970, and resulted in the expulsion of all Palestinian guerrilla groups from the country, was a harbinger of things to come. It was as if each Arab state had decided to turn back on itself, thereby increasing the political pressure on its own domestic constituency. The brief pan-Arab exaltation at the performance of the Egyptian and Syrian armies against Israel in 1973 was soon dissipated by the insistence of President Anwar Sadat, Nasser's successor, to reach a separate peace agreement with Israel. The civil war in Lebanon (1975–90) only served to confirm this drift in Arab societies. Urban violence seemed to be the sign of new times. It sometimes took the form of spontaneous riots brought about by straightforward economic factors as governments attempted to decrease their subsidies on essential items, such as flour, sugar and cereals. The phenomenon of so-called 'bread riots' reared its head on a massive scale in Egypt, Tunisia, Morocco and Algeria between 1977 and 1988.

Moreover, the balance of economic and political power in the Arab world began to shift from radical states in favour of the traditional monarchies of the Gulf. The meteoric rise in oil prices, precipitated by the 1973 war, gave these monarchies, with Saudi Arabia in the forefront, the means and facilities to engage the Arabs, both at the popular and official levels, in a new agenda of entrenched conservatism. It, moreover, operated in a different political space that had recently become available for new ventures of ideological experimentation. The Iran–Iraq war in the 1980s and the crisis over Kuwait in 1990–1, followed by a rigorous regime of sanctions against Iraq, reinforced the entrenchment of the Arab states as separate entities.

Ever since the early 1960s, Arab nationalism, embodied in its triad: Nasserism, the Arab Socialist Ba'th Party and the Movement of Arab Nationalists, started to experience wide-ranging debates aiming at reassessing its theoretical approach and political priorities. Socialism, slowly but inextricably, emerged as the dominant theme and the most urgent programme of action. As it did so, its erstwhile hostility towards Marxism was suddenly transformed into a 'fruitful dialogue'. Inevitably, certain Marxist notions of class struggle, the ownership of the means of production and the vanguard of the revolutionary masses, were incorporated into the mainstream of Arab nationalist discourse. It was at this juncture that the former close association between Arabism and Islam began to fade into the background and ceased to figure as a daily refrain of ideological pronouncements. In other words, Arabism at this stage of its history no longer felt the need to legitimize its ideology by using selective quotations from the Qur'an or by searching Islamic manuals for intellectual justification. Moreover, close cooperation between radical Arab states and the

Soviet Union, in addition to the rise and popularity of left-wing national liberation movements throughout the Third World, could not but reinforce this newly-found confidence in a reinvigorated secular ideology. So it was that a silent divorce took place between Islam and Arabism,[2] releasing the former from its association with a secular partner, thereby allowing it in due course to demarcate its own ideological space.

However, the perceived failure of the 'socialist' state as an efficient machine of national security began to take hold of people's imagination after the defeat of 1967. This defeat at the hands of the Israeli armed forces created the first wave of religiosity in the face of a devastating catastrophe. Its rippling effects, be they spontaneous or officially-inspired, were soon to develop a momentum of their own. Nasser's death only served to reveal the irreparable damage, marking a watershed in the unfolding drama of a state no longer capable of coping with the needs and demands of the urban masses which crowded into its cities and towns.

Despite the military successes of the Egyptian armed forces in 1973, and their undeniably brilliant crossing of the Suez canal, Nasser's protective shield had been forever removed, leaving an exposed domestic front that had to cope with the ravages of war, and consequently of economic failures. Sadat's rise to power, and his adoption of a socio-economic programme visibly hostile to the state as the ultimate guarantor of employment or social welfare, only served to hasten this process of erosion. In January 1977, the Egyptian urban masses made their last stand to prevent the collapse of their economic and political fence. In this year, and in conformity with the objectives of his open-door policies, Sadat reduced government subsidies on a wide range of commodities (sugar, rice, fuel and clothing), leading to price rises and fears of further measures. The food riots which lasted two days, caused widespread destruction and loss of life, and forced the government to withdraw its measures. Nevertheless, Sadat performed a tactical retreat on one front, only to make strategic advances into much wider landscapes. So much so that by his death in 1981 Egypt had been transformed in its social, economic and cultural structures, and firmly realigned with the West and the Arab Gulf states. Nasser's state had become a shadow of its former self, a lingering memory of a number of intellectuals and a newly-formed Nasserite political party.

The gradual recession of the state in the fields of health care, the labour market and housing, compelled various social groups to readjust their expectations or reorient their attitudes. These acts of reorientation and readjustment coincided, or were given further impetus, by opportunities made available both domestically and regionally. The pursuance of an open-door policy, based on market forces, paved the way for a number of Muslim organizations and associations to enter the world of capital accumulation by means of investment companies, Islamic banking and various ventures, often promising high and rapid rates of net profits to investors and shareholders. Professing to base their practices on 'no-interest earning transactions', their activites included the production of consumer goods, grocery shops and construction industries often funded by Islamic banks operating according to the same principles. These Islamic banks and companies were estimated in 1988 to have an accumulated capital of E£14 billion. Depositors were estimated to number millions of ordinary Egyptians.[3] The owners and organizers of these companies capitalized on another new trend: the migration of huge numbers of Egyptian workers and professionals to the Gulf, and sometimes to Europe and the United States, Australia and Canada. This new phenomenon in the social history of modern Egypt served to intensify the drive towards desecularization by linking wealth with an upright Islamic way of life. This was particularly the case of Egyptian expatriates working in the Gulf from the late 1970s onwards.

The adoption and application of open-door policies had become by the early 1980s a permanent feature of the official landscape throughout the Arab world. Both conservative and socialist states joined hands in this endeavour, whereby state ownership and management of business and industrial companies were either reduced or curtailed. Free market forces thus became the new watchword which cut across all political systems and slowly emerged in conjunction with the encouragement of foreign investments, the extension of tax benefits and the relaxation of controls over foreign exchange. Hence, privatization meant the reduction of the role of the public sector in the management of the economy and the encouragement of the private sector to assume a more dynamic role in generating wealth and prosperity. Liberalization was supposed to complete and enhance the performance of this process by inviting western governments, banks and agencies to invest their capital under favourable conditions so that the local economy would be integrated into the international market. In order to facilitate such an outcome, an ethos of economic competition rather than state restrictions took hold of Arab governments, whereby Egypt, Saudi Arabia, Algeria, Tunisia, Iraq, Syria and Jordan spoke almost the same language and introduced similar policies.[4]

These measures which seemed to grip all Arab governments with varying degrees of intensity and in such a manner as to create wide gaps in the actual application of such policies, were accompanied by the advent of consumerism and the rise of a new class of businessmen and intermediaries who became adept at linking their fortunes with international conglomerates and multinational companies. Consequently, local products were either driven out of the market or became a demoted commodity of questionable value. In other words, privatization and liberalization worked best and made permanent inroads into sectors such as services, rather than productive industries. This meant that whereas tourism flourished in Tunisia and Egypt, for example, manufacturing slumped or remained unattractive to the new investors. Furthermore, all Arab countries, including the oil-producing states, witnessed the escalation of their foreign debts, largely as a result of increasing military expenditure or widespread corruption and inefficient use of resources.

Moreover, economic liberalization operated in conjunction with the introduction of 'pluralistic' politics in most Arab countries. This approach was apparently embraced in response to domestic pressure and, more importantly, to the new international order. Although the pace of 'pluralistic politics' seemed to be accelerating in a number of countries, exemplified by holding regular national elections and the permission granted to a wide array of political parties to test their popularity, pluralism was soon to lose its constitutional and legal significance. So far no Arab government has lost power as a result of free elections or by failing to win a majority of votes. Hence, pluralistic politics has not yet progressed beyond the stage of nominal democracy whereby the ruling party, or its equivalent, always manages to hold onto power, and often with an increased majority. In this sense, the retreat of the state from the economic sphere, albeit in a partial or incomplete manner, has not yet translated itself into an easily recognizable system of genuine multi-party politics and proper democratic pluralism.

This state of affairs has generated[5] a number of popular and political responses to the new Arab order. These responses, as we have seen, range from riots in the streets to various efforts by Islamist groups to set up parallel agencies of government. Furthermore, the 1990s were largely characterized by an intense wave of violence unleashed by radical Islamists in Algeria, Tunisia, Egypt and elsewhere. As the twentieth century gave way to a new millennium the scale of violence seemed to have receded either as a result of harsh repressive measures or the adoption by some Islamist associations of a new strategy of peaceful struggle.

The collapse of the Soviet Union in 1991 was accompanied by the re-entry of the United States into the Middle East with a renewed vigour and determination. This was spectacularly demonstrated by its intervention to end the Iraqi occupation and annexation of Kuwait.

The Iraqi invasion of Kuwait on 2 August 1990 reactivated a number of interrelated issues, ranging from oil production and the Palestine question to Arab investments which were being increasingly filtered abroad.

The Palestinian *intifada* (uprising) which erupted towards the end of 1987 seemed to fail to stem the tide of Soviet Jews wishing to emigrate to Israel or to stop the relentless drive of its government to build new settlements in the West Bank and Gaza Strip. Being a largely spontaneous act of resistance, the Palestinian uprising galvanized Arab public opinion and was perceived as an example to be followed by other opposition groups. The brutal methods employed by the Israeli occupation forces to quell its renewed bouts of resurgence were correlated with the apparent failure of the Arab League to force Israel to curb its repressive measures or withdraw from the occupied territories in compliance with the United Nations Resolutions 224 and 338. The Intifada was originally precipitated by the 1982 Israeli invasion of Lebanon. The main purpose of the invasion was to destroy the political and military institutions of the Palestine Liberation Organisation (PLO) which it had established in Lebanon after the loss of its Jordanian base in 1970. For the first time in the history of the Israeli–Arab conflict, an Arab capital city was subjected to an Israeli military siege and a constant campaign of bombardments. The siege of Beirut lasted more than two months and claimed a large number of civilian casualties, while the rest of the Arab world stood and watched. The ensuing withdrawal of Palestinian forces and their dispersal throughout the Arab world signalled the end of the direct military role of the PLO. Operating from its new headquarters in the distant capital of Tunisia, the PLO, under the chairmanship of Yasser Arafat, embarked on a new strategy of political concessions, which culminated in the recognition of Israel as a legitimate state. Although the United States responded by entering into a dialogue with the PLO after 1988, it failed to convince Israel to budge from its refusal to offer significant concessions in return.

The Iran–Iraq war ended in 1988 with a stalemate and a considerable Iraqi burden of debt. However, Iraq's armed forces emerged with their reputation enhanced and their numbers multiplied to over one million. Iraq was thus being increasingly seen as the only Arab state able to reverse a series of humiliations and reversals of fortune. The Iraqi debts were mainly owed to the Arab Gulf States which had supported Saddam Husayn in his war with Iran. Kuwaiti rejection to reschedule owed debts and extend further credits, coupled with disputes over extracting oil from a neutral zone lying astride the Iraqi–Kuwaiti border, seemed to have triggered the invasion. Furthermore,

Kuwait and other Gulf states were accused of exceeding their production quota, thus serving to lower oil prices and deprive Iraq of much needed hard currency.

The US-led military intervention to liberate Kuwait, after an intense air bombardment which destroyed most of Iraq's infrastructure, succeeded in dislodging the Iraqi army from its positions and forced it to withdraw during the last week of February 1991. A number of Arab countries, including Syria and Egypt, participated in the campaign to end Iraqi occupation. The bitterness and recriminations which accompanied the war sharpened Arab divisions and reopened debates on the validity of 'Arab nationalism' as an official creed. At this juncture, the Middle East Peace process, long stalled, was revived under the direct patronage of the United States, as the sole superpower. The PLO leadership returned to the occupied territories fully recognised as the legitimate representative of the Palestinians. However, a final settlement leading to the establishment of a Palestinian state has not yet been agreed.

Neo-Arabism

Neo-Arabism was largely the product of a number of individual and collective initiatives embarked upon in the wake of Nasser's death. Their coalescence into a recognizable set of new concepts designed to go beyond the third social stage of pan-Arabism began to emerge in the 1980s. The initial period of reassessment was confined to criticisms of certain policies or the failures of a number of prominent individuals to live up to the ideals of Arab nationalism. However, as open-door policies accelerated, punctuated by the growing activities of militant Islamist groups, debates and reassessments widened to embrace the entire legacy of the 1950s and 1960s.

In the mid-1970s, a number of pan-Arabists decided to set up an independent research centre in Beirut in order to relaunch the idea of Arab nationalism on a more systematic basis. Directed by Khayr al-Din Hasib, a Cambridge graduate and former governor of the Central Bank of Iraq in the 1960s, the Centre established a monthly journal, *al-Mustaqbal al-'Arabi* (The Arab Future), and embarked on an ambitious programme of publishing scholarly monographs on issues related to Arab unity. It also began to sponsor a series of workshops and conferences, and which participants from all over the Arab world were invited to attend. Within a decade, the Centre for Arab Unity Studies established itself as the representative of a new voice in the Arab world, totally independent of governments and solely dedicated to a different approach. The fact that its publications include the names of most Arab intellectuals, who are anxious to reopen the debate on all problems relating to the contemporary national dilemma, testifies to its ambition to shift the political agenda to a different level.

In 1990, another organization, known as the Arab National Conference (*al-Mu'tamar al-Qawmi al-'Arabi*), was set up with the purpose of reviving the idea of Arab unity by holding annual meetings of its members and issuing a set of analytical studies known as 'State of the Arab Nation Reports'.[6] Its membership, ranging between 400 and 600, included a number of prominent pan-Arabists from each country in the Arab world. These reports tackle issues such as human rights, economic development, science and technology, the Arab-Israeli conflict and repercussions of corruption as a political and bureaucratic phenomenon. Its aims are defined as being: Arab unity, democracy, independent economic development, social justice and cultural renewal. Its stated ambition is to act as the ultimate reference point in dealing with pan-Arab issues.[7] It has so far refrained from turning itself into a political party, preferring apparently to act as a pressure group capable of influencing public opinion and Arab governments by highlighting the common tasks which face them in a persuasive and factual manner.

If one takes the publications of the Centre for Arab Unity Studies and the annual reports of the Arab National Conference as a barometer of a nascent neo-Arabism, a number of novel concepts and practices can be detected. Perhaps the most conspicuous of these and likely to persist for some time to come, is the insistence on restoring the autonomy of civil society.[8]

To simplify somewhat, civil society is conceived to consist of all institutions, associations and structures which fall outside the ambit of the state. Although there is no general agreement as to whether 'civil society' does exist as such in the Arab world or is capable of being regenerated, its desirable presence is no longer in question. There is also no doubt that the failure of various Arab states to offer adequate solutions to practical problems, such as housing, employment and health, or to correlate their control of education with high standards and subsequent satisfactory rewards, devalued their legitimacy and ability to deliver. Moreover, as the Arab state itself began to withdraw from direct economic control, it enlarged the pool of a variety of independent social strata. The fact that the ruling elites signalled their willingness to entertain pluralistic politics without a corresponding diminution of their power, hastened the discovery of a counter-elite, waiting to take over power, if only its civil society was allowed to have its say in a fair way. In this manner, the discovery of 'civil society' became linked to the ambitions and programmes of opposition forces not able to turn state institutions into instruments of economic development or effective political participation. In the case of pan-Arabists, this stance was carried further by considering the existing Arab states as the real barriers preventing, if not actively opposing, Arab unification. Not only does the Arab state, under its various forms and guises, hinder the emergence of civil society, its very history and development seemed to prove its hostility to all aspects of modern political practices.

According to the Syrian scholar Burhan Ghalyun, the incorporation of the Arab world into the international system in the nineteenth century caused its states and societies to diverge and develop at different rhythms and patterns of responses. What the emergent Arab state borrowed from the West was not modernity itself but its mere 'residues' or scraps. These 'scraps' manifested themselves in administrative and military techniques which were said to sum up political life in the modern age. To Ghalyun, the *raison d'être* of the modern state is 'political liberty' as an instrument of social emancipation and the achievement of equal citizenship. Its constitution as a state reflects the slow maturation of social and economic forces which are themselves historically generated. The modern state transcends society and achieves its autonomy by its ability to regulate the conflict of its interests and to govern its contradictions, so as to allow the alternation and circulation of political power in a peaceful manner. Hence, civil society announces the arrival of modernity and its democratic state.[9]

In the Arab world, Ghalyun explains, the post-independence state destroyed civil society in its erratic efforts to develop it. Its promises of quick victories, economic growth and continuous progress turned it into 'a normative state' which was expected to live up to its image. As it failed to do so by the early 1970s, it accentuated the distance between it and its society. Its increasing role as a dictatorial power in the hands of an isolated elite revealed its inadequacy to become a 'national state', as it pretended to be. Thus, despite its apparent might and stability, its use of naked force to quell opposition groups is a sign of its weakness and fragility. No longer able to represent its society and act as its agent, nor capable of withstanding international economic pressure, it has fallen back on its armed forces as its last resort of protection.[10]

Nevertheless, Ghalyun reiterates his belief in the existence of the Arab nation as a historical and cultural entity, while at the same time depriving existing Arab states of their legitimacy as true representatives of their society. Thus, the reactivation of civil society would not have a significant impact unless it cuts across internal borders. Civil society

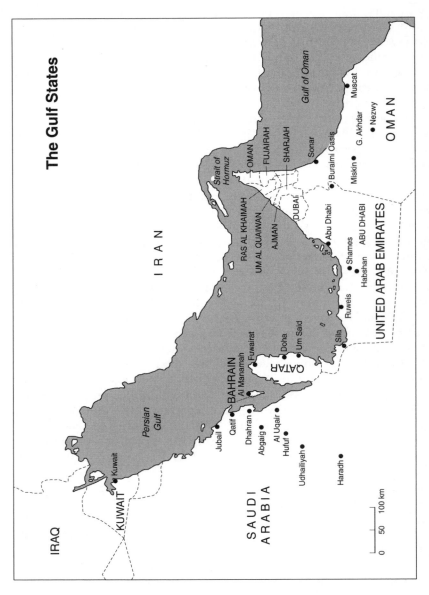

Map 7.1   The Gulf States

is rehabilitated in this instance inasmuch as it serves to create congruence between cultural identity and its political concomitance.[11]

Another pan-Arabist who has been converted to the idea of 'civil society' in its local context is the Moroccan academic and professor of philosophy, Muhammad 'Abid al-Jabiri. His point of departure is not Arab nationalism per se, but the need to build on its achievements, without neglecting to pinpoint its limits and failures. To him, Arab nationalism has largely fulfilled its mission as a national liberation movement. In other words, its main purpose was to underpin the struggles of various Arab countries to achieve their independence. It thus acted as a protective shield of solidarity and coordination rather than a systematic endeavour to build a unitary Arab state. Once independence had been achieved by almost all Arab countries, it began to lose its original purpose and fizzle out. This was particularly the case after Algeria, the last major Arab state, had become independent in 1962. However, Arab nationalism by concluding 'its historical function', as al-Jabiri avers, does not abrogate the project of Arab unity. Rather, it calls for a new approach that is in tune with contemporary requirements and the conditions of globalism.[12]

Thus, he takes the independence and separate political existence of all Arab states for granted. But he acknowledges the unity of the Arab nation as a cultural entity, despite its fragmentation. This unity is further refined by singling out four distinct 'Arab regions' which are said to qualify for immediate union: the Arabian Peninsula, the Fertile Crescent, the Nile Valley plus the Horn of Africa, and the Maghreb. These four regions, once unified, could coordinate their policies and devise means of cooperating with each other under the umbrella of the Arab League.[13] Moreover, the struggle for Arab unity, continues al-Jabiri, has to be conducted as part of establishing proper democratic institutions and practices in the separate Arab countries. In his opinion democracy would facilitate rather than postpone Arab unity. Given the fact that the Arabs have become culturally unified, and in view of their growing economic ties, most Arab citizens would freely choose to create a larger and more viable state.[14] In this sense, the prior establishment of democracy in a number of Arab states takes precedence over present endeavours for unity.[15]

By restoring democracy to the centre stage of Arab politics, pan-Arabists have thus rearranged priorities and discarded old notions of socialism and radical revolutionary struggle. Nevertheless, democracy has simply edged socialism out of the way and occupied its place as a new agent of change. What Nasserism stipulated in the early 1960s as the prerequisites of Arab unity, namely socialism, political independence and the free choice of the citizenry, has now been refined and redefined. Hence, there is a certain continuity which explains the survival of Nasserism as a basic model deemed to be capable of being developed and recast to meet the requirements of the democratic age. It is no wonder then to discover that when Egyptian Nasserites decided in the late 1980s to organize themselves into a political party, they chose to call it the Arab Democratic Nasserite Party. It was legally recognized by the Egyptian government in 1992.

In the last two decades, the idea of democracy and civil society has travelled far and wide in the Arab world. Its advocacy by groups of the intelligentsia and members of the middle classes adumbrates the re-emergence of pan-Arabism as a political force of opposition. Its future is yet to unfold as a popular force. While it may seem to rehearse programmes and concepts put forward at the turn of the twentieth century, it simply reclaims its vast and varied heritage. Democracy was then, albeit in a more restricted sense, taken for granted, and decentralization or self-determination slowly won the allegiances of a new generation of Arab activists. The story of their political projects and theoretical formulations has thus allowed us to explore the past until the end of the twentieth century.

As we enter the twenty-first century, neo-Arabism has yet to generate its own story with its own characters, plot and unforeseen end.

Notes

1   Nationalism and its Theories

1 See pp. 10–22.
2 Some scholars push this date further back to 1500 AD.
3 See, for example, Hugh Seton-Watson, *Nations and States*, Methuen, London, 1977, ch. 2.
4 'Nationality', *The Home and Foreign Review* 1, July 1862, pp. 146–74.
5 The best-known histories of nationalism in this period are those of Carleton Hayes, *The Historical Evolution of Modern Nationalism*, New York, 1931 and Hans Kohn, *The Idea of Nationalism: A study of its origins and background*, Macmillan, New York, 1944.
6 Hans Kohn, *Nationalism: its Meaning and History*, revised edition, An Anvil Original, Van Nostrand, Princeton, 1955, 1965.
7 Ibid., pp. 16–19.
8 Ibid., pp. 19–20.
9 Ibid., pp. 20–3.
10 Elie Kedourie, *Nationalism*, Hutchinson, London, 1974.
11 Ibid., p. 70.
12 Ibid., p. 74.
13 Elie Kedourie (ed.), *Nationalism in Asia and Africa*, London, 1971, pp. 22–92.
14 Lord Acton, *Essays on Freedom and Power*, Glencoe, Ill: The Free Press, 1948, pp. 166–95.
15 John Stuart Mill, *Utilitarianism*, Everyman, London, 1910, 1998, p. 394.
16 Ibid., p. 391. However, Mill goes on to qualify his statement by stating that 'several considerations are liable to conflict in practice with this general principle'.
17 Ibid., p. 391.
18 Ernest Renan, 'What is a nation?', in Homri, K. Bhaba, ed., *Nation and Narration*, Routledge, London and New York, 1990, p. 19. Renan's lecture 'Qu'est-ce qu'une Nation?' was first published in a collection of speeches, Ernest Renan, *Discours et conferences*, Paris, 1887, pp. 277–310.
19 Anthony Smith, *Theories of Nationalism*, London, 1971.
20 Ibid., p. 6.

21 John Plamenatz, 'Two types of nationalism', in Eugene Kamenka, ed., *National-ism. The Nature and Evolution of an Idea*, Edward Arnold, London, 1976, pp. 23–36.
22 Ibid., pp. 30–5.
23 Ernest Gellner, *Nations and Nationalism*, Oxford, 1984, p. 99.
24 Smith, *Theories of Nationalism*, pp. 6–7.
25 Ibid., pp. 162–4.
26 Ibid., p. 171.
27 Ibid., p. 175.
28 Anthony Smith, *The Ethnic Origins of Nations*, Blackwell, Oxford, 1994.
29 John Armstrong, *Nations before Nationalism*, University of North Carolina Press, 1982.
30 Smith, *The Ethnic Origins of Nations*, p. 91.
31 Ibid., p. 13. In his works, Smith makes numerous references to the 'Druze desire for independence'. As far as this author is aware, there does not exist such a desire among the Druze of either Lebanon, Syria or Israel.
32 Ibid., p. 131.
33 Ibid., pp. 131–4.
34 Ibid., p. 216.
35 Ibid., p. 215. In another passage, p. 207, Smith reiterates the need to qualify the 'modernity' of nations.
36 Gellner, *Nations and Nationalism*, ch. 2.
37 Ibid., pp. 14–18.
38 Ibid., pp. 19–28.
39 It is a regrettable fact that most authors on nationalism use the generic term 'man' to refer, one presumes, to both men and women. It is not clear why Gellner, an otherwise thoroughly egalitarian man, still uses Victorian phraseology in his sociological analysis.
40 Ibid., p. 31.
41 Ibid., p. 52.
42 See, for example, K. Minogue, 'Ernest Gellner and the dangers of theorising nationalism', in J. Hall and I. Jarvie, eds, *The Social Philosophy of Ernest Gellner*, Rodopi, Amsterdam, 1996.
43 Gellner, *Nations and Nationalism*, pp. 20–3.
44 In an obvious riposte to Kedourie, Gellner goes on to state: 'But this culturally creative, fanciful, positively invented aspect of nationalist ardour ought not to allow anyone to conclude, erroneously, that nationalism is a contingent, artificial ideological invention, which might not have happened, if only those damned busy-body interfering European thinkers, not content to leave things well alone, had not concocted it and fatefully injected it into the bloodstream of otherwise viable political communities', pp. 55–6.
45 Benedict Anderson, *Imagined Communities*, revised edition, Verso, London–New York, 1993. First published 1983.
46 Ibid., pp. 1–36.
47 Ibid., pp. 37–46.
48 Ibid., ch. 4.
49 Ibid., pp. 191–7
50 Ibid., p. xiii.
51 John Breuilly, *Nationalism and the State*, 2nd edn, Manchester University Press, 1993.
52 Ibid., pp. 96–115.

53 E. J. Hobsbawm, *Nations and Nationalism since 1780*, Cambridge University Press, Canto, 1991.
54 Ibid., ch. 6.
55 Gellner, *Nations and Nationalism*, pp. 41, 80.
56 Smith, *The Ethnic Origins of Nations*, pp. 143–4.
57 Breuilly, *Nationalism and the State*, pp. 149–50.
58 Ibid., p. 137.

2 Narrating the Nation

1 Jalal al-Sayyid, *Haqiqat al-Umma al-Arabiyya wa 'awamil hifziha wa tamziqiha*, Dar al-Yaqza al-'arabiyya, Beirut, 1973.
2 Youssef M. Choueiri, *Arab History and the Nation-State 1820–1980*, Routledge, London and New York, 1989.
3 See Anwar G. Chejne, 'The use of history by modern Arab writers', *Middle East Journal* 14, 1960, pp. 394–5.
4 *Durus al-tarikh al-'arabi, min aqdam al-azmina hatta al-an*. The first edition was published in Cairo in 1348h, which corresponds to 1929/1930. By 1939 it had gone into ten reprints, with some revisions and additions. Some editions were printed in Damascus and distributed by a Palestinian publisher. I have used the fourth edition 1353h/1934, which was reprinted in 1988 within a collection of Darawza's writings, and edited by Naji 'Allush. See, Muhammad 'Izzat Darawzah, *Mukhtarat qawmiyya*, Markaz dirasat al-wahdah al-'arabiyya, Beirut, 1988.
5 Muhammad 'Izzat Darawzah, *Mudhakkirat wa tasjilat*, vol. 1, Damascus, 1989.
6 Pp. 29–31, families mentioned include 'Abd al-Hadi, Tuqan, al-Nimr and al-Nabulsi.
7 M. Darwazah, *Durus al-Tarikh al-'Arabi*, pp. 52–60. See note 3.
8 In a multi-volume study, *Tarikh al-jins al-'arabi* (Cairo, 1958–64), Darwazah widened the scope of his Semitic theory to include in its successive waves of migration the Arabian Peninsula, the Fertile Crescent, North Africa and the Nile Valley.
9 Until its independence in 1956 the Sudan was considered by Egypt as an integral part of its territory and within what was called the unity of the Nile Valley. Between 1899 and 1956 both Cairo and London, under the Condominium Agreement (19 January 1899), exercised dual control over the Sudan, with Britain, needless to say, enjoying the upper hand as the colonial power in both countries.
10 Najd and al-Hijaz, the central and western regions of Arabia, respectively, were incorporated in the Kingdom of Saudi Arabia upon its foundation in 1932.
11 It is worth noting that most modern Arab historians stress the urban origins of Islam.
12 The exact date of the Prophet's birth is still a matter of dispute. However, most scholars take this year 570 AD to be the most probable one.
13 According to Darwazah, the Jews of Medina had originally fled from Palestine in the wake of their persecution by the Romans, and settled there as agriculturalists, artisans and money-lenders. *Ibid.*, pp. 86–7.
14 The starting point of the calendar falls on 15/16 July 622 AD, which corresponds not to the actual date of the month, but New Year's Day of the year in which it took place.
15 Darwazah singles out the existence of a wide range of foreign schools, colleges

and universities as a positive factor in the education of Christian and Muslim Syrians, without, however, neglecting the missionary character of these institutions (pp. 206–7).

16 Darwazah addresses himself to *al-fata* (the young boy) in the singular.

17 Darwish al-Miqdadi, *Tarikh al-Umma al-ʿarabiyya*, Iraqi Ministry of Education, Baghdad, 1939.

18 According to Nabih Amin Faris, 'The Arabs and their history', *The Middle East Journal* 8 (2), 1954, pp. 156–7, al-Miqdadi's book was 'selected as the text for the teaching of Arab history in the secondary schools of Palestine, Syria, and Iraq, where it continued to be the standard text of Arab youth for several student generations'.

19 The text has received the meticulous attention of the American scholar and student of Arabism, C. Ernest Dawn, in his article 'An Arab Nationalist view of world politics and history in the interwar perod: Darwish al-Miqdadi', in Uriel Dann, ed., *The Great Powers in the Middle East 1919–1939*, ch. 24, Holmes and Meier, New York and London, 1988. However, Dawn's analysis is primarily concerned with the 'anti-imperialist' thrust of the text.

20 Other sources consider Ghazala to be Shabib's wife.

21 He earned an honours degree in modern history from the University of Liverpool in 1919. In 1922, he returned to England to work for a higher degree under the supervision of Arnold Toynbee at the London Institute of Historical Studies.

22 Ghurbal had already published historical studies using primary sources on Lebanon in the nineteenth century and modern Tunisia. I have treated elsewhere Ghurbal's evolving attitude in my *Arab History and the Nation-state 1820–1980*, ch. 4. However, Ghurbal is here revisited from a different angle.

23 *Minhaj mufassal li-durus al-ʿawamil al-tarikhiyya fi binaʾ al-umma al-ʿarabiyya*, League of Arab States, Cairo, 1961.

24 However, Arab historical works, whatever their provenance, are less strident in their integrationist reach than abstract theoretical pronouncements.

25 Such as India, Central Asia, Egypt, Algeria and Tunisia.

26 Yet again, Ghurbal gives credit where credit is due. He praises Ottoman military performance in the war and considers it had a decisive influence on a number of fronts: cutting off Russia from its allies, engaging in numerous battles in the Dardanelles, Palestine, Syria, Iraq and Western Arabia, and sometimes scoring significant victories, p. 116.

27 See also chapter 5.

28 ʿAbd al-ʿAziz al-Duri, *al-takwin al-tarikhi li-al-Umma al-ʿarabiyya. Dirasa fi al-huwiyya wa al-waʿi*, Markaz Dirasat al-Wahda al-ʿArabiyya, Beirut, 1984. An English version is available under the title, A. A. Duri, *The Historical Formation of the Arab Nation. A study in Identity and Consciousness*, trans. Lawrence I. Conrad, Croom Helm, London, 1987. The translation was done under the auspices of the Centre for Arab Unity Studies, Beirut, its original publishers.

29 See, in particular, his booklet on Arab socialism, *al-Juzur al-tarikhiyya li-al-ishtirakiyya al-ʿArabiyya*, Baghdad, 1965. I would like to thank Dr Khayr al-Din Haseeb for making available to me a copy of this booklet.

30 Medina in Western Arabia, Kufa and Basra in Iraq, al-Fustat in Egypt and Qayrawan in Tunisia.

31 Anthony Smith, *The Ethnic Origins of Nations*, Blackwell, Oxford, 1994, p. 131.

32 Needless to say, al-Duri published his history one year before the appearance of Smith's book.

3 Cultural and Political Arabism

1   Benedict Anderson, *Imagined Communities*, revised edition, Verso, London and New York, 1993, ch. 3.

2   E. J. Hobsbawm, *Nations and Nationalism since 1780*, Canto, Cambridge University Press, 1991, ch. 1.

3   Ernest Gellner, *Nations and Nationalism*, Blackwell, Oxford, 1984, ch. 1.

4   See, among others, George Antonius, *The Arab Awakening*, Hamish Hamilton, London, 1938, pp. 20–38.

5   See, Abdul-Karim Rafeq, 'Arabism, society and economy in Syria, 1918–1920', in Youssef M. Choueiri, ed., *State and Society in Syria and Lebanon*, University of Exeter Press, 1993, pp. 2–3.

6   See, for example, Muhammad 'Izzat Darwazah, *Mukhtarat Qawmiyya*, pp. 367–72.

7   Linda Schatkowski Schilcher, *Families in Politics. Damascene factions and estates of the 18th and 19th centuries*, Franz Steiner-Verlag-Wiesbaden, Stuttgart 1985, p. 28.

8   Herbert L. Bodman, Jr., *Political Factions in Aleppo 1760–1826*, The University of North Carolina Press, 1963, pp. vii–viii.

9   Schilcher, *Families in Politics*, ch. 2.

10 On 10 July 1898, a French force under the command of Captain Marchand landed at Fashoda on the Upper Nile. Kitchener, the conqueror of the Sudan in the name of both Britain and Egypt, ordered the immediate withdrawal of the French expedition, thereby bringing the two countries to the brink of war. However, the French finally agreed to evacuate Fashoda and averted an Anglo-French confrontation.

11 Cf. Smith, *The Ethnic Origins of Nations*, p. 3.

12 Ibn Taymiyya, Taqi al-Din, *al-Siyasa al-Shar'iyya*, al-Matbu'a al-Khayriyya, Cairo, 1904, p. 21

13 'Abd al-Rahman al-Jabarti, *'Aja'ib al-athar fi al-tarajim wa al-akhbar*, vol. 1, Dar al-Faris, Beirut, n.d., pp. 14–15, 440–66.

14 Youssef M. Choueiri, *Arab History and the Nation-state 1820–1980*, Routledge, London and New York, 1989, p. 13; Rifa'a Rafi' al-Tahtawi, *Anwar Tawfiq al-Jalil*, Cairo, 1285/1868, p. 549.

15 al-Tahtawi, *Anwar Tawfiq al-Jalil*, p. 486.

16 See, Ibn Abi al-Diyaf, *Ithaf ahl al-Zaman*, vol. 1, Dar Tunis, Tunis, 1990, pp. 52–3, 58.

17 Ibid., vol.4, p. 21. According to Jamil M. Abun-Nasr, *A History of the Maghreb*, second edition, Cambridge University Press, 1975, p. 260, al-Riyahi paid his first visit to Istanbul in 1838 to plead Tunisia's poverty and inability to pay the required imperial tribute.

18 Ibn Taymiyya, *Iqtida' al-Sirat al-Mustaqim*, Dar al-Ma'rifa, Beirut, n.d., p. 145.

19 Literally 'sons of the Arabs', *awlad al-'arab*.

20 Mahmud Shukri al-Alusi, *Bulugh al-arab fi Muhawalat ma'rifat ahwal al-'Arab*, Matba'at dar al-Salam, Baghdad, 1896.

21 See, for example, Marcel Emerit, 'La crise Syrienne et l'expansion économique française en 1860', *La Reveue Historique*, 76ᵉ année, 1952, pp. 211–32.

22 'Adil al-Sulh, *Hizb al-istiqlal al-jumhuri – sutur min al-risala*, Dar al-Nahar, Beirut, 1970, p. 100.

23 In 1875 the British Prime Minister, Disraeli, bought Khedive Isma'il's holdings in the Suez Canal, making Britain the greatest of the shareholders.
24 Fakhri al-Barudi, *Mudhakkirat*, vol. 1, Dar al-Hayat, Beirut, 1951, pp. 29–32.
25 Mustafa al-Shihabi, *al-Qawmiyya al-'arabiyya*, The Arab League, Cairo, 1958, pp. 53–4.
26 These were Arif al-Nakdi, 'Adil Arslan, Muhammad al-Mihmasani and 'Abd al-Ghani al-'Uraysi.
27 Arab members of the Senior Circle included 'Abd al-Rahman Shahbandar whose career and politics are discussed in chapter 5, Shukri al-'Asali (1878–1916), 'Abd al-Wahhab al-Inglizi (1878–1916) and Salim al-Jaza'iri (1879–1916). As the date of their deaths indicates, the last three were all executed by Jamal Pasha, the Ottoman governor of Syria, on 6 May 1916.
28 See, Muhibb al-Din al-Khatib, *al-Doctor Salah al-Din al-Qasimi*, al-Matba'a al-Salafiyya, Cairo, 1959.
29 Ibid., pp. 43–9, 67–79. cf. David Dean Commins, *Islamic Reform. Politics and Social Change in Late Ottoman Syria*, Oxford University Press, 1990, pp. 100–2.
30 See the interesting work of the Tunisian scholar, Béchir Tlili, *Crises et mutations dans le monde islamo-méditerranéen contemporain*, Publications de l'Université de Tunis, Tunis, 1978.
31 Eliezer Tauber, *The Emergence of the Arab Movements*, Frank Cass, London, 1993, p. 43.
32 See, for example, L.B., 'La caricature en Turque', *Revue Du Monde Musulman*, vol. 16, 1908, pp. 10–13, which reproduces cartoons from the period. Abdulhamid's aids included Abu al-Huda al-Sayyadi, 'Izzat al-'Abid and Najib Malhamah (Melhama').
33 L. M., 'Empire Ottoman', *Revue Du Monde Musulman*, vol. 16, 1908, pp. 517–18, where the Society's programme is reproduced from the Egyptian newspaper, *al-Ahram*.
34 Passed by the Ottoman Parliament on 23 August 1909, it forbade the setting up of societies 'on the basis of nationalism' or 'race'.
35 On the significance of this term, see chapter 2.
36 Tawfiq Baru, *al-'Arab wa al-Turk 1908–1914*, Dar Tlas, Damascus, 1991, pp. 260–7.
37 Ahmad Qadri, *Mudhakkirati 'an al-thawra al-'arabiyya al-kubra*, Matabi' Ibn Zaydun, Damascus, 1956, pp. 6–7.
38 See, Antonius, *The Arab Awakening*, p. 187.
39 Tawfiq Baru, *al-'Arab wa al-Turk 1908–1914*, pp. 452–5.
40 'Abd al-Rahman al-Kawakibi, *Taba'i' al-istibdad*, al-Matba'a al-Rahmaniyya, Cairo, 1931.
41 See, Sylvia G. Haim, 'Alfieri and al-Kawakibi', *Oriente Moderno*, vol. XXXIV, 1954, pp. 321–34, and Ettore Rossi, 'Una traduzione turca dell' opera "*Della Tirannide*" di V. Alfieri Probabilmente conosciuta da al-Kawakibi', *Oriente Moderno*, vol. XXXIV, 1954, pp. 335–7.
42 Mustafa al-Shihabi, *al-Qawmiyya al-'Arabiyya*, p. 58.
43 al-Kawakibi mentions, al-Tahtawi, Khayr al-Din al-Tunisi, Ahmad Faris al-Shidyaq, Salim al-Bustani and Mab'uth al-Madani.
44 *The Characteristics of Tyranny* is, in fact, dedicated to the Egyptian Khedive 'Abbas II. To make matters worse, al-Kawakibi reminds his readers that the Khedive's first name is the same as that of the Prophet's uncle. Thus, no one could have missed the political connotation and allusion to an early authentic

Arab personality who gave his name to the most illustrious Muslim Caliphate, the 'Abbasid. Moreover, al-Kawakibi's book was first serialized in an Egyptian journal.

45 Christian and Jewish Arabs are called by al-Kawakibi 'Arabic-speaking non-Muslims'. At this stage, i.e. the first two decades of the twentieth century, Jews of Arab countries were considered part of the Arab nation.

46 al-Kawakibi specifies a ratio of three-quarters as the minimum requirement.

47 Commins, *Islamic Reform*, p. 58.

48 On al-Zahrawi, see Ahmed Tarabain, ''Abd al-Hamid al-Zahrawi', in Rashid Khalidi and others, eds, *The Origins of Arab Nationalism*, Columbia University Press, 1991, ch. 5.

49 'Abd al-Rahman al-Kawakibi, *Umm al-Qura*, 2nd edn, Dar al-Ra'id al-'Arabi, Beirut, 1982.

50 In this sense Hasan Kayali's revisionist study, *Arab and Young Turks. Ottomanism, Arabism, and Islamism in the Ottoman Empire 1908–1918*, University of California Press, 1997, fails to account for the continuing momentum of the Arabist tendency in the Ottoman empire. However, his chapter on western Arabia 1908–14 is a brilliant piece of analysis.

51 The Entente Libérale or Party of Liberty and Union formed a coalition government which included a number of members from outside the party.

52 On Talib al-Naqib see, Tawfiq Baru, *al-'Arab wa al-Turk*, pp. 399–409. Other, but less influential reform societies were set up in Hama, Mosul, Baghdad, Aleppo, Damascus and Jerusalem and Tripoli.

53 Muhibb al-Din al-Khatib, *al-Mu'tamar al-'Arabi al-Awwal*, Matba'at al-Bosphore, Cairo, 1913, pp. 42–3.

54 Muhammad 'Izzat Darwazah, *Mukhtarat Qawmiyya*, pp. 665–7; Akram Zu'aytir, 'al-mu'tamar al-islami', *Al-Hayat*, London, 20 June 1994.

55 The founders of the New Independence Party were: 'Awni 'Abd al-Hadi, Muhammad 'Izzat Darwazah, Mu'in al-Madi, Akram Zu'aytir, Rashid al-Hajj Ibrahim, Fahmi al-'Abboushi, Subhi al-Khadra' and Salim Salamah. All founders hailed from Palestine.

56 See, Akram Zu'aytir, Mudhakkirat – *Hizb istiqlali*, *Al-Hayat*, 21 June 1994, p. 7.

57 Yusuf Khuri, *al-Mashari' al-wahdawiyya al-'arabiyya*, Markaz Dirasat al-Wahda al-'Arabiyya, Beirut, 1990, pp. 93–100. The following discussion is based on this reference which includes the above-mentioned programme under the heading: *ila al-'arab min 'usbat al-'Amal al-Qawmi*.

58 The origins and activities of the first are still somewhat sketchy or shrouded in mystery. See, for example, Philip S. Khoury, *Syria and the French Mandate*, I. B. Tauris, London, 1987, pp. 401–6.

59 See chapter 2.

60 Qustantin Zurayq, *al-'Amal al-Fikriyya al-'Amma*, vol. 1, Markaz Dirasat al-Wahdah al-'Arabiyya – Mu'assasat 'Abdul Hamid Shuman, Beirut, 1996, pp. 35–6.

61 The following information on the ANP is based on an unpublished paper kindly lent to me by my colleague, Dr Raghid al-Sulh: 'The Arab Nationalist Movement in the thirties'.

62 Salah al-Din al-Sabbagh, Kamil Shabib, Mahmud Salman and Fahmi Said. For their views and activities see the memoirs of Salah al-Din al-Sabbagh, *Fursan al-'Uruba*, Ala-Shabab al-'Arabi, Baghdad, 1956.

63 See below, pp. 96–7.

64 Fallah 'Abdallah al-Mudayris, *Malamih awwalliyya hawla nash'at al-tajamu'at wa*

al-tanzimat al-siyasiyya fi al-Kuwayt 1938–1975, Dar Qirtas, al-Kuwayt, 1994, pp. 6–9.

65 See note 61.

66 Jill Crystal, *Oil and Politics in the Gulf*, Cambridge University Press, 1995, pp. 53–4.

67 Fallah 'Abdallah al-Mudayris, *Malamih Awwalliyya*, pp. 9–12.

68 See, Fuad Khalil Mufarrij, ed., *al-Mu'tamar al-'Arabi al-Qawmi fi Bludan*, Maktabat 'Arafa, Damascus, 1937, p. 1. This is a documentary collection of the Bludan Conference proceedings.

69 Anthony Eden, *Freedom and Order: Selected Speeches, 1939–1945*, Faber & Faber, London, 1947, pp. 104–5.

70 Wm. Roger Louis, *The British Empire in the Middle East 1945–1951*, Clarendon Press, Oxford, 1988, p. 123.

71 Although King Faruq of Egypt (1936–52) orchestrated a propaganda campaign to promote his claims to the Caliphate, by the late 1930s, his efforts turned out to be 'an ephemeral episode in the evolution of Egypt's regional relations'. See, Israel Gershoni and James P. Jankowski, *Redefining the Egyptian Nation 1930–1945*, Cambridge University Press, 1995, pp. 158–63.

72 See, for example, Yehoshuah Portath, *In Search of Arab Unity, 1930–1945*, Frank Cass, London, 1986, chs 4 and 5.

4   Educating the Nation: Sati' al-Husri

1 Two works on Sati' al-Husri stand out for their comprehensive nature and critical evaluations. The first, William L. Cleveland, *The Making of an Arab Nationalist. Ottomanism and Arabism in the life and thought of Sati' al-Husri*, Princeton University Press, Princeton, 1971, is a relatively sympathetic and largely descriptive assessment. The second, Bassam Tibi, *Arab Nationalism. A Critical Enquiry*, trans. and edited by Marion Farouk Sluglett and Peter Sluglett, Macmillan, Basingstoke, 1981, was originally published in German in 1971. Although it has a wider theoretical scope than that of Cleveland, it is a highly critical account of al-Husri's works and his role as an Arab nationalist thinker. See also, L. M. Kenny, 'Sati' al-Husri's views on Arab Nationalism', *Middle East Journal*, vol. XVII (1963), no. 3, pp. 231–56. See also the proceedings of a symposium recently held on the thirtieth anniversary of al-Husri's death: Ahmad Yusuf Ahmad et al, *Sati' al-Husri: Thalathun 'aman 'ala al-rahil*, Markaz-Dirasat al-Wahdah al-'Arabiyya, Beirut, 1999.

2 William L. Cleveland, *The Making of an Arab Nationalist. Ottomanism and Arabism in the life and thought of Sati 'al-Husri*, Princeton University Press, Princeton, 1971, p. ix.

3 Bassam Tibi, *Arab Nationalism. A Critical Enquiry*, trans. and ed. Marion Farouk Sluglett and Peter Sluglett, Macmillan Press, London and Basingstoke, 1981, p. 173. It is worth noting that Tibi takes al-Husri to task for attributing to ideas a life of their own.

4 The biographical data in this section is largely based on Cleveland, *The Making of an Arab Nationalist*, pp. 12–33; Tibi, *Arab Nationalism*, pp. 92–6; Albert Hourani, *Arabic Thought in the Liberal Age*, Oxford University Press, 1970, pp. 311–12; and Sati' al-Husri, *al-'Amal al-Qawmiyya* (Collected Works on Nationalism), vol. 1, Markaz Dirasat al-Wahdah al-'Arabiyya, 1990, pp. i–xii. The last is a biographical note written by his son Khaldun al-Husri.

5 Niyazi Berkes, *The Development of Secularism in Turkey*, McGill University Press, Montreal, 1964, p. 405.
6 Ibid., pp. 409–11.
7 Sati' al-Husri, *al-'Amal al-Qawmiyya*, vol.1, pp. 731–6.
8 See, Shakib Arslan, *Sirah dhatiyya* (An autobiography), Dar al-Tali'a, Beirut, 1969, pp. 221–6 and 236–92.
9 On Shakib Arslan, see William L. Cleveland, *Islam Against the West. Shakib Arslan and the Campaign for Islamic Nationalism*, Al-Saqi Books, London, 1985.
10 Sati' al-Husri, *Mudhakkirati fi al-Iraq 1921–1941* (My memoirs in Iraq, 1921–1941), vol. 1, Dar al-Tali'a, Beirut, 1967, pp. 17–22; *idem, Ara' wa ahadith fi al-qawmiyya al-'arabiyya*, Markaz Dirasat al-Wahdah al-'Arabiyya, Beirut, 1985, pp. 12–15 and 69–73.
11 Details of his activities can be found in Sati' al-Husri, *Mudhakkirati*, vol. 1, pp. 183–247.
12 Ibid., p. 557.
13 Ibid., pp. 325–7. The textbook was composed by Hibat al-Din al-Shahrastani, a former Shi'ite Minister of Education in Iraq.
14 Suddenly in his memoirs, *ibid*, pp. 611–18, al-Husri departs from his normal restrained and somewhat dry chronology of his career, revealing his bitter attitude towards his detractors and their outmoded tactics to hamper his efforts.
15 See, Sati' al-Husri, *Mudhakkirati*, vol. 2, 1968, pp. 143–61.
16 Excerpts from the speech were translated into English by Sylvia G. Haim, *Arab Nationalism. An Anthology*, University of California Press, 1962, 1976, pp. 97–9. Shawkat's speech was addressed to the students of the Central Secondary School, Baghdad, whose headmaster was the historian Darwish al-Miqdadi.
17 Ibn Khaldun's *Prolegomenon* has been translated into English and edited by F. Rosenthal under the title: *The Muqaddima, an Introduction to History*, 3 vols, Pantheon Books, New York, 1958. Although it was not rediscovered and widely debated by educated Arab circles until the second half of the nineteenth century, Ottoman officials, were well-acquainted with its contents, particularly after its translation from Arabic into their language in 1749.
18 Sati' al-Husri, *Mudhakkirati*, vol. 2, pp. 160–1.
19 Sati' al-Husri, *Dirasat 'an Muqaddimat Ibn Khaldun* (Studies on the Muqaddimah of Ibn Khaldun), second and enlarged edition, Maktabat al-Kanaji, Cairo, 1961. He named his first-born son Khaldun and was thus known as Abu Khaldun or the father of Khaldun, which is not quite the same as Ibn Khaldun or the son of Khaldun.
20 Sati 'al-Husri's works on nationalism and education were republished in 1985 and reprinted in 1990 in three volumes by the Centre of Arab Unity Studies, thereby testifying to the continuing popularity and apparent relevance of his writings to the contemporary Arab world. Hereafter all references are to these three volumes divided into 17 parts which is the number of separate books published by al-Husri on nationalism or education.
21 According to the Syrian leader, Akram Hawrani, al-Husri succeeded in silencing his opponents by accusing them of being agents of French colonialism. He also singles out his tenacity, stubbornness and reputation as a flawless nationalist. He deplores, however, the fact that al-Husri did not make sociology a compulsory subject in view of its relevance to understanding nationalism in an objective manner. See, Akram Hawrani, *Mudhakkirat* (Memoirs), vol. 1, Maktabat Madbuli, Cairo, 2000, p. 346.
22 See chapter 4.

23 It is to be noted that Egyptian notions of Arabism were still at this stage centred on some form of Arab alliance, rather than complete political unity.

24 See, Yusuf Khuri, *al-mashari' al-wahdawiyya al-'arabiyya 1913–1918,* pp. 144–53 and Nuri al-Sa'id, *al-Kitab al-Azraq* (The Blue Book), Matba'at al-Hukuma, Baghdad, 1943.

25 Ibid., p. 150.

26 Ibid., p. 152.

27 TransJordan remained an Amirate until 1946 when its ruler became King and the Amirate of TransJordan was officially recognized as the Hashemite Kingdom of Jordan.

28 Ibid., p. 166.

29 Sati 'al-Husri, vol. III, part 17, p. 127.

30 These criticisms which also included al-Husri's growing disenchantment with the bureaucracy of the Arab League were made public in a book he published in 1961, ibid., pp. 137–56. Unless otherwise indicated, all future references will be to al-Husri's works fully listed in the bibliography.

31 Sa'dun Hammadah's criticism was included in his introduction to a collection of articles by the founder of the Ba'th Party, Michel 'Aflaq. See, Michel 'Aflaq, *Fi Sabil al-B'ath*, Dar al-Tali'a, Beirut, 1963, p. 7.

32 However, there were certain shifts of emphasis in al-Husri's enormous output between 1923 and 1961, and these will be duly noted.

33 Sati' al-Husri, vol. 1, part 2, p. 43.

34 He discussed the benefits of military service in fostering discipline, altruism, love of the fatherland and the welfare of the nation on two occasions during his Iraqi episode in 1928 and 1934. See, ibid., pp. 34–5 and 37–41.

35 Vol. 1, part 5, pp. 27–170.

36 Vol. 1, part 1, pp. 9–11.

37 Ibid., pp. 11–12. In all these examples al-Husri does not make a single reference to the Arab case. A point to be explained below.

38 In keeping with his general approach, al-Husri normally assigns cultural and political developments more significance than socio-economic factors. Much later, al-Husri made a cautious attempt to bridge the gap in his historical exposition. See, in particular, vol. 2, part 13, p. 158.

39 Vol. 1, part 1, pp. 12–16.

40 See, in particular, vol. I, part 4, pp. 103–6; vol. II, part 10, pp. 37–43, and vol. III, part 14, pp. 237–54. However, in the last reference which was first published in 1961, al-Husri modifies his rejection of geographic factors in the genesis of nations by alluding to the factor of 'interaction' between nature and man.

41 Vol.1, part 5, pp. 14–16.

42 Ibid., p. 17.

43 Ibid., p. 19.

44 Ibid., pp. 22–3.

45 For a sympathetic and highly nuanced treatment of Herder, see Isaiah Berlin, *Vico and Herder. Two Studies in the History of Ideas*, Chatto and Windus, London, 1976, pp. 145–216.

46 Herder is referred to by al-Husri in a number of his works, but always with a qualifying statement. See, in particular, his article on the connection between nationalism and language: 'Irtibat al-qawmiyya bi-al-lugha', in vol. II, part 13, pp. 45–62. Herder's theory is discussed on pp. 47–9.

47 Ibid., pp. 50–1.

48 Vol. III, part 14, pp. 63–4. He alludes to the slavery trade between Africa and the Americas which goes back to the seventeenth century and the Dutch and Portuguese colonial settlements along the Indian Ocean as well as in Indonesia.

49 Ibid., p. 218.

50 Ibid., pp. 219–21.

51 All earlier works of al-Husri harp on this particular theme. See, for example, vol. I, part 1, pp. 21–2.

52 Vol. II, part 13, pp. 56–7.

53 Ibid., pp. 59–63. Examples given by al-Husri include Hungarians resisting Germanization, Bulgarians replacing Greek with their own language, and French policies to uproot Arabic as the mother tongue of Algerians.

54 Vol. I, part 1, pp. 22–3, 30–1, 68–72.

55 Vol. II, part 8, pp. 32–4.

56 Ibid., p. 32.

57 See, for example, Sati' al-Husri, *Yawm maysalun; Safhah min tarikh al-'arab al-hadith*, New edition, Dar al-Ittihad, Beirut, 1964, trans. into English by Sidney Glazer, *The Day of Maysulun: a page from the modern history of the Arabs*, The Middle East Institute, Washington, D.C., 1966. This is, however, a translation of an earlier edition first published in 1947.

58 Vol. I, part 1, pp. 23–8; vol. II, part 9, pp. 73–9; vol. II, part 11, pp. 153–8; vol. I, part 1, pp. 105–6.

59 Vol. I, part 1, pp. 126–7.

60 Sati' al-Husri, *al-Bilad al-'arabiyya wa al-dawla al-'uthmaniyya*, Dar al-'Ilm li-al-Malayyin, Beirut, 1960.

61 Ibid., p. 95.

62 Vol. I, part 1, pp. 18–20.

63 Vol. III, part 14, pp. 237–54.

64 Vol. I, part 5, pp. 47–51. Al-Husri points out that at some point in his early career he was completely won over by the eloquence of Renan's arguments, and it took him a long time before he realized its tenuous premises. See also, vol. II, part 13, pp. 99–109.

65 Vol. I, part 4, pp. 59–108 and vol. II, part 9, pp. 47–97.

66 Vol. II, part 7, pp. 7–15 and Vol. I, part 1, pp. 89–91.

67 Vol. I, part 1, p. 15.

5   In Search of Theory

1 Article 22, Provision 4, of the Covenant of the League of Nations defined, among other things, the character of the Mandate in Greater Syria and Iraq as follows: 'Certain communities formerly belonging to the Turkish Empire have reached a stage of development where their existence as independent nations can be provisionally recognized subject to the rendering of administrative advice and assistance by a Mandatory until such time as they are able to stand alone. The wishes of the communities must be a principal consideration in the selection of the Mandatory.'

2 Italics in the original.

3 The full text of the Memorandum can be found in *Great Britain and Palestine 1915–1945*, Information Papers No. 20, Royal Institute of International Affairs, London and New York, 1946, pp. 155–8. At the time of the Memorandum's publication in 1922, the population of Palestine consisted of a total of 752,048,

divided into 589,177 Moslems, 71,464 Christians, 83,790 Jews and 7,617 listed under Others. Ibid., p. 61.

4   See, for example, Walid Kazziha, *Revolutionary Transformation in the Arab World*, Charles Knight & Company Ltd., London, 1975, p. 11.

5   Q. Zurayq, *al-wa'i al-Qawmi*, Dar al-Makshuf, Beirut, 1939.

6   Zurayq illustrates the urgency of such a task by alluding to his embarrassment every time he was asked by a friendly westerner to supply him with a list of references where the theory of Arab nationalism was fully expounded (p. 8).

7   The adopted slogan declared: 'One Arab nation with an eternal mission.'

8   See, Q. Zurayq, *al-'Amal al-fikriyya al-'amma*, vol. 1, Markaz Dirasat al-wahdah al-'arabiyyah-Mu'assasat Shuman, Beirut, 1996, pp. 57–62, and 'Abdallah Hanna, *al-Ittijahat al-fikriyya fi suriyya wa lubnan 1920–1945*, Dar al-Taqaddum al-'Arabi, Damascus, 1973, pp. 42–8.

9   al-Shaykh 'Abdallah al-'Alayili, *Dustur al-'Arab al-Qawmi*, 2nd edition, Beirut, Dar al-Jadid, 1996.

10 In the introduction to Syliva G. Haims's, ed., *Arab Nationalism. An Anthology*, University of California Press, 1962, 1976, p. 42, she refers to al-'Alayili's text as being 'a difficult book, dealing with unfamiliar subjects in an unfamiliar way, and written in an involved and sometimes obscure manner'.

11 Al-'Alayili cites the foundation by Benjamin Disraeli (1804–81), the Conservative Prime Minister, of Young England as a political group armed with a clear doctrine. This he did through the medium of fiction in the 1840s.

12 The Arab Revolt was first proclaimed in Mecca under the leadership of Sharif Husayn, a descendant of the Prophet Muhammad. Islam originated in the same city.

13 See, Haim, ed., *Arab Nationalism. An Anthology*, pp. 41–2.

14 Between 1833 and 1855 Gobineau published his *Essai sur l'inégalité des races humaines*, in which he praised the creative ability of the German race and the 'purity of blood' as the sign of superiority.

15 See in particular pp. 116–17 where common interests are said to include economic, social, political, spiritual and rational dimensions.

16 Lebanon and Syria were nominally independent in 1941 but were still under French and British occupation.

17 The newly-built railway connecting Baghdad with Europe was cited as an example.

18 The two founders of the Ba'th Party published in 1944 a work entitled *Arab Nationalism and its attitude towards Communism*, Damascus (*al-Qawmiyya al-'Arabiyya wa mawqifuha min al-shuyu'iyya*).

19 This dualistic definition of democracy anticipates a similar idea adopted by the Egyptian President Gamal 'Abd al-Nasir (Nasser) in the 1960s.

20 Alexandretta enjoyed a limited autonomy under the provisions of the French Mandate. In 1936 its population of 200,000 consisted of an Arab majority (50 per cent), a sizeable Turkish minority (40 per cent), and the rest were Armenians whose sympathies were largely pro-Syrian.

21 Sulayman al-'Isa, 'al-Bidayat', *al-M'arifa*, no. 113, July, 1971, pp. 25–6.

22 Ibid., pp. 31–2.

23 Zaki al-Arsuzi, *al-'Abqariyya al-'Arabiyya fi lisaniha*, Damascus, 1943. It was published in 1957 in a revised edition, and republished as part of his collected works by the Printing Press of the Syrian Armed Forces – Political Administration, in 1972. It is to the last edition entitled *al-mu'allafat al-kamila*, Damascus, 6 vols, 1972–6, that references are made.

24 Elie Kedourie, ed., *Nationalism in Asia and Africa*, Frank Cass, London, 1971, p. 25.
25 Zaki al-Arsuzi, *al-Mu'allafat al-Kamila*, vol. 2, Damascus, 1973, p. 225.
26 See, Descartes, *Discours de la méthode*, Bordas, Paris, 1984, pp. 45–6. Descartes' full statement runs as follows: "Le bon sens est la chose du monde la mieux partagée . . . la puissance de bien juger, et distinguer le vrai qu'avec le faux, qui est proprement ce qu'on nomme le bon sens ou la raison, est naturellement égale en tous les hommes . . ."
27 Zaki al-Arsuzi, vol. 2, p. 225. This was originally published in 1954 in a booklet entitled *Ba'th al-umma al-'arabiyya* (The Resurrection of the Arab Nation).
28 Al-Arsuzi, vol. 2, pp. 47–8, 224–5.
29 Ibid., p. 228.
30 Ibid., pp. 225–6. The belief in the Great Chain of Being dominated both Christian and Islamic cultures until well into the modern period. See, Arthur Koestler, *The Sleepwalkers*, Pelican Books, Harmondsworth, 1972, pp. 97–116, and A. D. Lovejoy, *The Great Chain of Being*, Cambridge, MA., 1936.
31 al-Arsuzi, vol. 2, pp. 226–7, 319–25.
32 Al-Arsuzi, vol. 1, 1972, pp. 45–55.
33 Ibid., pp. 145–69, 176–82, 226–30.
34 For further details, see W. K. C. Guthrie, *A History of Greek Philosophy*, vol. V, Cambridge University Press, 1978, pp. 1–31.
35 'Abdurrahman Badawi, *La transmission de la Philosophie Grecque au Monde Arabe*, Librairie Philosophique J. Vrin., Paris, 1968, p. 36. As for Arab grammarians, see Ibn Jinni, *al-Khasa'is*, vol. 1, Dar al-Huda, Beirut, n.d., pp. 40–7. Ibn Jinni (d. 392H/1002 AD), had an ambivalent attitude, not dissimilar to Plato's. It is worth mentioning that conservative Muslim thinkers such as the Ash'arites, believed that language was God-inspired, while less traditionalist ones, namely the Mu'tazilites, thought that language was conventional.
36 Mustafa al-Shihabi, *al-Qawmiyya al-'Arabiyya*, The Arab League, Cairo, 1958, pp. 51–5.
37 See the English version of 'the Declaration' in George Antonious, *The Arab Awakening*, Hamish Hamilton, London, 1938, pp. 433–4. An Arabic version of the text is included in Amin Sa'id, *Asrar al-Thawra al-Arabiyya al-Kubra*, Dar al-Katib al-'Arabi, Beirut, n.d., pp. 244–46.
38 In addition to Shahbandar, the other six, who hailed from what is now the Republics of Lebanon and Syria, were: Rafiq al-'Azm, Mukhtar al-Sulh, Kamil Qassab, Fawzi al-Bakri, Hasan Hamadah and Khalid al-Hakim.
39 Antonius, *The Arab Awakening*, pp. 270–1.
40 Hasan al-Hakim, *'Abd al-Rahman al-Shahbandar: Hayatuhu wa jihaduhu*, al-Dar al-Muttahida, Beirut, 1985, pp. 109–13.
41 Ibid., p. 112. Shahbandar believed that Europe was in the grip of class struggles pitting capitalists against the workers. Syria, on the other hand, was heading under the French for total bankruptcy.
42 Shahbandar's exploits in what was termed 'the Great Revolt' were described in detail in his memoirs: 'Abd al-Rahman Shahbandar, *Mudhakkirat*, Dar al-Irshad, Beirut, 1967, pp. 149–218.
43 These were later collected and published in bookform in 1936 under the title 'The Big Social Issues in the Arab World': *al-Qadaya al-ijtima'iyya al-Kubra fi al-'alam al-Arabi*, al-Muqtataf al-muqattam Press, Cairo, 1936.
44 Ibid., pp. 91–103.
45 Ibid., p. 132.

46 Ibid., pp. 134–5. It is worth noting that Shahbandar joins both Darwazah and Miqdadi (see chapter 2) in his allusion to the weakness and limited appeal of Arab nationalism before the fall of the Ottoman Empire.

47 Ibid., pp. 141–2.

48 Ibid., pp. 143–4.

49 Ibid., p. 146.

50 These included the exclusion of Lebanon, with which a similar treaty was negotiated, joint Franco-Syrian control of foreign and defence policy and an alliance of the two countries for 25 years.

51 Akram Hawrani, *Mudhakkirat*, vol. 1, pp. 185–6.

52 Ibid., pp. 215–6.

53 M. 'Aflaq, *fi sabil al-Ba'th*, Dar al-Tali'a, Beirut, 1963, p. 35. al-Husri took 'Aflaq to task for stipulating 'faith' as a pre-condition of understanding Arab nationalism. See, Sati' al-Husri, *al-Iqlimiyya*, Beirut, 1985, pp. 87–98.

54 Salim Khayyatta, Mustafa al-'Aris, Yusuf Khattar al-Hilu and others.

55 This section is partly based on an article by Fayyiz Sarah in *Al-Hayat*, Wednesday, 29 April 1992, p. 14 and on conversations with former Ba'thists who wish to remain anonymous.

56 However, the Constitution of the Arab Ba'th party, endorsed by the founding conference of 1947, did spell out concrete measures to be implemented over the short and long term.

57 Cf. Renan's phrase: 'A nation is a soul, a spiritual principle, a rich legacy of memories and present-day consent.'

58 'Aflaq's analogy bears a striking resemblance to Shahbandar's diagnosis, alluded to in the previous section.

59 Hani al-Fukayki, *Awkar al-hazima*, Dar Riad al-Rayyes, London, 1993, p. 79. Al-Fukayki was a member of the Ba'th Regional Command in Iraq in the 1960s.

60 Sati' al-Husri, a thoroughly secular Arab nationalist, took 'Aflaq to task for this arbitrary distinction.

61 Michel 'Aflaq, *Fi Sabil al-Ba'th*, pp. 83–91.

62 In addition to its Sunnite majority, Syria is home to a number of other Muslim sects – 'Alawites, Druze, Isma'ilis – as well as Christians and Jews.

6   Socialism and Pan-Arabism

1 It will be recalled that Algeria did not gain its independence until July 1962.

2 Full text of 'Resolution Adopted by the Tangier Conference for the Unification of the Maghrib Countries', dated April 30 1958, in Muhammad Khalil, *The Arab States and the Arab League. A Documentary Record*, vol. II, Khayat, Beirut, 1962, p. 469.

3 Algeria rejected this move by Morocco and Mauritania and continued its support for the Polisario Front, which since 1973 has been fighting for an independent state in Western Sahara.

4 The full text of the 1989 Agreement in Yusuf Khuri, *al-Mashari' al-wahdawiyya al-Arabiyya 1913–1989* (Arab Unity Projects. A documentary record), pp. 751–3.

5 See Ibid., pp. 522–50. Tunisia's Constitution declares the country to be an integral part of 'the Maghreb and the Arab family'.

6 Ibid., pp. 552–99.

7 On Azzam's pan-Arabist credentials, see, Ralph M. Coury, *The Making of an Egyptian Arab Nationalist*, Ithaca Press, London, 1998.

8 On the function of the *majlis* in its Saudi context see, Tim Niblock, 'Social structure and the development of the Saudi Arabian political system' in Tim Niblock, ed., *State, Society and Economy in Saudi Arabia*, Croom Helm, London, 1981, pp. 75–105.

9 Philip Mansel, *Constantinople, City of the World's Desire, 1453–1924*, John Murray, London, 1995, p. 421.

10 In the 1950s and 1960s the American school of modernization theory and other scholars produced a considerable amount of literature on the role of the military in politics. See, for example, John J. Johnson, ed., *The Role of the Military in Underdeveloped Countries*, Princeton University Press, 1962, and S. Fisher, ed., *The Military in the Middle East*, Ohio State University Press, Columbus, 1963.

11 Prominent Jewish families included the Sasuns (or Sasoons) in Iraq and the Qattawis (or Cattaouis) in Egypt, and Jewish merchants in nineteenth-century Morocco handled the Sultan's trade.

12 See, for example, Albert Hourani, *A History of the Arab Peoples*, Faber, London, 1994, ch. 24.

13 This view has been forcefully stated in two articles by Fouad Ajami, 'The end of pan-Arabism', *Foreign Affairs* 57, Winter 1978–9, pp. 355–73, and 'The end of Arab nationalism', *The New Republic*, 12 August 1991.

14 In 1946 the Independence Party (Istiqlal) was established in Iraq by Muhammad Kubba as a pan-Arabist organization. It remained the principal Arab Nationalist Party in Iraq until it was superseded by the Ba'th in the late 1950s.

15 Ronald P. Dore, *Land Reform in Japan*, Schocken Books, New York, 1985, pp. 132–7.

16 At the time the radio had become an effective instrument of propaganda and which Nasser made use of by setting up the 'Voice of the Arabs' to transmit his message to the Arab world at large. The 'Voice of the Arabs' began its transmission in 1953.

17 Bandung was the first gathering of the bloc of non-aligned states in Asia and Africa.

18 At the time the Canal's annual revenue amounted to some $100 million gross, out of which Egypt received $3 million.

19 Text of speech in, Jamal 'Abd al-Nasir, *al-Majmu'a al-Kamila*, Vol. II, Markaz Dirasat al-Wahda al-'Arabiyya, 1996, pp. 363–77. Reference to Syria, p. 365. English text, Muhammad Khalil, *The Arab States and the Arab League*, vol. I, pp. 742–71.

20 Article One of the Egyptian decree of nationalization stated: 'The shareholders and the holders' shares shall be compensated for the stock and shares which they own . . .'.

21 See Anthony Nutting, *Nasser*, Constable, London, 1972, p. 164.

22 See, Patrick O'Brien, *The Revolution in Egypt's Economic System. From Private Enterprise to Socialism 1952–1965*, Oxford University Press, 1966, ch. 4.

23 The Arab Socialist Union was dissolved in 1977 by his successor, Anwar Sadat, and replaced by the National Democratic Party which, in its turn, has continued as the ruling party despite the introduction of 'pluralistic' politics.

24 'Abd al-Nasir, *al-Majmu'a al-Kamila*, vol. II, p. 571.

25 See, for example, ibid., pp. 607–13.

26 Candidates were vetted and screened by the National Union.

27 The United Arab Republic.

28 Ahmad Hamrush, *Mujtama' 'Abd al-Nasir*, Vol. 3, Dar al-Mawqif al-'Arabi, 1982, ch. 9.

29 Robert Stephens, *Nasser*, Penguin, Harmondsworth, 1973, p. 371.
30 Text of Eisenhower's message to Congress, in Muhammad Khalil, *The Arab States and the Arab League. A Documentary Record*, vol. II, pp. 909–15.
31 Jamal 'Abd al-Nasir, *al-Mithaq*, Dar al-Masira, Beirut, 1976. English trans. *The Charter*, UAR Information Department, Cairo, 1962.
32 For al-Husri's analysis of nationalism, see chapter 4.
33 This was an allusion to South Yemen and the Arab Gulf which were still under British control.
34 On the events surrounding the merger of the two parties see, Akram Hawrani, *Mudhakkirat* (Memoirs), vol. 2, pp. 1492–6. For the political origins of the Ba'th and its theory of Arab nationalism, as articulated by 'Aflaq and al-Arsuzi, see ch. 5.
35 Hanna Batatu, *Syria's Peasantry, the Descendants of its Lesser Rural Notables, and their Politics*, Princeton University Press, 1999, chapter 12. Batatu refers to the Military Committee as 'the transitional Ba'th'.
36 Ibid., p. 145.
37 The second National Congress was held as far back as 1954. Since that date the Party was organized on the basis of Regional Commands in a number of Arab countries – Syria, Jordan, Iraq and Lebanon – and a 'National Command' which had charge of the general policy of the Party. Each regional command was divided into branches, divisions, companies and cells. The cell constituted the primary structure with a membership ranging from three to seven. The company was, in its turn, composed of three to seven cells. The division was composed of at least two companies, whereas the branch could include two or more companies. Whereas the regional command is elected by its local convention, the National Congress, composed of the membership of the regional commands and other delegates, elects the National Command, normally 13 members, and the Secretary-General of the Party.
38 See, *Nidal al-Ba'th*, vol. IV, Dar al-Tali'a, Beirut, 1976, pp. 53–4. This is a documentary collection of the Party's conventions and Congresses.
39 Ibid., pp. 98–100.
40 Ibid., p. 116.
41 Those who managed to escape to Syria and later to Egypt included Fu'ad al-Rikabi, the first head of the Iraqi regional command and Saddam Husayn, the future President of Iraq.
42 Majid Khadduri, *Republican 'Iraq. A Study in Iraqi politics since the Revolution of 1958*, Oxford University Press, 1964, p. 198. See, also, Hanna Batatu, *The Old Social Classes and the Revolutionary Movements of Iraq*, Book III, Princeton University Press, 1978, ch. 55.
43 *Nidal al-Ba'th*, pp. 224–5.
44 Hani al-Fukayki, *Awkar al-Hazima*, p. 329.
45 'Ali Salih al-Sa'di remained a member of the Iraqi command until 11 November 1963, when he was ousted by other Ba'thist opponents and sent to Spain together with his supporters.
46 Ibid., p. 329. For the full text of the theoretical resolutions, see, *Nidal al-Ba'th*, vol. 4, pp. 169–212. English text: 'Arab Socialist Ba'th Party, National Command', *Some of the theoretical starting-points adopted by the 6th National Congress, Held in October 1963*, Bureau of Publication and Information Press, 1980.
47 Hani al-Fukayki, *Awkar al-Hazima*, pp. 331–2.
48 Ibid., pp. 332–3.
49 Walid Kazziha, *Revolutionary Transformation in the Arab World. Habash and his*

comrades from Nationalism to Marxism, Charles Knight & Company Ltd., London, 1975, pp. 109–10.

7   Epilogue: Civil Society and Democracy

1   Although the war itself lasted six days, Israel's blitzkrieg on Monday, 5 June 1967, wiped out the Egyptian air force on the ground and left the Egyptian army in Sinai without air cover. Hence, the Egyptian, Syrian and Jordanian armies were at the mercy of the superior Israeli air force.

2   It was largely 'silent' in the sense that Islam was rarely questioned or attacked, but simply ignored.

3   For further details, see Nazih Ayubi, *Political Islam*, Routledge, London and New York, 1991, ch. 8.

4   See, for example, Iliya Harik and Denis J. Sullivan, eds, *Privatization and Liberalization in the Middle East*, Indiana University Press, 1992.

5   For further details, see Youssef Choueiri, *Islamic Fundamentalism*, Pinter, London and Washington, 1997, pp. 170–80.

6   For some of the studies published in 1999, see, al-Mu'tamar al-Qawmi, *al-'Arabi, Hal al-Umma al-'Arabiyya*, Beirut, 1999 (published by the Centre for Arab Unity Studies).

7   Ibid., p. 549.

8   This section is largely based on the proceedings of a conference organized by the Centre for Arab Unity Studies in January, 1992, and published under the title 'Civil Society in the Arab Homeland': *al-mujtama' al-madani fi al-Watan al-'Arabi*, Markaz Dirasat al-Wahda al-'Arabiyya, Beirut, 1992.

9   Ibid., pp. 733–55.

10   Burhan Ghalyun, *al-Mihna al-'Arabiyya: al-Dawla did al-Umma* (The Arab Ordeal: State against Nation), Markaz Dirasat al-Wahda al-'Arabiyya, Beirut, 1994.

11   Ibid., pp. 99–100, 102, 106.

12   Muhammad 'Abid al-Jabiri, *Mas'alat al-Huwiyya: al-'Uruba wa al-Islam wa al-gharb* (The Question of Identity: Arabism, Islam and the West), Markaz Dirasat al-Wahdah al-'Arabiyya, Beirut, 1997, pp. 59–65.

13   The division of the Arab world into four distinct regions was proposed by the veteran Moroccan statesman 'Allal al-Fasi, in the 1940s, and by a number of political parties including the Syrian Social Nationalist Party of Antun Sa'adah.

14   Ibid., pp. 84–5.

15   Muhammad 'Abid al-Jabiri, *al-Dimuqratiyya wa huquq al-insan*, Markaz Dirasat al-Wahdah al-'Arabiyya, Beirut, 1997, pp. 106–8.

Dynasties

'Abbasids	750–1258
Aghlabids	800–909
Almohads	1147–1269
Almoravids	1053–1149
Alawis of Morocco	1672–
Ayyubids	1171–1250
Buwayhids	945–1055
Fatimids	969–1171
Mamluks	1254–1517
Ma'nids	1517–1697
Marinids	1269–1465
Muhammad 'Ali's Dynasty	1805–1953
Ottomans	1281–1924
Seljuks	1055–1194
Umayyads of Damascus	661–750
Umayyads of Spain	756–1031

Further Reading

Theories of nationalism

Balakrishnan, Gopal (ed.) *Mapping the Nation*. London and New York, 1996.

Bhabha, Homi K. (ed.) *Nation and Narration*. London and New York, 1990.

Hall, John A. (ed.) *The State of the Nation. Ernest Gellner and the Theory of Nationalism*. Cambridge, 1998.

Hutchinson, John and Anthony D. Smith (eds) *Nationalism*. Oxford, 1994.

Jankowski, James and Israel Gershoni (eds) *Rethinking Nationalism in the Arab Middle East*. New York, 1997.

Seton-Watson, Hugh. *Nations and States. An Enquiry into the Origins of Nations and the Politics of Nationalism*. London, 1977.

General studies on the Arab world

Bromley, Simon. *Rethinking Middle East Politics*. Polity Press, 1994

Findlay, Allan M. *The Arab World*. London, 1994.

Hitti, Philip K. *History of the Arabs*. London, 1990.

Hourani, Albert. *A History of the Arab Peoples*. London 1991.

Hudson, Michael C. *Arab Politics. The Search for Legitimacy*. New Haven, 1977.

Laroui, 'Abdallah. *The History of the Maghrib*. Princeton, 1977.

Luciani, G. (ed.) *The Arab State*. London, 1990.

Morsy, Magali. *North Africa 1800–1900*. London and New York, 1984.

Owen, Roger. *The Middle East in the World Economy 1800–1914*. London, 1990.

Cultural Arabism

Buheiry, Marwan R. (ed.) *Intellectual Life in the Arab East 1890–1939*. Beirut, 1981.

Commins, David Dean. *Islamic Reform. Politics and Social Change in Late Ottoman Syria*. Oxford, 1990.

Escovitz, Joseph. 'He was the Muhammad 'Abduh of Syria: A Study of Tahir al-Jaza'iri and his Influence'. *International Journal of Middle East Studies*, 18, 1986:293–310.

Green, A. H. *The Tunisian Ulama 1873–1915. Social Structure and Response to Ideological Currents*. Leiden, 1979.

Hourani, Albert. *Arabic Thought in the Liberal Age 1798–1939*. Cambridge, 1983.

Khuri, R. *Modern Arab Thought. Channels of the French Revolution to the Arab East*. Princeton, 1983.

Sharabi, Hisham. *Arab Intellectuals and the West*. Baltimore, 1970.

Ziadat, A. A. *Western Science in the Arab World. The Impact of Darwinism 1860–1930*. London, 1986.

Political Arabism

Antonius, George. *The Arab Awakening*. London, 1938.

Cleveland, William L. *The Making of an Arab Nationalist*. Princeton, 1971.

Dawn, C. Ernest. *From Ottomanism to Arabism: Essays on the Origins of Arab Nationalism*. Urbana Il., 1973.

Eppel, Michael. *The Palestine Conflict in the History of Modern Iraq: The Dynamics of Involvement*. London, 1994.

Gershoni, Israel and James P. Jankowski. *Redefining the Egyptian Nation 1930–1945*. Cambridge, 1995.

Haddad, Mahmoud. 'The Rise of Arab Nationalism Reconsidered'. *International Journal of Middle East Studies*, vol.26, no.2, 1994:201–222.

Khalidi, R. et al. (eds.) *The Origins of Arab Nationalism*. New York, 1991.

Khoury, Philip S. 'Divided Loyalties: Syria and the Question of Palestine 1919–1939'. *Middle East Studies*, 21, 1983:324–348.

—— *Urban Notables and Arab Nationalism. The Politics of Damascus, 1860–1920*. Cambridge, 1983.

Marr, Phebe. 'The Development of a Nationalist Ideology in Iraq, 1920–1941'. *Muslim World*, 75, April 1985:85–101.

Porath, Y. *In Search of Arab Unity 1930–1945*. London, 1986.

Zeine, Zeine N. *The Emergence of Arab Nationalism*. Third edition, New York, 1973.

Social Arabism

Batatu, Hanna. *The Old Social Classes and the Revolutionary Movements of Iraq*. Princeton, 1978.
—— *Syria's Peasantry: The Descendants of its Lesser Rural Notables and Their Politics*. Princeton, 1999.
Binder, Leonard. *The Ideological Revolution in the Middle East*. New York, 1964.
Devlin, John F. *The Ba'th Party. A History from its Origins to 1966*. Stanford, 1976.
Drysdale, Alasdair. 'The Syrian Political Elite, 1966–1976: A Spatial and Social Analysis'. *Middle Eastern Studies*, vol.17, no.1, 1981:3–30.
Gordon, Joel. *Nasser's Blessed Movement. Egypt's Free Officers and the July Revolution*. Oxford University Press, 1992.
Hinnebusch, Raymond A. *Authoritarian Power and State Formation in Ba'thist Syria: Army, Party and Peasant*. San Francisco, 1990.
Hopwood, Derek. *Syria 1945–1986: Politics and Society*. London, 1988.
Kaylani, Nabil M. 'The Rise of the Syrian Ba'th, 1940–1958: Political Success, Party Failure'. *International Journal of Middle East Studies*, 3, 1972:3–23.
Kerr, Malcolm H. *The Arab Cold War. Gamal Abd al-Nasir and His Rivals 1958–1970*. Third edition, London, 1977.
Kienle, Eberhard. *Ba'th v Ba'th: The Conflict Between Syria and Iraq 1968–1989*. London, 1990.
Olson, Robert. *The Ba'th and Syria 1947 to 1982. The Evolution of Ideology, Party and State*. Princeton, 1982.
Seale, Patrick. *The Struggle for Syria*. New Haven, 1986.
Stephens, Robert. *Nasser. A Political Biography*. London, 1973.
Van Dam, Nikolaos. *The Struggle for Power in Syria: Politics and Society Under Asad and the Ba'th*. Third edition, London, 1995.
Waterbury, John. *The Egypt of Nasser and Sadat*. Princeton, 1983.

Neo-Arabism: civil society and democracy

Abu Khalil, As'ad. 'A New Arab Ideology? The Rejuvenation of Arab Nationalism'. *Middle East Journal*, vol.46, no.1, 1992:22–36.
Farah, Tawfic E. (ed.) *Pan-Arabism and Arab Nationalism*. Boulder, Colorado, Westview Press, 1987.
Harik, Iliya and Denis J. Sullivan (eds.) *Privatization and Liberalization in the Middle East*. Indiana University Press, 1992.
Polk, William R. *The Arab World Today*. Harvard University Press, 1991.
Springborg, Robert. *The Political Economy of Mubarak's Egypt*. Boulder, Colorado, 1988.

Bibliography

Arabic: Books

'Abd al-Nasir, Jamal, *al-Majmuʿa al-kamila*, vol. 2, Markaz Dirasat al-wahdah al-Arabiyya, Beirut, 1996.
——, *Al-Mithaq*, Dar al-Masira, Beirut, 1976.
'Aflaq, Michel, *Fi Sabil al-Baʿth*, Dar al-Taliʿa, Beirut, 1963.
al-Alayili, al-Shaykh 'Abdallah i, *Dustur al-ʿArab al-Qawmi*, 2nd edition, Beirut, Dar al-Jadid, 1996, first published 1941.
al-Alusi, Mahmud Shukri, *Bulugh al-arab fi Muhawalat maʿrifat ahwal al-ʿArab*, Matbaʿat dar al-Salam, Baghdad, 1896.
al-Arsuzi, Zaki, *al-ʿAbqariyya al-ʿarabiyya fi lisaniha*, Damascus, 1943.
——, *Al-Muʾallafat al-kamila*, vols. 1–6, Damascus, 1973–6.
Baru, Tawfiq, *al-ʿArab wa al-Turk 1908–1914*, Dar Tlas, Damascus, 1991.
al-Barudi, Fakhri, *Mudhakkirat*, vol. 1, Dar al-Hayat, Beirut, 1951.
Darawzah, Muhammad 'Izzat, *Mudhakkirat wa tasjilat*, vol. 1, Damascus, 1989.
——, *Mukhtarat qawmiyya*, Marakaz Dirasat al-Wahdah al-ʿArabiyya, Beirut, 1988.
al-Diyaf, Ibn Abi, *Ithaf ahl al-Zaman*, vol. 1, Dar Tunis, Tunis, 1990.
al-Duri, 'Abd al-'Aziz, *al-Juzur al-tarikhiyya li-al-ishtirakiyya al-ʿArabiyya*, Baghdad, 1965.
——, *al-Takwin al-tarikhi li-al-Umma al-ʿarabiyya. Dirasa fi al-huwiyya wa al-waʿi*, Markaz Dirasat al-Wahda al-ʿArabiyya, Beirut, 1984.
al-Fukayki, Hani, *Awkar al-hazima*, Dar Riad al-Rayyes, London, 1993.
Ghalyun Burhan, *al-Mihna al-ʿArabiyya: al-Dawla did al-Umma* (The Arab Ordeal: State against Nation), Markaz Dirasat al-Wahda al-ʿArabiyya, Beirut, 1994.
Ghurbal, Shafiq, *Minhaj mufassal li-durus al-ʿawamil al-tarikhiyya fi binaʾ al-umma al-ʿarabiyya*, League of Arab States, Cairo, 1961.
al-Hakim, Hasan, *ʿAbd al-Rahman al-Shahbandar: Hayatuhu wa jihaduhu*, al-Dar al-Muttahida, Beirut, 1985.

Hamrush, Ahmad, *Mujtama' 'Abd al-Nasir*, vol. 3, Dar al-Mawqif al-'Arabi, 1982.

Hanna, 'Abdallah, *al-Ittijahat al-fikriyya fi suriyya wa lubnan 1920–1945*, Dar al-Taqaddum al-'Arabi, Damascus, 1973.

Hawrani, Akram, *Mukhakkirat*, vols. 1–2, Maktabat Madbuli, Cairo, 2000.

al-Husri, Sati', *Dirasat 'an Muqaddimat Ibn Khaldun* (Studies on the Muqaddimah of Ibn Khaldun), second and enlarged edition, Maktabat al-Kanaji, Cairo, 1961.

——, *Ara' wa ahadith fi al-qawmiyya al-'arabiyya*, Markaz Dirasat al-Wahdah al-'Arabiyya, Beirut, 1985.

——, *Yawm maysalun; Safhah min tarikh al-'arab al-hadith*, new edition, Dar Ittihad, Beirut, 1964, trans. into English by Sidney Glazer, *The Day of Maysalun: a page from the modern history of the Arabs*, The Middle East Institute, Washington, D.C., 1966.

——, *al-'Amal al-Qawmiyya*, (Collected Works on Nationalism, vols 1–3, Markaz Dirasat al-Wahdah al-'Arabiyya, 1990.

——, *al-Iqlimiyya*, Beirut, Marakaz dirasat al-wahdah al-'arabiyya, Beirut, 1985.

——, *Mudhakkirati fi al-Iraq 1921–1941* (My memoirs in Iraq, 1921–1941), vols 1–2, Dar al-Tali'a, Beirut, 1967–8.

Ibn Jinni, *al-Khasa'is*, vol. 1, Dar al-Huda, Beirut, n.d.

Ibn Taymiyya, *Iqtida' al-Sirat al-Mustaqim*, Dar al-Ma'rifa, Beirut, n.d.

——, *al-Siyasa al-Shar'iyya*, al-Matbu'a al-Khayriyya, Cairo, 1904.

al-Jabarti, 'Abd al-Rahman, *'Aja'ib al-athar fi al-tarajim wa al-akhbar*, vol. 1, Dar al-Faris, Beirut, n.d.

al-Jabiri, Muhammad 'Abid, *al-Dimuqratiyya wa huquq al-insan*, Markaz Dirasat al-Wahdah al-'Arabiyya, Beirut, 1997.

al-Kawakibi, 'Abd al-Rahman, *Umm al-Qura*, 2nd edition, Dar al-Ra'id al-Arabi, Beirut, 1982.

——, *Taba'i' al-istibdad*, al-Matba'a al-Rahmaniyya, Cairo, 1931.

al-Khatib, Muhibb al-Din, *al-Doctor Salah al-Din al-Qasimi*, al-Matba'a al-Salafiyya, Cairo, 1959.

——, *al-Mu'tamar al-'Arabi al-Awwal*, Matba'at al-Bosphore, Cairo, 1913.

al-Khuri, Yusuf, *al-mashari' al-wahdawiyya al-'arabiyya 1913–1918*, Markaz Dirasat al-Wahda al-'Arabiyya, Beirut, 1990.

al-Miqdadi, Darwish, *Tarikh al-Umma al-'arabiyya*, Iraqi Ministry of Education, Baghdad, 1939.

Al-Mu'tamar al-Qawmi al-arabi, *Hal al-Umma al-'Arabiyya*, The Centre for Arab Unity Studies, Beirut, 1999.

Mudayris, Fallah 'Abdallah, *Malamih awwalliyya hawla nash'at al-tajamu'at wa al-tanzimat al-siyasiyya fi al-Kuwayt 1938–1975*, Dar Qirtas, al-Kuwayt, 1994.

Mufarrij, Fuad Khalil, editor, *al-Mu'tamar al-'Arabi al-Qawmi fi Bludan*, Maktabat 'Arafa, Damascus, 1937.

Nidal al-Ba'th, vol. IV, Dar al-Tali'a, Beirut, 1976.

Qadri, Ahmad, *Mudhakkirati 'an al-thawra al-'arabiyya al-kubra*, Matabi' Ibn Zaydun, Damascus, 1956.

al-Sa'id, Nuri, *al-Kitab al-Azraq* (The Blue Book), Matba'at al-Hukuma, Baghdad, 1943.

Sabbagh, Salah al-Din, *Fursan al-'Uruba*, Ala-Shabab al-'Arabi, Baghdad, 1956.

al-Sayyid, Jalal, *Haqiqat al-Umma al-'Arabiyya wa 'awamil hifziha wa tamziqiha*, Dar al-Yaqza al-'Arabiyya, Beirut, 1973.

Shahbandar, Abd al-Rahman, *Mudhakkirat*, Dar al-Irshad, Beirut, 1967.

——, *al-Qadaya al-ijtima'iyya al-Kubra fi al-'alam al-'Arabi*, (The Big Social Issues in the Arab World), al-Muqtataf al-muqattam Press, Cairo, 1936.

Shakib Arslan, *Sirah dhatiyya* (An autobiography), Dar al-Tali'a, Beirut, 1969.

al-Shihabi, Mustafa, *al-Qawmiyya al-'arabiyya*, The Arab League, Cairo, 1958.

al-Sulh, 'Adil, *Hizb al-istiqlal al-jumhuri – sutur min al-risala*, Dar al-Nahar, Beirut, 1970.

al-Tahtawi, Rifa'a Rafi', *Anwar Tawfiq al-Jalil*, Cairo, 1285/1868.

Zurayq, Qustantin, *al-'Amal al-fikriyya al-'amma*, vol. 1, Markaz Dirasat al-wahdah al-'arabiyyah-Mu'assasat Shuman, Beirut, 1996.

Zurayq, Qustantin, *al-wa'i al-Qawmi*, Dar al-Makshuf, Beirut, 1939.

Arabic: Articles

'Isa, Sulayman, 'al-Bidayat', *al-M'arifa*, no. 113, July, 1971.

Zu'aytir, Akram, 'al-mu'tamar al-islami', *Al-Hayat*, London, 20 June 1994.

——, 'Hizb istiqlali, *Al-Hayat*, London, 21 June, 1994.

Other Languages: Books

Abun-Nasr, Jamil M., *A History of the Maghrib*, second edition, Cambridge University Press, 1975.

Acton, Lord, *Essays on Freedom and Power*, Glencoe, IL: The Free Press, 1948.

Anderson, Benedict, *Imagined Communities*, revised edition, Verso, London and New York, 1993. First published 1983.

Antonious, George, *The Arab Awakening*, Hamish Hamilton, London, 1938. Albert L. Bodman, Jr?

Badawi, 'Abdurrahman, *La transmission de la Philosophie Grecque au Monde Arabe*, Librairie Philosophique J. Vrin., Paris, 1968.

Batatu, Hanna, *Syria's Peasantry, the Descendants of its Lesser Rural Notables, and their Politics*, Princeton University Press, 1999.

——, *The Old Social Classes and the Revolutionary Movements of Iraq*, Book III, Princeton University Press, 1978.

Berlin, Isaiah, *Vico and Herder. Two Studies in the History of Ideas*, Chatto and Windus, London, 1976.

Bodman, Herbert L. Jr., *Political Factions in Aleppo 1760–1826*, The University of North Carolina Press, 1963.

Breuilly, John, *Nationalism and the State*, 2nd edition, Manchester University Press, 1993.

Choueiri, Youssef M., *Arab History and the Nation-State 1820–1980*, Routledge, London and New York, 1989.

——, *Islamic Fundamentalism*, Pinter, London and Washington, 1997.

Cleveland, William L. *Islam Against the West. Shakib Arslan and the Campaign for Islamic Nationalism*, Al-Saqi Books, London, 1985.

——, *The Making of an Arab Nationalist. Ottomanism and Arabism in the life and thought of Sati' al-Husri*, Princeton University Press, 1971.

Commins, David Dean, *Islamic Reform. Politics and Social Change in Late Ottoman Syria*, Oxford University Press, 1990.

Crystal, Jill, *Oil and Politics in the Gulf*, Cambridge University Press, 1995.

Dawn, C. Ernest, 'An Arab Nationalist view of world politics and history in the interwar period', in Uriel Dann, ed., *The Great Powers in the Middle East 1919–1939*, Holmes and Meier, New York and London, 1988.

Descartes, R., *Discours de la méthode*, Bordas, Paris, 1984.

Duri, A. A., *The Historical Formation of the Arab Nation. A Study in Identity and Consciousness*, trans. Lawrence I. Conrad, Croom Helm, London, 1987.

Eden, Anthony, *Freedom and Order: Selected Speeches, 1939–1945*, Faber & Faber, London, 1947.

Gellner, Ernest, *Nations and Nationalism*, Blackwell, Oxford, 1984.

Gershoni, Israel and Janowski, James P., *Redefining the Egyptian Nation 1930–1945*, Cambridge University Press, 1995.

Great Britain and Palestine 1915–1945, Information Papers No. 20, Royal Institute of International Affairs, London and New York, 1946.

Guthrie, W. K. C. *A History of Greek Philosophy*, vol. V, Cambridge University Press, 1978.

Haim, Sylvia G., ed., *Arab Nationalism. An Anthology*, University of California Press, 1962, 1976.

Harik, Iliya and Sullivan, Denis J., eds, *Privatization and Liberalization in the Middle East*, Indiana University Press, 1992.

Hayes, Carleton, *The Historical Evolution of Modern Nationalism*, New York, 1931.

Hobsbawm, E. J., *Nations and Nationalism since 1780*, Cambridge University Press, 1991.

Hourani, Albert, *A History of the Arab Peoples*, Faber & Faber, London, 1991.

——, *Arabic Thought in the Liberal Age*, Oxford University Press, 1970.

Inalcik, Halil, *The Ottoman Empire: the Classical Age 1300–1600*, Weidenfeld and Nicolson, London, 1975.

Kayali, Hasan, *Arab and Young Turks. Ottomanism, Arabism, and Islamism in the Ottoman Empire 1908–1918*, University of California Press, 1997.

Kazziha, Walid, *Revolutionary Transformation in the Arab World. Habash and his Comrades from Nationalism to Marxism*, Charles Knight & Company Ltd., London, 1975.

Kedourie, Elie, *Nationalism*, Hutchinson, London, 1960, 1974.

——, ed., *Nationalism in Asia and Africa*, London, 1971.

Khadduri, Majid, *Republican 'Iraq. A Study in Iraqi Politics since the Revolution of 1958*, Oxford University Press, 1964.

Khalil, Muhammad, *The Arab States and the Arab League. A Documentary Record*, vol. II, Khayat, Beirut, 1962.

Khoury, Philip S., *Syria and the French Mandate*, I.B. Tauris, London, 1987.

Koestler, Arthur, *The Sleepwalkers*, Pelican Books, Harmondsworth, 1972.

Kohn, Hans, *Nationalism: its Meaning and History*, revised edition, An Anvil Original, Van Nostrand, Princeton, 1955, 1965.

Louis, Wm. Roger, *The British Empire in the Middle East 1945–1951*, Clarendon Press, Oxford, 1988.

Lovejoy, A. D., *The Great Chain of Being*, Cambridge, MA, 1936.

Mill, John Stuart, *Utilitarianism*, Everyman, London, 1910, 1998.

Minogue, K, 'Ernest Gellner and the dangers of theorising nationalism', in J. Hall and I. Jarvie, eds, *The Social Philosophy of Ernest Gellner*, Rodopi, Amsterdam, 1996.

Niyazi, Berkes, *The Development of Secularism in Turkey*, McGill University Press, Montreal, 1964.

Nutting, Anthony, *Nasser*, Constable, London, 1972.

O'Brien, Patrick, *The Revolution in Egypt's Economic System. From Private Enterprise to Socialism 1952–1965*, Oxford University Press, 1966.

Plamenatz, John, 'Two types of nationalism', in Eugene Kamenka, ed., *Nationalism. The Nature and Evolution of an Idea*, Edward Arnold, London, 1976.

Portath, Yehoshuah, *In Search of Arab Unity, 1930–1945*, Frank Cass, London, 1986.

Rafeq, Abdul-Karim, 'Arabism, society and economy in Syria, 1918–1920', in Youssef M. Choueiri, ed., *State and Society in Syria and Lebanon*, University of Exeter Press, 1993.

Renan, Ernest, 'What is a nation?', in Homri, K. Bhaba, ed., *Nation and Narration*, Routledge, London and New York, 1990.

Schilcher, Linda Schatkowski, *Families in Politics. Damascene factions and estates of the 18th and 19th centuries*, Franz Steiner-Verlag-Wiesbaden, Stuttgart, 1985.

Seton-Watson, Hugh, *Nations and States*, Methuen, London, 1977.

Smith, Anthony, *The Ethnic Origins of Nations*, Blackwell, Oxford, 1994.

——, *Theories of Nationalism*. London, Duckworth, 1971.

Stephens, Robert, *Nasser*, Harmondsworth, Middlesex, 1973.

Tarabain, Ahmed, ''Abd al-Hamid al-Zahrawi', in Rashid Khalidi et al., eds, *The Origins of Arab Nationalism*, Columbia University Press, 1991.

Tauber, Eliezer, *Emergence of the Arab Movements*, Frank Cass, London, 1993.

Tibi, Bassam, *Arab Nationalism. A critical enquiry*, trans. and ed. Marion

Farouk Sluglett and Peter Sluglett, Macmillan Press, London and Basingstoke, 1981.

Tlili, Béchir, *Crises et mutations dans le monde islamo-méditerranéen contemporain*, Publications de l'Université de Tunis, Tunis, 1978.

Other Languages: Articles

Acton, Lord 'Nationality', *The Home and Foreign Review*, 1 July 1862.

Chejne, Anwar G. 'The use of history by modern Arab writers', *Middle East
Journal* 14, 1960.

Faris, Nabih Amin, 'The Arabs and their history', *The Middle East Journal*, 8
(2), 1954.

Haim, Silvia G., 'Alfieri and al-Kawakibi', *Oriente Moderno* 34, 1954.

Kenny, L. M., 'Sati' al-Husri's views on Arab Nationalism', *Middle East
Journal* 17, 1963.

L. B., 'La caricature en Turque', *Revue Du Monde Musulman*, vol. 16, 1908.

L. M., 'Empire Ottoman', *Revue Du Monde Musulman*, vol. 16, 1908.

Rossi, Ettore, 'Una traduzione turca dell' opera "*Della Tirannide*" di V.
Alfieri Probabilmente conosciuta da al-Kawakibi', *Oriente Moderno*,
vol. 34, 1954.

Index